AI Search Playbook

Master answer engine optimization and generative engine optimization using technical and content strategies

Pedro Gustavo Torres

www.bpbonline.com

First Edition 2027

ISBN: 978-81-69619-370

Dedicated to

My family and my career mentors

About the Author

Pedro Gustavo Torres is biased towards action; impact-driven engineering leader who excels at building and scaling high-performing teams across startups, scaleups, and enterprise organizations. His leadership philosophy centers on empowering people with clarity, competence, and autonomy, enabling them to deliver meaningful results.

With over 25 years of experience across North America and Europe, he has led and coached hundreds of software engineers and helped raise three unicorns in the tech industry. Passionate about people, technology, and products, he thrives on driving impact through collaboration and innovation.

A strong advocate of AI, agile, Lean, DevOps, and SRE practices, he champions systems and cultures that foster high performance and continuous improvement. Over the past 15 years, he has built and led engineering organizations of more than 200 engineers in both blue-chip enterprises and dynamic startups, striking the right balance between structure and agility.

With a foundation in software engineering, he maintains a hands-on understanding of technology that informs his strategic and people-centered leadership. He is also an international speaker, community co-founder, and podcast co-host, sharing insights on leadership, engineering culture, and the future of technology.

About the Reviewer

Dmitry Vostokov is a software diagnostics, observability, and AI practitioner with extensive experience in cloud-native systems, security monitoring, anomaly detection, data engineering, ML pipelines, GenAI architectures, and agentic AI workflows. His work integrates deep systems engineering with methods for interpreting complex technical behavior, from execution artifacts and telemetry to large-scale operational signals. He has a long-standing interest in the relationship between software behavior, diagnostic evidence, information retrieval, and intelligent automation. Dmitry's perspective on AI search, answer engine optimization, generative engine optimization, the Semantic Web, optimization, and scaling is informed by this broader concern with how information is structured, retrieved, interpreted, ranked, and operationalized in modern intelligent systems. He brings practical engineering experience and an analytical interest in making AI-driven discovery more reliable, explainable, observable, and useful at scale for technical, business, and knowledge-oriented audiences.

Acknowledgement

I am deeply grateful to all those who inspired me to write this book.

My family has always been the cornerstone of my determination, and the mentors I had throughout my career and my peers also played a fundamental role in the professional I became.

I am grateful to BPB Publications, the reviewers, the technical experts, and the editors for their guidance and expertise in bringing this book to fruition. Their support and assistance were invaluable in navigating the complexities of the publishing process.

I also want to express my gratitude to the readers who have shown interest in my book. Your support and encouragement have been deeply appreciated.

Thank you to everyone who has played a part in bringing this book to life.

Preface

Search is being rewritten. For two decades, the rules of digital discovery remained remarkably stable. Brands invested in keywords, backlinks, and page speed. Marketing teams measured success in rankings and click-through rates. The playbook was clear, the metrics were familiar, and while Google's algorithm updates were sometimes disruptive, they operated within a framework everyone understood. That era is ending.

This book was written at a moment of genuine inflection. AI agents (large language models powering ChatGPT, Claude, Gemini, and Perplexity) are reshaping how consumers discover, evaluate, and decide. They do not rank pages. They synthesize answers. They do not send traffic. They deliver verdicts. And increasingly, they do so without the consumer ever visiting a website.

The *AI Search Playbook* is a practical guide for brand leaders, product experience managers, marketers, and technical teams navigating this transition. It introduces two complementary disciplines (answer engine optimization and generative engine optimization) and builds a complete operational framework for each, from content strategy and schema markup to product data architecture, competitive measurement, and automation at scale.

The book is organized as a journey. Early chapters establish what has changed and why it matters. The middle chapters provide the tactical and technical foundations for optimizing content, product data, and infrastructure for AI-driven discovery. Later chapters address scale, competitive intelligence, and organizational capability. The final chapter looks ahead, examining multimodal search, Agent-to-Agent commerce, ethical AI, and how to build a discovery stack that does not depend on any single platform.

Comprising ten chapters, the book moves from strategic orientation to operational execution. It is designed for practitioners who need to act, not just understand. Every framework is actionable. Every concept is grounded in how AI systems actually behave. Every chapter builds toward the same goal: ensuring your brand is not just indexed but cited, recommended, and trusted by the AI agents that are becoming the primary gatekeepers of consumer attention.

The search box is not going away. However, it is no longer where discovery begins. The AI Search Playbook is your guide to the landscape that has replaced it.

Chapter 1: The Rise of AI Agents- This chapter establishes the foundational shift driving everything that follows. It traces the transition from traditional SEO, where brands competed for ranked links on search results pages, to AI-first discovery, where large language models synthesize answers and deliver them in a conversational style, often without sending users to any website at all. The chapter introduces AI agents as the new gatekeepers of consumer attention, examines the technical mechanisms behind retrieval-augmented generation, and explains why the click, the fundamental unit of digital marketing for two decades, is no longer the primary measure of value. It also addresses the measurement crisis posed by zero-click responses, introduces new north-star metrics for the AI era, and maps the behavioral and generational shifts accelerating adoption. By the end of this chapter, readers will understand why the transition to AI-first discovery is structural rather than incremental, and why organizations that treat it as a future concern rather than a present imperative risk being invisible before they realize the shift has happened.

Chapter 2: Understanding and Mastering AEO- This chapter introduces answer engine optimization as the first operational response to AI-first discovery. Where traditional SEO optimizes for rankings and clicks, AEO optimizes for selection and synthesis, becoming the source that AI agents extract, cite, and recommend. The chapter defines AEO in practical terms, situates it within the modern marketing stack, and introduces a maturity model to assess organizational readiness. It examines the shift from ranking to source-of-truth status, provides tactical guidance on answer-first content structures and question-based page organization, and delivers a deep treatment of schema markup as the technical foundation of AEO. The chapter closes with voice search and digital assistant optimization, addressing the unique requirements of conversational query formats. By the end of this chapter, readers will be able to design content and implement structured data that makes their brand genuinely extractable and citable by AI agents across major platforms.

Chapter 3: GEO Strategies Foundations- This chapter introduces generative engine optimization as the strategic layer above AEO. Being extracted is not the same as being recommended. GEO addresses the qualitative dimensions of AI representation: how AI agents perceive your authority, characterize your brand, and position your products as they synthesize responses. The chapter establishes the three pillars of GEO (authority perception, narrative control, and information primacy) and explains how AI agents assess credibility across sources. It introduces the product curation hierarchy, a five-tier framework for understanding how prominently brands appear in AI responses, and provides strategies for achieving primary authority positioning. The chapter also introduces the concept of information gain, the unique value your content provides that cannot be obtained elsewhere, and explains how brand entities are represented in AI knowledge graphs. By the end of this chapter, readers will have a clear framework for moving from being mentioned in AI responses to being recommended as the authoritative choice.

Chapter 4: Structuring Product Data for AI-driven Recommendations- This chapter addresses the product data imperative at the heart of AI-driven commerce. When a consumer asks an AI agent for a product recommendation, the agent must parse catalogs, extract specifications, compare attributes, and synthesize a response. If your product data is not structured for this kind of analysis, you are invisible regardless of product quality. The chapter traces the transformation from traditional SKU-centric catalogs to semantic product catalogs designed for machine understanding, provides a comprehensive treatment of product schema implementation, and develops the concept of attribute-based search optimization. It addresses how to handle complex technical specifications for AI comparisons, manage product variants, and structure data for software and digital products. A dedicated section on freshness and verifiability establishes data currency as a trust signal. By the end of this chapter, readers will have a practical framework for transforming product information into recommendation-ready assets.

Chapter 5: Technical Frameworks for Implementing Agent-ready Catalogs- This chapter addresses the infrastructure layer that makes AI optimization strategies operational. The most brilliantly structured product catalog achieves nothing if AI agents cannot access it reliably. The chapter opens with a detailed treatment of llms.txt, the emerging protocol for AI agent discovery, covering its structure, advanced implementation strategies, security considerations, and integration with existing discovery mechanisms. It then addresses robots.txt configuration for AI-specific user agents, explaining the critical distinction between training crawlers and retrieval crawlers and the strategic implications of each. A section on page speed examines how technical performance influences AI citation rates through crawl efficiency, extraction quality, and reliability signals. The chapter closes with frameworks for integrating AI visibility metrics into technical dashboards and establishing data governance for AI-ready content at scale. By the end of this chapter, readers will be able to design and operate the technical infrastructure that enables AI optimization to be durable and systematic.

Chapter 6: Advanced AEO and Optimizing LLM Citations- This chapter moves from foundational optimization to advanced techniques for organizations seeking competitive leadership in AI-driven discovery. It opens with a technical breakdown of retrieval-augmented generation, explaining how AI agents retrieve, rank, extract, synthesize, and validate information, and identifying optimization opportunities at each stage of the pipeline. The chapter then introduces a systematic framework for reverse-engineering competitive visibility: understanding why specific competitors dominate AI responses, analyzing citation patterns, and identifying gaps with precision. Detailed guidance on creating quotable insights addresses the characteristics of content that AI agents preferentially cite, with frameworks for statistical content, expert attribution, and named methodologies. A section on semantic punctuation examines how formatting, structure, and linguistic patterns influence machine parsing and extraction accuracy. The chapter closes with an advanced treatment of E-E-A-T signals for AI systems. By the end of this chapter, readers will have the techniques to move from being included in AI responses to being positioned as the primary authority.

Chapter 7: PXM Evolution and Managing AI Experience- This chapter introduces product experience management as the organizational and strategic framework for AI-ready product data. PXM extends traditional product information management from a system of record to a system of engagement, encompassing how product information translates into experiences across every channel where customers encounter products, including AI discovery channels that never send traffic to your website. The chapter defines PXM in the AI era, provides a phased twelve-month transformation roadmap from basic PIM to AI-ready PXM, and examines the critical distinction between functional and emotional product data. Both dimensions matter for AI recommendations: functional specifications answer technical queries, while emotional and experiential attributes answer qualitative ones. The chapter addresses how to systematically capture emotional data through review mining, expert assessment, and user research, and how to structure it for AI-driven extraction. A section on data quality as a ranking signal establishes accuracy, completeness, and freshness as strategic competitive advantages. Case studies ground the framework in real implementation patterns. By the end of this chapter, readers will understand how to treat product data as a strategic asset that compounds in value over time.

Chapter 8: Dominating Agentic Shelf with Digital Shelf Analytics- This chapter introduces the Agentic Shelf as the defining competitive battleground of AI-driven commerce. When a consumer asks an AI agent for a recommendation, there is no shelf to browse and no page of results to scroll. There are often just three options, or one. Any brand not selected does not exist for that consumer. The chapter develops Share of Model as the critical new KPI for brand health in AI discovery, providing a comprehensive measurement framework that includes citation frequency, prominence scoring, primary recommendation rate, context coverage, and competitive displacement analysis. It then introduces a four-layer competitive intelligence framework to understand not just who wins AI recommendations but also why, enabling precise diagnosis of authority gaps, data quality deficits, and positioning weaknesses. A detailed treatment of price and availability as hard signals explains how these binary filters can disqualify a brand from consideration before any other factor is evaluated. The chapter closes with a gap-closing framework that prioritizes quick wins, medium-effort initiatives, and strategic investments. By the end of this chapter, readers will have the measurement and competitive intelligence frameworks needed to systematically improve their position on the Agentic Shelf.

Chapter 9: Scaling GEO and Automating Visibility Across AI Platforms- This chapter addresses the scaling paradox at the heart of AI optimization: the more successful your optimization becomes, the more products, content types, and platforms you need to optimize, creating an expanding workload that manual processes cannot sustain. The chapter provides a complete architecture for a six-stage automation pipeline covering data ingestion, enrichment, content generation, quality assurance, publishing, and monitoring, explaining how each stage converts raw product data into AI-ready content at scale. Platform-specific optimization frameworks address the distinct retrieval behaviors, content preferences, and ranking signals of ChatGPT, Claude, Gemini, and Perplexity, alongside a three-tier content strategy that delivers platform-specific enhancements without multiplying manual effort. A detailed framework for creating and maintaining an AI brand voice ensures that the characterizations AI agents generate remain intentional and aligned with brand positioning. The chapter also covers automated audit processes and a four-pillar data-integrity framework to maintain quality during high-frequency updates. By the end of this chapter, readers will have the operational architecture to scale AI optimization across large catalogs without a proportional increase in headcount.

Chapter 10: Future-proofing Brands for the Next AI Shift- The final chapter looks beyond current AI optimization to the structural transformations ahead. It traces the three-stage evolution toward Agent-to-Agent commerce, where AI systems research, negotiate, and transact entirely on behalf of human buyers, and examines the strategic implications for brands as the competitive model shifts from persuasion to verifiability. The chapter then addresses the next wave of multimodal search, providing detailed optimization frameworks for visual, voice, and video search across all dimensions, from image metadata to conversational content structure to chapter markers and cross-modal consistency. A section on ethical AI and data privacy addresses the privacy paradox, principles of responsible AI optimization, and the evolving regulatory landscape across major jurisdictions. The chapter introduces a resilient discovery stack architecture that distributes presence across AI platforms, traditional search, social media, marketplaces, owned channels, and industry platforms, reducing the risk of dependency on any single source. It closes with a comprehensive, continuous audit guide organized across daily, weekly, monthly, quarterly, and annual cycles. By the end of this chapter, readers will have the strategic frameworks and operational checklists needed to remain visible, competitive, and adaptable through whatever the next AI shift brings.

Code Bundle and Coloured Images

Please follow the link to download the
Code Bundle and the ***Coloured Images*** of the book:

https://rebrand.ly/evjsvh5

The code bundle for the book is also hosted on GitHub at
https://github.com/bpbpublications/AI-Search-Playbook.
In case there's an update to the code, it will be updated on the existing GitHub repository.

We have code bundles from our rich catalogue of books and videos available at https://github.com/bpbpublications. Check them out!

Errata

We take immense pride in our work at BPB Publications and follow best practices to ensure the accuracy of our content to provide an indulging reading experience to our subscribers. Our readers are our mirrors, and we use their inputs to reflect and improve upon human errors, if any, that may have occurred during the publishing processes involved. To let us maintain the quality and help us reach out to any readers who might be having difficulties due to any unforeseen errors, please write to us at: errata@bpbonline.com

Your support, suggestions and feedback are highly appreciated by the BPB Publications' Family.

Piracy

If you come across any illegal copies of our works in any form on the internet, we would be grateful if you would provide us with the location address or website name. Please contact us at business@bpbonline.com with a link to the material.

If you are interested in becoming an author

If there is a topic that you have expertise in, and you are interested in either writing or contributing to a book, please visit www.bpbonline.com. We have worked with thousands of developers and tech professionals, just like you, to help them share their insights with the global tech community. You can make a general application, apply for a specific hot topic that we are recruiting an author for, or submit your own idea.

Reviews

Please leave a review. Once you have read and used this book, why not leave a review on the site that you purchased it from? Potential readers can then see and use your unbiased opinion to make purchase decisions. We at BPB can understand what you think about our products, and our authors can see your feedback on their book. Thank you!

For more information about BPB, please visit www.bpbonline.com.

Join our Discord space

Join our Discord workspace for latest updates, offers, tech happenings around the world, new releases, and sessions with the authors:

https://discord.bpbonline.com

Table of Contents

CHAPTER 1
The Rise of AI Agents

Introduction

The search landscape is being rewritten. For two decades, the rules of digital discovery remained remarkably stable, with brands investing in keyword optimization, backlink profiles, and page speed improvements. Product experience management teams structured their data for search engine crawlers. Marketing leaders measured success in rankings, impressions, and click-through rates. The playbook was well-established, the metrics were clear, and Google's algorithm updates, while sometimes disruptive, operated within a familiar framework. That era is ending.

We are witnessing a fundamental transformation in how consumers discover, evaluate, and make decisions about products and services. This shift is not merely an evolution of search engine technology. It represents a wholesale reimagining of the relationship between information seekers and information providers. At the center of this transformation are AI agents: large language models that do not just index and rank content, but understand, synthesize, and deliver it in conversational formats that often eliminate the need to visit your website at all.

This is the **notorious shift** that will define the next decade of digital marketing. For brand leaders, product experience management professionals, and product managers, this shift demands urgent attention. The strategies that drove organic traffic and conversions over the past 20 years are becoming less effective at an alarming rate. Meanwhile, a new set of imperatives is emerging. Many organizations are unprepared to address them.

Structure

The chapter covers the following topics:

- Shift from SEO to AI-first discovery
- LLM summarization and synthesis of web content

- AI agents as the new gatekeepers of attention
- Collapse of click-through metrics
- Notorious shift in consumer search behavior

Objectives

This chapter examines the forces reshaping digital discovery. We will explore the technical mechanisms behind AI-powered search, the behavioral shifts driving adoption, and the profound implications for how brands must think about visibility, authority, and conversion in an age where the click is no longer king.

Shift from SEO to AI-first discovery

The transition from traditional SEO to AI-first discovery represents a structural change in how attention, information, and commercial intent flow across the web. For more than two decades, brands learned to compete within a stable system in which search engines surfaced ranked lists of links, and success depended on earning clicks. To understand why AI-driven discovery fundamentally changes the rules, it is important first to revisit the model it is beginning to replace.

Traditional SEO model

To grasp the scale of current shifts, we must recognize the system they are replacing. Classic search engine optimization was based on a simple principle: search engines scanned and categorized web content, ranking it according to its relevance and credibility. People would then perform a search, view a ranked list of these pages, and visit the websites to get the information they needed.

This model created clear incentives. Brands optimized title tags and meta descriptions to improve click-through rates from search results pages. They built content hubs targeting specific keyword clusters. They earned backlinks from authoritative domains to boost their rankings. For product catalogs, they implemented schema markup for prices, availability, and reviews. They ensured product detail pages loaded quickly and displayed correctly on mobile devices. Success was measured in organic traffic, keyword rankings, product detail page views, and ultimately conversions from search-driven visitors.

The search engine mediated the relationship between searcher and information provider, but the fundamental transaction remained intact: the search engine directed attention, and websites captured it.

The AI-first paradigm

The AI-first discovery model breaks this transaction. When a user asks ChatGPT, Claude, Gemini, or Perplexity a question about products, they increasingly receive a comprehensive answer without leaving the AI interface.

Consider this real scenario: A user asks Perplexity, "What is the best standing desk for a home office under $800?" The AI responds with:

- A comparison of four specific models with detailed specifications.
- Pros and cons for each based on size, adjustability, and build quality.
- Current pricing from multiple retailers.
- Specific recommendations based on room size and user height.
- Assembly difficulty ratings.
- Warranty information.

The user's research phase is complete. They might ask a follow-up question about cable management or stability, get that answered, and then search directly for the recommended brand to purchase. The manufacturer's analytics show a single direct visit before conversion, but the entire research journey, the phase that traditionally generated multiple organic sessions, happened invisibly inside an AI conversation.

This represents more than a new search interface; it is a fundamental restructuring of the value chain. The AI agent becomes both the search engine and the destination. It does not merely point users toward information; it delivers the data itself, often with reasoning, context, and personalization that far exceed what a traditional search results page could provide. The shift is visualized in the following figure:

***Figure 1.1**: The gatekeeper shift from the search engine model (left) to the AI-first model (right)*

For brands, this creates a profound challenge. Your meticulously optimized product pages, your detailed specification sheets, your carefully constructed comparison content. All of it risks becoming invisible if the AI can extract and repackage your information without sending users to your site. The traffic you have built your growth models around may simply evaporate.

From indexation to citation

In the era of traditional search, success meant being indexed and ranking well. In the AI-first era, success means being cited: having your products, your brand, and your information actively featured in the answers AI agents generate. Being indexed is no longer enough. If AI agents can extract information from your competitors but not from you, if they recommend other brands while omitting yours, you have become invisible, regardless of how well-optimized your website is for traditional search.

Technical underpinnings of this shift

Understanding why this shift is happening requires examining the technical capabilities that enable AI-first discovery. Three key developments have converged to allow for this transformation, which will be discussed in the following section.

Advancement in natural language understanding

Modern large language models can interpret the intent behind queries with unprecedented accuracy. Unlike traditional search engines that matched keywords, LLMs understand context, nuance, and implicit requirements.

The traditional search approach includes the following:

- **Query:** "project management tool remote designers".
- Matches pages containing these keywords.
- Returns a ranked list of pages.
- User evaluates what might be relevant.

An AI-first approach includes:

- **Query:** "What is the best project management tool for a remote team of designers?"
- **Understands:** Small creative team, needs visual collaboration, likely values interface design, remote-specific features needed.
- Synthesizes information from multiple sources about tools that fit these criteria.
- Delivers specific recommendations with reasoning.

For product discovery, this means AI agents can understand complex, multi-dimensional requirements that keyword-based search handles poorly. *Dishwasher for small apartment, very quiet, energy efficient, under $600* becomes a precisely understood set of constraints rather than a keyword salad.

Retrieval-augmented generation

AI agents do not rely solely on their training data. They can retrieve real-time information from the web and use it to generate responses. This hybrid approach (combining the reasoning capabilities of large language models with access to up-to-date information) makes AI agents far more powerful and reliable than earlier conversational AI systems.

For product catalogs, this is critical. An AI agent can retrieve current pricing, inventory status, and recent reviews, then synthesize that information with product specifications and category knowledge to make timely recommendations. Your product launched last week? The AI can include it in today's recommendations if it can retrieve the information effectively.

Multimodal integration

Increasingly, AI agents can process and reason about images, documents, and structured data alongside text. This capability is transformative for product discovery.

AI agents can now:

- Extract specifications from product images and infographics.
- Parse technical details from PDF spec sheets.
- Interpret product lifestyle images to understand use cases and contexts.
- Analyze comparison tables to understand competitive positioning.
- Process video transcripts to gather installation or usage information.

However, this capability creates a critical vulnerability: *if your product information is embedded in formats AI cannot easily extract, your products may be excluded from recommendations.*

Common AI extraction failures for product data are listed as follows:

- Specifications displayed only in JavaScript-generated comparison tables.
- Key features embedded in carousel images without alt text.
- Technical details in downloadable PDFs not linked in HTML.
- Product dimensions or materials shown only in styled infographics.
- Pricing or availability requiring interaction with dynamic elements.

E-commerce sites that rely heavily on visual presentation and interactive elements often inadvertently hide their product information from AI extraction. A beautifully designed product page that requires users to click through image galleries, expand hidden sections, or interact with comparison tools may appear nearly empty to an AI agent attempting to gather information.

These technical capabilities create a user experience that feels qualitatively different from traditional search. Instead of scanning through multiple search results, reading snippets, clicking links, and piecing together information across tabs, users engage in a dialogue. They ask questions, receive answers, ask follow-up questions, and iteratively refine their understanding. All within a single conversational thread.

LLM summarization and synthesis of web content

To understand how to optimize for AI-first discovery, we need to examine the technical process by which large language models consume, process, and present web content. This process operates very differently from traditional search engine crawling and indexing.

Retrieval process

When a user asks an AI agent a question that requires current information, the system initiates a retrieval process. Unlike traditional search engines that maintain a comprehensive index of the web, AI agents typically use a combination of approaches:

- **Real-time web search**: The AI system formulates search queries from the user's question and retrieves relevant web pages from search APIs (typically the Bing Search API or Google Search API). These queries may differ significantly from what a human would type into a search box, because the AI optimizes for retrieving high-quality source material rather than mimicking human search behavior.

  Importantly, most AI platforms do not crawl the web themselves. They rely on existing search infrastructure, which means traditional search ranking factors still matter, but as a filter for what gets retrieved, not as a direct ranking factor for what gets presented to users.

- **Document fetching**: Once relevant URLs are identified, the system fetches the full content of these pages. This is where the first crucial difference from traditional SEO emerges: the AI is not looking at your meta description or title tag to decide whether to present your page to the user. Instead, it is retrieving your full content to extract information.

- **Content extraction and parsing**: The AI system extracts the meaningful content from each page, stripping away navigation elements, ads, and other non-essential material. For text-heavy pages with semantic HTML structure, this works relatively well.

  For product pages, however, extraction can fail in critical ways:

  - Product specifications displayed in images are often invisible to extraction.
  - JavaScript-rendered content may not be captured.
  - Interactive comparison tools do not transfer into extracted text.
  - Pricing and availability behind dynamic loading may be missed.
  - Product dimensions in styled tables without proper HTML markup can be lost.

A beautifully designed product detail page optimized for human shoppers may appear to the AI as: "Product name. Add to cart. Related products." The specifications, features, use cases, and differentiators that drive purchase decisions are nowhere to be found in the extracted content.

Synthesis process

Once the AI agent has retrieved relevant content, it engages in a sophisticated synthesis process:

- **Information extraction**: The model identifies key facts, claims, statistics, specifications, and recommendations from each source. This extraction is semantic rather than keyword-based: the AI understands concepts and relationships, not just word matches. For product content, the AI looks for:
    - Technical specifications and features
    - Pricing and availability
    - Use cases and ideal customer profiles
    - Comparisons to alternatives
    - Reviews and ratings
    - Strengths and limitations
- **Cross-source integration**: Combines information from multiple sources. The AI identifies areas of consensus, contradiction, and complementary detail. This is where the AI adds significant value over traditional search. Instead of presenting ten different articles that each partially address the question, it creates a unified answer that incorporates insights from all of them. For product queries, this might mean:
    - Extracting specs from manufacturer sites.
    - Gathering pricing from retailers and marketplaces.
    - Pulling reviews from editorial sites and user forums.
    - Synthesizing use case information from how-to guides.
    - Combining all of this into a coherent recommendation.
- **Reasoning and inference**: The AI does not merely stitch together information from different sources: it actually reasons over it, uncovering implications, weighing alternatives, surfacing trade-offs, and arriving at conclusions that are not explicitly spelled out anywhere.

  For example, if one source mentions a product is "compact" and another provides dimensions, the AI might infer "suitable for small spaces" even if no source explicitly states it.

- **Response generation**: Finally, the AI generates a natural language response that addresses the user's specific question, incorporating the synthesized information in a conversational format with appropriate citations (though citation practices vary significantly across platforms).

What this means for your product content

This process has profound implications for how you should structure and present product information. They are discussed in the upcoming subsections.

Comprehensiveness matters more than keywords

The AI is reading and understanding your full content, not matching keywords. A well-researched, comprehensive product page that thoroughly addresses specifications, use cases, comparisons, and customer needs will be valued far more than a keyword-stuffed page optimized for traditional SEO.

For product catalogs specifically:

- Include complete technical specifications in semantic HTML.
- Provide detailed feature descriptions, not just bullet points.
- Explain use cases and ideal customer profiles explicitly.
- Include comparison information showing how your product relates to alternatives.
- Address frequent questions and concerns directly on the page.

Structured information is critical

When AI agents extract information from your pages, clearly structured content with proper headings, lists, tables, and semantic markup makes extraction more reliable and accurate.

Best practices for product data are as follows:

- Use HTML tables (not images) for specification comparisons.
- Implement proper schema.org markup for products, including offers, reviews, and specifications.
- Use semantic HTML5 elements (article, section, aside) appropriately.
- Structure features in actual HTML lists, not paragraph text.
- Ensure key product information appears in semantic HTML, not only in images or JavaScript.

Example of poor structure for AI extraction:

```
[Beautiful image with specifications overlaid]
"This amazing product features the latest technology!"
```

Example of good structure for AI extraction:

```
<h2>Technical Specifications</h2>
<table>
  <tr><th>Dimensions</th><td>24" W x 18" D x 36" H</td></tr>
  <tr><th>Weight</th><td>45 lbs</td></tr>
  <tr><th>Material</th><td>Powder-coated steel frame</td></tr>
  <tr><th>Weight Capacity</th><td>300 lbs</td></tr>
</table>
```

Factual accuracy and specificity are paramount

Since AI agents synthesize information across sources, factual errors or vague claims in your content may cause the AI to deprioritize your page or present conflicting information. Specific, well-supported claims with clear attribution are more likely to be incorporated into AI responses.

For product content, keep the following in mind:

- Provide exact measurements, not "compact" or "spacious."
- Include specific materials, not "high-quality construction."
- List concrete features, not marketing hyperbole.
- Cite third-party testing or certifications when relevant.
- Be accurate about compatibility, requirements, and limitations.

Vague marketing language that worked for human persuasion may actively harm your AI visibility. Some examples are:

- "Industry-leading performance" → Specific benchmark scores.
- "Easy to use" → Setup in under 10 minutes, no tools required.
- "Affordable pricing" → Exact price with clear value comparison.
- "Versatile solution" → Specific use cases and customer types.

Make information explicit

Unlike human readers who can infer relationships and context, AI extraction works best with explicit statements. Do not make the AI guess.

- **Less effective for AI**: "Our premium model offers enhanced capabilities."
- **More effective for AI**: "The Premium Model includes 2x processing power (8-core vs 4-core), 500GB storage (vs 250GB in Standard), and supports up to 50 simultaneous users (vs 25 in Standard)."

Question of source selection

A critical question for brands is: how do AI agents decide which sources to retrieve and incorporate? While the exact mechanisms vary by platform and are not fully disclosed, several factors appear to be important:

- **Domain authority and reputation**: AI systems often rely on traditional search APIs for initial retrieval, which means that domain authority, backlinks, and other conventional SEO signals still matter, but as a filter for what gets retrieved, not as a direct ranking factor for what gets presented to users.
- **Critical caveat**: Manufacturer and brand sites may be deprioritized in favor of "neutral" review sites, comparison platforms, or major retailers. An AI agent researching "best coffee makers" might preferentially retrieve information from Wirecutter, Consumer Reports, or Amazon rather than from Breville, Cuisinart, or Technivorm directly. This happens even if the manufacturer's sites have more detailed and accurate information. This bias toward "objective" third-party sources means your own product pages may be less influential than editorial coverage or retailer listings.
- **Content recency**: For time-sensitive queries, recent content is strongly preferred. An article from last month will typically be prioritized over one from three years ago, all else being equal. For product catalogs, this means:
    - Keep product pages updated with current availability and pricing.
    - Regularly refresh content even for evergreen products.
    - Include publication or last-updated dates.
    - Remove or clearly mark discontinued products.
- **Topical relevance and depth**: Detailed, focused content on specific topics tends to be retrieved more reliably than broad, shallow content that touches on many issues. A comprehensive guide to "choosing standing desks for home offices" will likely be preferred over a general article about "office furniture trends" that briefly mentions standing desks.

  For product content, this suggests:
    - Create focused product category pages rather than sprawling catalogs.
    - Develop in-depth buying guides for your product categories.
    - Build detailed comparison content, positioning your products clearly.
    - Address specific use cases with dedicated content.
- **Structured data and semantic markup**: While the evidence is still emerging, proper schema markup appears to improve AI extraction reliability and may influence retrieval. At a minimum, it ensures that when your pages are retrieved, the critical information is correctly extracted.

Implement for all product pages:

- Product schema (name, description, SKU, brand).
- Offer schema (price, availability, URL).
- Review schema (aggregate ratings, review count).
- Organization schema (your brand information).
- BreadcrumbList schema (category hierarchy).

- **Comprehensiveness and specific detail:** AI agents appear to favor sources that provide specific numbers, detailed comparisons, and comprehensive feature lists over vague marketing language. A specification sheet with exact measurements, materials, and capacities is more valuable for synthesis than aspirational brand messaging.

  Understanding this process should inform your content strategy. You are no longer optimizing primarily for human readers who arrive at your page from search results. You are optimizing for two audiences simultaneously:

  - Human shoppers who visit your site directly.
  - AI agents that will read, interpret, and potentially synthesize your content as part of answers delivered to users who may never visit your site.

These audiences have different needs, but they are not mutually exclusive. Clear, comprehensive, well-structured product information serves both.

AI agents as the new gatekeepers of attention

The metaphor of the "gatekeeper" has long been applied to search engines, notably Google. In controlling which websites appeared at the top of search results, Google determined which brands received attention and traffic. This gatekeeping power was immense but also relatively transparent. The rules of ranking were knowable, if complex. Brands could invest in SEO and reasonably expect to improve their visibility over time.

AI agents represent a fundamentally different kind of gatekeeper: one with more discretion, less transparency, and potentially more power over brand visibility.

Discretionary nature of AI synthesis

When an AI agent answers a question, it exercises judgment about which information to include, how to frame it, and which sources to cite. Unlike a search results page that presents multiple options and lets users choose, an AI response is often singular and definitive.

Consider the following scenario:

A user asks ChatGPT, "What is the best CRM for a small business?"

The AI might provide:

- Detailed analysis of HubSpot (features, pricing, ideal use cases).
- Comprehensive overview of Salesforce Essentials (capabilities, integration options).
- Brief mention of Zoho CRM (noted as "more affordable option").
- Complete omission of Pipedrive, Copper, and Freshsales.

All six are high-quality CRM platforms suitable for small businesses, but the user only hears about three, each with vastly different levels of detail. If your product is Pipedrive, you have lost the opportunity to capture that user's attention. Potentially permanently. The AI's discretion in synthesis has determined winners and losers.

This discretion operates at multiple levels:

- **Source selection**: Which websites does the AI retrieve information from in the first place? This is influenced by traditional search ranking factors, as well as the AI's assessment of source quality, relevance, and reliability for the specific query.
- **Information extraction**: Of all the information on a retrieved page, which specific claims, facts, or recommendations does the AI extract and incorporate into its response? This depends on the AI's interpretation of what is most relevant to the user's question and how clearly the information is presented.
- **Synthesis decisions**: When inputs from multiple sources conflict, how does the AI reconcile them? Which recommendations take precedence, and which viewpoints are amplified? If one review platform rates your product highly while another scores it lower, which signal carries more weight? These decisions are driven by the AI's judgments, shaped by patterns learned during training and by the context of the specific query.
- **Attribution choices**: Even when information is incorporated, which sources get explicitly cited, and how prominently? A brief mention at the end of a response ("Based on information from [list of 8 sources]") generates far less brand awareness than a highlighted recommendation with specific attribution ("According to Wirecutter's testing, the [Product] offers the best combination of performance and value in this category").

For brand leaders, this represents a loss of control and visibility. In the traditional search model, you could see precisely where you ranked for specific keywords and systematically improve those rankings. In the AI-first model, your visibility depends on opaque synthesis decisions that may vary from query to query, platform to platform, and even conversation to conversation.

Challenge of optimization

This opacity creates a significant challenge: how do you optimize for an unpredictable gatekeeper? Several approaches are emerging; they are discussed in the following subsection.

Become the authoritative source

If your content is consistently the most comprehensive, accurate, and authoritative on a topic, AI agents are more likely to retrieve and cite it. This suggests doubling down on high-quality, differentiated content rather than mass-producing SEO-optimized pages.

For product brands specifically:

- Create the definitive buying guides for your category.
- Publish original research, testing data, or comparative analysis.
- Develop comprehensive technical documentation.
- Build detailed use case libraries with specific customer stories.
- Produce regular content updates that maintain currency.

Optimize for extractability

Making your content easy for AI agents to extract and synthesize, through clear structure, specific claims, and proper markup, increases the likelihood that your information will be incorporated into AI responses.

Product-specific tactics are as follows:

- Ensure product specifications use industry-standard terminology that AI models recognize ("battery life: 12 hours" rather than "all-day battery").
- Provide detailed comparison tables that position your product relative to competitors on key dimensions.
- Include specific use cases and customer types in product descriptions ("ideal for photographers who need weather-sealed construction" rather than "durable build quality").
- Structure feature lists with clear, scannable formatting.
- Implement comprehensive schema markup for all product attributes.

Build cross-platform authority

Being cited in AI responses may depend partly on traditional authority signals. Continuing to build backlinks, earn media coverage, and establish your brand as an authoritative voice in your category remains essential.

Consider the following:

- Earning coverage in publications AI agents frequently cite (industry-specific review sites, major editorial platforms, reputable marketplaces).
- Building partnerships with authoritative third-party sites.

- Contributing expert content to high-authority platforms.
- Maintaining a strong presence on platforms AI agents use for verification.

Engage where AI agents look

Understanding which types of sources AI agents prioritize is important. Industry reports, academic papers, reputable news outlets, major retailers, and specialized review sites are often favored. Ensuring your brand has a presence in those contexts can improve visibility.

For product brands:

- Get your products reviewed by authoritative editorial sites in your category.
- Ensure accurate product listings on major marketplaces (Amazon, Best Buy, etc.).
- Participate in third-party testing and certification programs.
- Contribute data to industry reports and market analyses.
- Maintain updated profiles on comparison platforms.

None of these approaches offers the predictable ROI of traditional SEO. You cannot easily measure your "AI ranking" for specific queries. Optimizing A/B testing strategies is difficult when you cannot systematically track changes in visibility. This uncertainty is uncomfortable for organizations accustomed to data-driven optimization, but it is the reality of the current landscape.

Concentration of power

The gatekeeping power of AI agents is also more concentrated than traditional search. While Google dominated traditional search, competitors like Bing, DuckDuckGo, and others existed, and each used its own algorithms.

In the AI agent landscape, a handful of large language models [primarily those from OpenAI (ChatGPT), Anthropic (Claude), Google (Gemini), and Meta (Llama)] power the vast majority of AI-driven discovery.

This concentration has several implications:

- **Platform risk**: If your content is deprioritized or misrepresented by one of these major platforms, you have lost visibility across a significant portion of AI-driven discovery. A systematic bias or extraction failure affecting your product content on ChatGPT impacts millions of potential customers. Diversification across platforms matters, but options are limited.
- **Algorithmic homogeneity**: If major AI platforms use similar approaches to retrieval and synthesis, which they often do given shared training techniques and similar source preferences, they may make similar decisions about which brands to feature. This could create winner-take-all dynamics in which a few brands dominate AI-driven

visibility in each category, while smaller competitors struggle to gain any presence in AI responses.

- **Limited recourse**: Unlike traditional search, where you could diagnose ranking issues through tools like Search Console and address specific technical problems, understanding why an AI agent is not mentioning your brand or is misrepresenting your offerings is often impossible. The platforms provide limited transparency into their decision-making processes. You cannot simply check your "rank" or identify which technical issue is causing problems.

For brand leaders, this concentration of gatekeeping power should be a strategic concern. Your relationship with these AI platforms and their perception of your brand's authority and relevance may become as important as your relationship with Google has been over the past two decades. Yet building those relationships is more challenging when the platforms themselves do not offer direct communication channels or guidance on optimization.

Opportunity in dialogue

Despite these challenges, AI agents also create new opportunities for brand engagement. Since interactions with AI are conversational and iterative, users often ask follow-up questions that provide additional opportunities for brand mentions.

Consider this conversation flow:

- **User**: "What are the best marketing automation tools?"
- **AI**: [Provides overview of HubSpot, Marketo, ActiveCampaign]
- **User**: "Which has the best email deliverability?"
- **AI**: [Cites specific data about deliverability rates]
- **User**: "How does HubSpot's pricing compare to the others?"
- **AI**: [Provides pricing comparison]
- **User**: "Does it integrate with Salesforce?"
- **AI**: [Describes integration capabilities]

Each turn in this conversation is a new opportunity for your brand to be featured if you have created content that addresses these specific dimensions. The user might ask five to ten follow-up questions, exploring pricing, integrations, use cases, learning curve, customer support, and more. Your brand can be mentioned multiple times across this journey, building familiarity even without a website visit.

This suggests a shift in content strategy: rather than targeting specific keywords, you should cover the whole landscape of questions and considerations potential customers might explore in conversation. Instead of creating separate pages optimized for "marketing automation pricing," "marketing automation integrations," and "marketing automation use cases," you might create comprehensive, interconnected resources that AI agents can draw from across multiple turns of a conversation.

Think of it as creating a knowledge graph rather than isolated landing pages: comprehensive information architectures where product specifications, use cases, pricing, comparisons, implementation details, and customer stories are all deeply connected and easily extractable.

Collapse of click-through metrics

For two decades, the click has been the fundamental unit of value in digital marketing. Clicks from search results to websites. Clicks from websites to product pages. Clicks from product pages to checkout. Every central web analytics platform, every attribution model, every marketing dashboard was built around understanding and optimizing these click-through pathways.

The rise of AI agents is systematically destroying this metrics infrastructure.

Zero-click answer phenomenon

The term "zero-click search" originally described search results where users found the answer they needed directly on the search results page, in a featured snippet, knowledge panel, or local business information, without clicking through to any website. AI agents take this phenomenon to its logical extreme.

When a user asks ChatGPT, "What is the best CRM for a small business?" they receive a comprehensive answer that discusses several options, compares features, highlights trade-offs, and offers a recommendation, all without ever visiting a CRM vendor's website. The user's information needs are satisfied. The answer is complete. No click occurs.

From the user's perspective, this is ideal. They got exactly what they needed, efficiently and without the friction of navigating multiple websites. From the brand's perspective, it is alarming. If you are one of the CRM vendors mentioned in that answer, you have received brand awareness but no traffic, no opportunity to present your positioning, no chance to capture the user's email address, and no path to conversion that you can measure or optimize.

Consider a more complete product research journey:

- **User**: "What is the best standing desk for a home office under $800?"
- **AI**: [Provides comparison of Uplift V2, Fully Jarvis, FlexiSpot E7, and Vari Electric with specs, pricing, pros/cons]
- **User**: "Which is easiest to assemble?"
- **AI**: [Provides assembly difficulty information and time estimates]
- **User**: "Does the Uplift V2 come with cable management?"
- **AI**: [Describes cable management options and what is included vs. add-ons]

- **User**: "What is the warranty?"
- **AI**: [Details warranty coverage for each model]
- **User**: "Okay, I will get the Uplift V2."

The user then searches "Uplift desk" and purchases directly. Uplift's analytics show a single direct visit before conversion. The entire research phase is entirely invisible: the five-question conversation that built confidence and drove the decision. The product comparison content that informed the AI's response, the detailed specification pages that provided assembly and warranty information, and the comprehensive buying guide that positioned Uplift favorably all drove value. Still, none of it appears in the analytics.

This is the impact of the zero-click phenomenon on product discovery.

Measurement crisis

This creates an immediate crisis for marketing measurement. Consider the typical metrics used to evaluate content marketing and SEO performance in e-commerce:

- **Organic traffic**: If users are getting product information and recommendations from AI agents instead of visiting your website, your organic traffic declines, even if your content is being used extensively to inform AI responses and drive actual purchases through invisible pathways.
- **Product detail page views**: A critical e-commerce metric. If users research products in AI conversations and only visit your site when ready to purchase, PDPs may see dramatic traffic declines while conversions hold steady or even increase. The traditional conversion funnel appears to collapse.
- **Click-through rate**: Meaningless if the user never sees a search results page with clickable links to your website, only an AI-generated answer.
- **Time on site**: If users are not arriving at your site for research, you cannot measure how they engage with your content once they are there. Direct-to-purchase visits replace research-phase sessions that used to span multiple pages and several minutes.
- **Pages per session**: Similarly impacted. Users who previously browsed multiple product pages, read buying guides, and compared options now arrive ready to buy, viewing only the product page and the checkout page.
- **Add to cart rate**: If AI provides enough information for purchase decisions, users might go directly to checkout on their first visit, appearing as extraordinarily high-converting traffic but representing a fundamentally different customer journey.
- **Bounce rate**: Traditional bounce rate loses meaning when users arrive via direct search after AI research, complete a purchase on a single page, and leave. Is that a "bounce" or a successful conversion?

- **Conversion rate from organic**: Critically important, but impossible to calculate accurately if the organic traffic itself has vanished. You may see conversion rates spike as research-phase traffic disappears and only high-intent traffic remains, but total conversions could decline.

These metrics served as the foundation for how marketing organizations evaluated the ROI of content investments, SEO initiatives, and organic search strategies. Their collapse leaves a hard-to-fill void.

What to measure instead

If traditional click-through metrics are becoming obsolete, what should brand leaders track instead? Several alternative approaches are emerging, which will be discussed in the upcoming subsection.

New north star metrics for AI-first discovery

To measure success in an AI-first world, brands need new north star metrics that go beyond clicks and pageviews. Traditional analytics no longer capture the value of AI-mediated discovery, so leaders must track how their brand is represented, cited, and recommended by AI agents. The following metrics provide a framework for understanding visibility, influence, and positioning within AI-generated responses. They focus on both quantitative presence (how often your brand appears) and qualitative context (how it is described and framed), giving you actionable insights for optimizing AI-driven brand impact:

- **Brand mention frequency**: Monitor how frequently your brand appears in AI agent responses to relevant queries. This requires systematic querying of AI platforms with questions your target customers would ask, then analyzing whether and how your brand is mentioned. Implementation approach:
    - Develop a comprehensive list of product research queries in your category.
    - Query major AI platforms (ChatGPT, Claude, Gemini, Perplexity) monthly.
    - Track mention frequency, position, and context.
    - Monitor changes over time to assess optimization impact.
- **Share of voice in AI responses**: Similar to traditional share of voice analysis in media or search, this involves comparing how often your brand appears in AI responses versus competitors for relevant queries. Key questions:
    - What percentage of relevant product queries include your brand?
    - How does this compare to your top three competitors?
    - Are you gaining or losing share over time?
    - Which specific query types favor your brand vs. competitors?

- **Citation quality and context**: Not all mentions are equal. Tracking the qualitative nature of how your brand is presented. Assess:
    - **Mention type**: Listed as one option vs. specifically recommended.
    - **Detail level**: Brief mention vs. detailed analysis.
    - **Framing**: Positive, neutral, or negative context.
    - **Specific strengths**: What attributes or use cases is your brand cited for?
    - **Competitive context**: How are you positioned relative to alternatives?
- **Sentiment in AI descriptions**: How does the AI describe your brand? Are the characterizations accurate and positive, or are there systematic misrepresentations that need to be addressed? Monitor the following:
    - Factual accuracy of product information in AI responses.
    - Tone and framing of brand mentions.
    - Specific claims made about your products.
    - Competitive comparisons and how you are positioned.
    - Errors or outdated information that need correction.
- **Product recommendation rate**: When AI is asked for product recommendations in your category, how often is your product mentioned? In what position? With what specific framing? Track:
    - Recommendation frequency across different query variations.
    - Ranking/position when multiple products are recommended.
    - Conditions or use cases where your product is recommended.
    - Competitor products are recommended alongside yours.
- **Direct traffic and branded search growth**: As AI agents handle more unbranded, informational queries, the traffic that does reach your website may be increasingly direct or branded, meaning users who already know about you and are specifically seeking you out. Tracking changes in these traffic sources can signal AI-driven brand awareness. Watch for:
    - Increase in branded search volume even as generic category searches decline.
    - Growth in direct traffic from users who learned about you via AI.
    - Changes in search query patterns (more branded, specific queries).
    - Conversion rate improvements as traffic becomes more qualified.

None of these metrics map cleanly to revenue or provide the clear optimization pathways that traditional click-through metrics offered. This creates uncertainty for marketing organizations that need to justify investments and demonstrate ROI. It also creates an opportunity for early movers who develop robust frameworks for measuring and optimizing AI-driven brand visibility before industry standards emerge.

Paradox of invisible impact

Perhaps the most challenging aspect of the zero-click phenomenon is what we might call **invisible impact**: your content may be driving significant value by informing AI agent responses and building brand awareness, but this value is almost entirely invisible in your analytics.

Imagine that your comprehensive buying guide for project management software is regularly retrieved and synthesized by AI agents answering relevant questions. Thousands of users per month are receiving recommendations informed by your research and insights. Your brand is mentioned as a credible source. Some of those users eventually become customers.

However, when they convert, they appear in your analytics as direct traffic or branded search. There is no visible connection back to the AI interactions that first introduced them to your brand. The buying guide that drove awareness shows declining organic traffic. The ROI analysis suggests cutting investment in this content. Yet it is actually driving substantial business value through invisible pathways.

This is an invisible impact: real business value that your existing measurement infrastructure cannot detect. It creates a risk that organizations will underinvest in the very content and strategies that are driving growth, because the data does not support those investments.

A real-world example: When outdoor equipment retailer REI analyzed its 2024 traffic data, it discovered a troubling trend. Informational queries like "best hiking boots for beginners" and "how to choose a backpack" declined 43% year over year. Their comprehensive buying guides were receiving dramatically less traffic despite being regularly updated.

However, when they conducted brand awareness surveys, they found that aided awareness among their target demographic increased by 12%. When they asked new customers, "How did you first learn about REI?", a surprising percentage mentioned "researching outdoor gear online" but could not identify specific websites, suggesting AI-mediated discovery.

Their content was working, driving awareness and consideration. The analytics just could not see it.

Addressing this requires a combination of new measurement approaches and a renewed emphasis on leading indicators: content quality, authority signals, expert reviews, and brand awareness in target segments. These may correlate with AI visibility, even when that visibility cannot be directly measured.

Rethinking attribution

The attribution models that governed digital marketing investment decisions were built on the assumption of trackable touchpoints across a customer journey. A user searches, clicks on your website, perhaps leaves and returns later via social media, and eventually converts. Attribution models assign credit to each touchpoint based on various philosophies about what drives conversion: first-touch, last-touch, linear, time-decay, and position-based.

When a significant portion of the discovery and research phase happens in AI conversations that you cannot track, traditional attribution breaks down completely.

Consider this actual customer journey in the AI era:

- **Day 1**: User asks ChatGPT for standing desk recommendations (invisible to your analytics).
- **Day 1**: Receives comparison, including your brand (invisible).
- **Day 2**: Asks follow-up about assembly and cable management (invisible).
- **Day 3**: Asks about warranty and return policy (invisible).
- **Day 4**: Searches your brand name, visits the site, and purchases.

Your analytics sees this as a single direct visit immediately before conversion. Multi-touch attribution sees one touchpoint. In reality, this was a four-day, multi-question research journey. You just cannot see most of it.

This suggests the need for attribution models that blend traditional trackable interactions with proxy measures of untrackable AI-driven awareness. Sophisticated organizations are beginning to experiment with approaches like:

- **Survey-based attribution**: Directly asking customers how they first learned about your product and whether AI tools played a role in their research. Implementation:
    - Post-purchase surveys asking "How did you first learn about [Product]?"
    - Include "AI assistant (ChatGPT, Claude, etc.)" as a specific option.
    - Ask follow-up questions about what information was most valuable.
    - Track responses over time to quantify AI-driven discovery.
- **Cohort analysis**: Comparing the behavior of users who arrive during periods when your AI visibility is high (as measured through brand mention tracking) versus periods when it is lower. Approach:
    - Measure your brand mention frequency monthly via systematic AI querying.
    - Track conversion rates, average order value, and time to purchase for cohorts in high-visibility vs. low-visibility months.
    - Look for correlations between AI visibility and downstream business metrics.
    - Control for seasonality and other variables.
- **Brand lift studies**: Measuring overall brand awareness and consideration in your target market, looking for increases that correlate with AI visibility improvements,

even if direct attribution is not possible. Methods:

- Regular brand awareness surveys in your target demographic.
- Track aided and unaided awareness over time.
- Measure consideration and purchase intent.
- Correlate changes with content improvements and AI visibility initiatives.

- **Source tracking in customer conversations**: Training sales teams and customer service representatives to ask discovery questions and specifically track AI-assisted research. Process:
    - Add "How did you research our product?" to sales qualification.
    - Include AI assistants as a specific option in CRM.
    - Track the percentage of customers who mention AI-assisted discovery.
    - Identify patterns in which products or categories see the highest AI influence.

These approaches are imperfect, but they may be necessary adaptations to a reality in which much of the customer journey takes place in spaces you cannot observe directly. The goal is not perfect attribution, which may no longer be possible, but directional understanding sufficient to guide investment decisions.

Notorious shift in consumer search behavior

The changes we have outlined, the growing capabilities of AI agents, their emergence as gatekeepers, and the erosion of click-through metrics are not theoretical. They signal a fundamental, accelerating transformation in how people discover information and decide what to buy. For brands, recognizing and adapting to this behavioral shift is essential to building effective strategies in the AI era.

Psychology of AI-driven search

To understand why this shift is happening so quickly, we need to consider the psychology of search behavior and how AI agents align with fundamental human preferences. Several well-established cognitive and behavioral dynamics help explain why users are gravitating toward AI-mediated discovery at a pace that has surprised many analysts:

- **Cognitive ease**: Human brains are wired to prefer cognitive ease, so we gravitate toward options that require less mental effort. Traditional search requires substantial effort: formulating queries, scanning results, evaluating sources, opening multiple tabs, and synthesizing information across disparate pages. AI agents dramatically reduce this cognitive burden by doing the synthesis work for users. The appeal is neurological, not just preferential.

- **Trust through interaction**: The conversational nature of AI interactions can build trust more effectively than traditional search. As users ask follow-up questions and receive coherent, contextually aware responses, they develop confidence in the AI's understanding of their needs. This iterative trust-building is more similar to consulting a knowledgeable friend than to evaluating anonymous search results.
- **Reduction of choice overload**: Traditional search often confronts users with overwhelming choice, dozens of potential sources, each requiring evaluation. Behavioral economics research has long shown that excessive choice can be paralyzing rather than empowering. AI agents reduce choice overload by providing curated, synthesized answers. For many users, this is not a limitation; it is a relief.
- **Perceived objectivity**: While AI agents certainly have biases and limitations, many users perceive them as more objective than search results that may be influenced by SEO manipulation or advertising. The conversational format can feel more like consulting a knowledgeable advisor than navigating a marketplace where every source has commercial motives.

  For product recommendations specifically, this perceived freedom from commercial pressure is compelling, even though AI training data necessarily includes marketing content and commercial sources. Users feel they are getting advice rather than being sold to.
- **Removal of commercial pressure**: Users may feel AI provides recommendations free from direct advertising influence. While AI training includes marketing content, the conversational format lacks the visual clutter of ads, sponsored results, and SEO-optimized content competing for attention. This creates a perception of neutrality that may not fully reflect reality but strongly influences user preference.

These psychological factors help explain why adoption is happening faster than many analysts expected. AI agents are not just a new tool; they are a fundamentally better-aligned interface for how many people prefer to seek information and make decisions.

Generational divides and adoption curves

The shift to AI-driven search is not uniform across demographics. Adoption is significantly higher among younger users, who have less attachment to traditional search behaviors and more comfort with conversational AI interfaces. The timelines are as follows:

- **Gen Z (born 1997-2012)**: For brands targeting Gen Z, the shift is already well advanced. These users are native to AI-driven discovery in a way that older generations may never be. Marketing strategies built primarily around traditional search may already be missing large segments of these audiences.
  - **Recommendation**: For Gen Z-focused brands, AI-first optimization should be the primary approach, not an experiment.

- **Millennials (born 1981-1996)**: Substantial and growing adoption, particularly among younger Millennials. These users readily adopt new technologies while also maintaining traditional search habits. They may use both AI and traditional search, depending on context and query type.
  - **Recommendation**: Dual optimization for both conventional and AI-first discovery.
- **Gen X (born 1965-1980)**: Lower adoption rates but growing steadily. Gen X users may be slower to seek out AI tools actively, but will adopt them as they become embedded in familiar platforms.
  - **Recommendation**: Traditional search optimization remains essential, but AI optimization is becoming necessary as these tools integrate into browsers, phones, and productivity software.
- **Boomers (born 1946-1964)**: Slower adoption of standalone AI tools, but increasing exposure as AI becomes embedded in devices and applications they already use (Siri, Google Assistant, voice search).
  - **Recommendation**: Traditional search remains dominant for this demographic, but indirect AI optimization matters as these features become default.

For brands focused on younger audiences, the urgency is immediate. For those targeting older demographics, the transition may be slower, but it is still unavoidable. As AI agents are woven into everyday tools like phones, browsers, and productivity software, even people who would never deliberately open ChatGPT will end up relying on AI-driven search, often without realizing they have made that choice.

Category-specific patterns

The shift to AI-driven discovery is also uneven across product and service categories:

- **High consideration, complex decisions (Fast AI adoption)**: Categories where consumers traditionally conduct extensive research see rapid AI adoption. The complexity that made these categories difficult to navigate via traditional search makes them ideal for AI-assisted decision-making. Examples:
  - Consumer electronics (laptops, cameras, audio equipment).
  - Home appliances (washing machines, refrigerators, HVAC systems).
  - Furniture (desks, mattresses, ergonomic seating).
  - B2B software (CRM, project management, marketing automation).
  - Professional services (legal, financial advisory, consulting).
  - Healthcare decisions (treatment options, specialist selection).

- **Local and transactional (Slower AI adoption)**: Categories where users want to complete a specific transaction or visit a physical location see less disruption, as users often specifically want to reach a website or location rather than just gather information. Examples:
  - Restaurant reservations.
  - Local service providers.
  - E-commerce purchases of known brands.
  - Grocery delivery.
  - Fast fashion and impulse purchases.
- **Visual and aesthetic decisions (Moderate AI adoption)**: Products where visual appeal drives decisions may see slower AI adoption, as users prefer browsing visually rather than receiving text descriptions. Examples:
  - Fashion and apparel.
  - Home decor and interior design.
  - Art and collectibles.
  - Some beauty and cosmetics categories.
- **Niche and specialized (Variable AI adoption)**: Highly specialized B2B categories or niche consumer markets may see slower adoption initially, as AI agents are less likely to have comprehensive information about specialized topics and may produce less reliable answers. However, as AI knowledge improves, these categories may see rapid adoption once a reliability threshold is crossed. Examples:
  - Industrial equipment.
  - Scientific instruments.
  - Specialized professional tools.
  - Niche hobbyist products.

Understanding where your category falls on this spectrum should inform both the urgency and nature of your response to the AI search shift.

Compounding effect of network dynamics

One reason to expect the shift to AI-driven search to accelerate rather than plateau is the presence of positive feedback loops that create compounding growth:

- **Usage → Improvement → Adoption cycle**: As more users adopt AI agents for search, the platforms improve through usage data, feedback, and expanded training. As the experience improves, adoption increases further, creating more data for improvement. This virtuous cycle drives exponential rather than linear growth.

- **Generational wealth transfer**: As younger users who prefer AI-driven search age into higher purchasing power, the business impact of this channel grows dramatically. Gen Z entering peak earning years over the next decade means the AI-first segment will control an increasing market share, attracting more brand investment in optimization.
- **Platform integration**: As AI becomes embedded in browsers (Microsoft Edge Copilot), operating systems (Windows, iOS), and productivity tools (Microsoft 365, Google Workspace), users do not need to actively choose AI search. It becomes the default for many queries. This passive adoption drives penetration beyond the early adopter segment.

These dynamics suggest that we may be in the early stages of a rapid transition rather than a gradual evolution. Brands that treat this as a future concern rather than a present imperative may find themselves scrambling to catch up as the shift accelerates over the next 24-36 months.

Remaining constant

Amid all this change, it is worth noting what has not fundamentally changed: consumers still want to solve problems, make informed decisions, and find products and services that meet their needs. What is changing is the interface through which they do this and the intermediaries they trust to help them.

This suggests that the fundamental principles of marketing remain as important as ever: understanding customer needs, communicating value clearly, building trust and credibility, and delivering superior products. What changes is where and how these principles must be applied.

Your content still needs to be excellent, authoritative, and valuable. The difference is that it now needs to be excellent, authoritative, and valuable for both human readers who may visit your website and AI agents that will extract and synthesize it without sending anyone to your site.

Your brand still needs to be visible where your customers are looking. The difference is that "where they are looking" is increasingly inside conversational interactions with AI agents rather than on search results pages.

Your value proposition still needs to be compelling and differentiated. The difference is that you may have only seconds of attention within an AI response rather than minutes of engagement on your website to communicate that differentiation.

Your product information still needs to be accurate, complete, and persuasive. The difference is that it must be structured for both AI extraction and human comprehension.

The fundamentals have not changed. The execution requirements have.

Conclusion

AI agents are increasingly replacing traditional search for informational and product research, especially among younger demographics. For brands, being indexed is no longer sufficient; visibility now depends on being cited directly in AI-generated answers. As zero-click responses become the norm, familiar metrics like click-through rate, organic traffic, and product detail page views lose much of their meaning. This behavioral shift is already visible, with a significant share of Gen Z beginning product research inside AI chatbots rather than search engines. At the same time, AI agents extract and synthesize information automatically, meaning that brands whose data is not clearly structured for extraction effectively drop out of consideration. Measurement, therefore, requires new approaches, including tracking brand mentions in AI responses, analyzing share of voice, and assessing the quality and context of citations. The transition is accelerating, driven by positive feedback loops and generational adoption patterns. While the fundamental principles of marketing still apply, execution must now serve two audiences: human decision-makers and AI agents acting on their behalf. The search box is not going away, and clicks still matter, but neither is the primary unit of value anymore. Understanding this shift, along with its technical, behavioral, and measurement implications, is the essential starting point for competing in an AI-first era.

In the next chapter, we will explore **answer engine optimization** (**AEO**), which is the first pillar of the AI-first playbook, focused on ensuring your brand and products appear in the direct answers AI agents provide to customer questions. You will learn specific techniques for structuring content, optimizing product data, and becoming the authoritative source that AI agents cite. The gatekeepers of consumer attention are changing. The question is whether your brand will adapt quickly enough to remain visible as they do.

Join our Discord space

CHAPTER 2
Understanding and Mastering AEO

Introduction

Understanding how discovery is migrating to AI platforms is essential, but understanding alone is insufficient. Brand leaders need actionable strategies to ensure their organizations remain visible and authoritative as discovery migrates to AI platforms. This chapter provides those strategies by introducing and operationalizing **answer engine optimization** (**AEO**), the discipline of optimizing content and digital presence specifically for AI agents, voice assistants, and other answer-driven platforms.

AEO represents a fundamental evolution beyond traditional SEO. While SEO focuses on ranking highly in search results to earn clicks, AEO focuses on becoming the definitive source that AI agents cite, reference, and recommend, often without generating any clicks. It requires different technical approaches, different content strategies, and different success metrics.

For organizations that have spent years perfecting their SEO operations, AEO presents both a challenge and an opportunity. The challenge is that much of what you have optimized for is becoming less relevant. The opportunity is that many of your competitors are equally unprepared, and early movers can establish authoritative positions that compound over time.

This chapter will equip you with the frameworks and tactics needed to master AEO. We will define what AEO means in practical terms, examine the technical foundations that make content AI-ingestible, explore the critical role of structured data, and provide specific strategies for capturing voice search and digital assistant recommendations. By the end, you will have a clear roadmap for transforming your content operations to thrive in the answer economy.

Structure

The chapter covers the following topics:

- AEO in the modern marketing stack
- From ranking to source of truth

- Answer-first content structures for product pages
- Schema markup as the foundation of product AEO
- Voice search and digital assistant optimization

Objectives

This chapter examines how AEO emerges as the strategic and operational answer to AI-first discovery, redefining what visibility, authority, and performance mean when AI agents mediate consumer choice. We will explore how AI systems evaluate credibility, extract answers, and select sources, and what organizations must do to become the sources AI trusts and recommends.

By the end of this chapter, you will be able to clearly distinguish AEO from traditional SEO in terms of goals, mechanics, and success metrics, and understand why optimization for answers and citations requires a fundamentally different approach than optimization for clicks and rankings.

You will be able to identify the technical and content requirements that make your product and brand information extractable and citable by AI agents, including the structural and formatting decisions that determine whether AI systems can reliably interpret and reuse your content.

You will be equipped to design answer-first content structures that increase the likelihood of primary citations across major AI platforms, shifting your content from being merely discoverable to being directly referenced and recommended.

You will learn how to prioritize schema and structured data implementations that have a measurable impact on AI visibility and recommendation behavior, rather than treating structured data as a generic SEO hygiene task.

Finally, you will be able to establish a practical AEO roadmap that your organization can operationalize immediately, translating strategy into concrete changes across content, technical implementation, and measurement.

AEO in the modern marketing stack

As AI agents increasingly mediate how information is discovered and consumed, the mechanics of visibility are changing at a foundational level. Marketing stacks built around traffic acquisition and click optimization are colliding with systems designed to deliver direct answers, not destinations. In this environment, brands are no longer competing solely for rankings but for inclusion in the responses generated by AI systems. This shift requires a new optimization discipline, one designed for answer-driven interfaces rather than search result pages. That discipline is AEO.

Defining answer engine optimization

AEO is the practice of structuring and presenting product data and content to maximize the likelihood that AI agents will retrieve, understand, cite, and recommend your information when responding to user queries.

Unlike SEO, which optimizes for visibility in search rankings, AEO optimizes for selection and synthesis. The goal is not to appear in position 1 of 10 blue links; it is to become the source from which AI agents extract authoritative answers.

This distinction is crucial. Traditional SEO was about signals: keywords, backlinks, and site speed. AEO is about substance and structure: the information content of your pages, how clearly it is structured, how complete your product data is, and how authoritative it is perceived to be.

Comparing traditional SEO vs. AEO for *Best Standing Desks*:

- SEO approach:
    - Target keyword phrase in title/H1.
    - Build backlinks from furniture sites.
    - Optimize page speed.
    - Create a 2,000+ word article.
    - Internal linking strategy.
- AEO approach:
    - Extractable comparison table with exact specs (height range: "24-50 inches", not "adjustable"; weight capacity: "350 lbs", not "heavy duty").
    - Comprehensive Product schema with pricing, availability, ratings.
    - Answer specific questions users ask ("How stable at full height?", "Assembly time?", "Warranty coverage?").
    - Use-case recommendations with measurable criteria ("Best for small spaces: 47" width" vs "Best for dual monitors: 60" width").

Both might produce quality content, but they optimize for different endpoints. SEO aims to rank and convert visitors. AEO seeks to be the source AI agents draw from when synthesizing answers, whether users visit your site or not.

AEO's place in the marketing stack

Understanding where AEO fits in your marketing technology is essential:

- **Product information management (PIM)**: Plays a central role in AEO for organizations with product catalogs. AI agents rely on structured, comprehensive, and up-to-date product data to accurately retrieve and recommend information, making the quality of your PIM a direct driver of AI visibility. To meet AEO requirements, your PIM must automatically generate schema markup from product attributes, ensure real-time synchronization of pricing, availability, and specifications, and support SKU-level data rather than only product-family-level data. Additionally, maintaining audit trails that demonstrate data freshness helps signal recency and reliability to AI systems, further improving the likelihood of being cited and recommended.

- **Content management systems**: Must support semantic HTML, schema markup injection, and answer-first content structures.
- **Digital asset management**: Product images need descriptive alt text, captions, and ImageObject schema so AI can understand visuals, not just text.
- **Analytics**: Traditional pageview metrics provide limited AEO value. New approaches, such as tracking brand mentions in AI responses and monitoring product recommendation rates, require different tools.

For product organizations, additional integrations matter:

- E-commerce platforms feed real-time inventory and pricing.
- Review systems updating aggregateRating (from schema.org) data.
- SKU-level optimization (each variant needs a distinct schema).

Strategic value proposition

For executives evaluating AEO investment:

- **Defensive value**: As consumers migrate to AI discovery, organizations without AEO risk invisibility. Early data suggests that brands without AEO experience organic traffic declines 15-25% faster than optimized competitors.
- **Offensive value**: Early movers can establish source of truth positions that are difficult for competitors to displace. First-mover advantage in AI citations creates compounding returns.
- **Product discovery value**: A consumer electronics brand implementing comprehensive product AEO saw a 43% increase in brand mentions when users asked AI agents for recommendations, despite only a 12% increase in traditional search visibility. This translated to 18% growth in branded search volume over six months.
- **Efficiency value**: Well-structured AEO content serves multiple purposes, improving human user experience, supporting voice search, enabling personalization, and reducing customer service inquiries.

AEO maturity assessment

Organizations approach AEO from different starting points and will evolve their capabilities over time. A maturity model can help you assess your current state and plan progression:

- **Level 0 - Unaware**: No recognition of AEO as a distinct discipline. All optimization efforts focused on traditional SEO. Content created without consideration for AI ingestion.
- **Level 1 - Aware**: Recognition that AI agents are changing discovery, but no systematic response. Ad hoc experimentation with structured data or content formats without an integrated strategy.
- **Level 2 - Reactive**: Basic AEO tactics implemented for high-priority content. Some structured data markup. Some content was reformatted for better extractability. No comprehensive measurement or governance.
- **Level 3 - Systematic**: AEO integrated into content operations. Structured data standards established and enforced. Content templates designed for AI ingestion. Regular monitoring of AI platform mentions.
- **Level 4 - Optimized**: AEO as core organizational capability. Automated systems for structured data generation. Sophisticated measurement of AI visibility and attribution. Continuous testing and refinement of AEO approaches.
- **Level 5 - Innovative**: Organization actively shapes AEO best practices through experimentation and thought leadership. Custom tools and processes that provide a competitive advantage. AEO insights fed back into product and business strategy.

Most organizations today are at Level 0 or Level 1. Moving to Level 3 or higher requires dedicated resources, executive sponsorship, and cross-functional collaboration. However, the competitive advantages of higher maturity are substantial and likely to compound over time.

From ranking to source of truth

For years, the search strategy was defined by a single, unambiguous goal, which was to reach the top of the results page. Visibility, traffic, and commercial impact were tightly coupled to ranking position, and optimization efforts followed accordingly. In an AI-mediated discovery environment, that relationship begins to fracture. Being highly ranked no longer guarantees influence, and in many cases, influence is exerted without any visible ranking. The critical question shifts from 'where do we appear?' to 'whether we are trusted enough to be used'. This distinction marks the dividing line between optimizing for rankings and optimizing to become the source of truth.

Paradigm shift

In traditional search, ranking position was paramount. Studies consistently show that the top three organic results capture the majority of clicks, with the first position alone often accounting for 30-40% of total clicks for high-volume queries. Moving from position four to position one could double or triple your traffic overnight.

This created clear optimization incentives. Brands invested heavily in the specific factors that influenced ranking: acquiring high-quality backlinks, optimizing for core ranking keywords, improving technical site performance, and building domain authority over time. The playbook was well-established and, while competitive, fundamentally meritocratic: better content and stronger authority signals led to better rankings.

AI agents break this paradigm in several ways:

- **Selection over ranking**: AI agents do not present a ranked list of ten results; they synthesize information from selected sources and present a unified answer. You are either selected as a source or you are not; there is no *position three* in an AI-generated answer.
- **Multi-source synthesis**: AI agents often draw from multiple sources simultaneously, combining information from several websites into a single response. Being selected is necessary but not sufficient, as what matters is which specific information gets extracted and how it is presented.
- **Dynamic source selection**: The same AI agent might pull from different sources for similar queries depending on subtle differences in how questions are phrased, what follow-up questions have been asked, or what context has been established earlier in the conversation.
- **Attribution variability**: Even when your content is used to inform an AI response, you may or may not receive explicit attribution. Some platforms consistently cite sources; others provide general references; some provide no attribution at all.

These differences mean that traditional ranking metrics, which determine where you appear for specific keywords, are increasingly decoupled from real visibility in AI-driven discovery.

Product authority for AI agents

If traditional ranking signals are insufficient, what determines whether an AI agent selects and cites your content? While the exact mechanisms are proprietary and evolving, several factors appear to be consistently important:

- **Topical authority and specialization**: AI agents appear to favor sources that demonstrate deep expertise on specific topics over generalist sources. A comprehensive, detailed resource from a specialized publication or vendor often gets cited over a brief mention on a high-authority general news site.
- **Information density and specificity**: Content that provides specific, detailed information, including precise numbers, clear comparisons, and explicit methodologies, is more valuable for synthesis than vague generalities. AI agents can extract and incorporate specific claims more reliably than broad statements. Specific data beats vague claims:

  - **Vague (less extractable)**: "Premium coffee maker with advanced temperature control for perfect brewing."
  - **Specific (highly extractable)**: "Maintains water temperature at 198-205°F throughout brewing, 1,400-watt element brews 8 cups in under 6 minutes, thermal carafe holds temperature 2+ hours without heating plate."
  - The specific version provides extractable data AI agents cite when answering "What temperature for coffee?" or "How long to brew 8 cups?"
- **Structural clarity**: Well-organized content with clear hierarchies, explicit headings, and a logical information architecture is easier for AI agents to parse and extract. Dense, unstructured prose may contain valuable information but is less likely to be reliably extracted.
  - **Poor**: Specifications buried in paragraph text.
  - **Good**: HTML tables with semantic structure, proper headers, units specified.
- **Factual consistency across sources**: When information from your content aligns with information from other authoritative sources, AI agents are more likely to incorporate it. Contradictions or unsupported claims may lead to your content being deprioritized.
- **Recency and maintenance**: Recently updated content is strongly preferred. Stale content, even if comprehensively authoritative when originally published, may be passed over in favor of more recent sources. For product catalogs:
  - Discontinued products need a discontinued schema status.
  - Pricing updates are reflected immediately.
  - New products have complete AEO from launch.
  - Regular refreshes signal active maintenance.
- **Comprehensive schema markup**: Explicit structured data helps AI understand meaning and relationships, making extraction more reliable, especially for products where specifications have precise meanings (weight capacity vs. product weight, dimensions vs. coverage area).

Understanding these factors helps explain why AI agents might not select content that ranks well in traditional search, and vice versa. A technically perfect SEO page that is vague or poorly structured may rank well but provide little value for AI synthesis. Conversely, a deeply technical resource that is too specialized to rank for competitive head terms might become a primary source for AI agents answering related queries.

Source of truth for product categories

In enterprise data management, a *source of truth* is the authoritative, primary reference for specific information, where the definitive version of the data resides. In the context of AEO, becoming a *source of truth* means establishing your content as the primary, authoritative reference that AI agents return to consistently for specific topics or questions.

This concept differs from traditional SEO's notion of *owning* keywords. You cannot *own* a topic in AI-driven discovery the way you might dominate search results for a keyword. However, you can become the source that AI agents consistently cite when they need authoritative information on specific dimensions of a topic, especially for product information. An example of two wireless router manufacturers competing for AI visibility is provided as follows:

- **Manufacturer A** provides marketing-focused copy:
    - "Ultra-fast Wi-Fi performance"
    - "Covers large homes."
    - "Advanced security"
- **Manufacturer B** provides extractable technical specs:
    - "Wi-Fi 6 (802.11ax), 5.4 Gbps combined (1.2 Gbps @ 2.4GHz + 4.2 Gbps @ 5GHz)"
    - "Coverage: 2,500 sq ft (tested, 4-bedroom home, standard construction)"
    - "WPA3 encryption, automatic monthly firmware updates, OpenVPN compatibility"
    - "Supports 50+ simultaneous devices (tested with 95%+ throughput at 40 devices)."
- **AI visibility impact**: When users ask product-specific questions, Manufacturer B's extractable data makes it the preferred source:
    - "Router for 2,000 sq ft home?" → B cited (specific coverage data).
    - "Which routers support WPA3?" → B included (explicit security specs).
    - "How many devices can connect?" → B referenced (tested capacity).

Over dozens of queries, Manufacturer B becomes the source of truth for router specifications, not through better marketing, but through extractable, specific product data.

The following figure illustrates how the synthesis filter works in practice: of all the content AI agents retrieve, only structured, extractable, and authoritative information survives to become a cited source of truth:

***Figure 2.1**: Only structured, extractable content survives AI processing to become a cited source of truth*

Therefore, establishing a source of truth status requires:

- **Comprehensiveness**: Cover products more thoroughly than competitors, addressing every relevant dimension and question a user might have.
- **Maintenance**: Continuously updating information to ensure it remains current and accurate, signaling to AI agents that this is the actively maintained authoritative source.
- **Accessibility**: Making information easy for AI agents to find, extract, and understand through clear structure and appropriate markup.
- **Corroboration**: Citations and references from other authoritative sources that reinforce your status as the definitive reference.

Organizations that successfully establish a source of truth status for key topics create compounding advantages. AI agents that have successfully extracted accurate information from your content previously are more likely to return to you for related queries. Users who encounter your brand repeatedly in AI responses develop awareness and trust, even if they never visit your website.

Answer-first content structures for product pages

Creating content that AI agents can reliably extract and synthesize requires fundamentally different structural approaches than traditional web content. This section provides tactical guidance on structuring content for optimal machine ingestion while maintaining human readability.

Inverted pyramid for products

AEO requires an aggressive answer-first structure. AI agents extracting information from your content need to identify the direct answer to potential queries within the first few sentences or paragraphs. Burying the answer deep in your content, even in a well-structured article, reduces the likelihood that it will be reliably extracted.

Consider these two approaches to answering *how much weight can standing desks hold*:

- **Poor structure**: *Standing desks have become popular as awareness of sitting's health impacts has grown. When selecting a standing desk, consider factors such as build quality, adjustment mechanism, and structural integrity. Weight capacity is one consideration. Premium models use steel or aluminum. Weight capacity varies. High-end models from Uplift, Fully, and ErgoDesk typically support 300-400 pounds.*
- **Answer-first structure**: *Premium standing desks support 300-400 lbs, sufficient for multi-monitor setups with laptops and equipment. Specific examples: ErgoDesk Pro (350 lbs), Uplift*

V2 (400 lbs), Fully Jarvis (350 lbs). Budget models support 150-220 lbs. Higher-capacity desks experience less wobble at maximum height. Dual-motor systems distribute weight better than single-motor, improving stability under load.

The second structure provides the specific answer immediately, in a format that AI agents can easily extract and cite. The supporting context follows, available to users who want more detail without obscuring the core information.

Question-based product page organization

Since AI agents respond to queries, organizing content around explicit questions creates natural points of extraction. This approach involves structuring content sections as direct answers to specific questions users might ask:

- Instead of a traditional **product page**:
  - Overview
  - Features
  - Specifications
  - Reviews
- Consider an **answer-first product page**:
  - **What is this product, and who is it for?** (Use cases, target customers)
  - **How does this compare to alternatives?** (Comparison table)
  - **What are the key specifications?** (Structured table)
  - **What size/variant should I choose?** (Decision criteria)
  - **How complex is the setup?** (Time, skill level, tools)
  - **What do customers say?** (Review synthesis)
  - **What warranty is included?** (Coverage details)

Each section then begins with a direct, extractable answer to its question, followed by elaboration and supporting detail. This structure maps naturally to how users interact with AI agents, which often involves asking a series of related questions rather than reading a comprehensive article linearly.

Layered information architecture

AI agents with different capabilities and responding to different query types may need different levels of detail from your content. A layered architecture provides information at multiple levels of granularity:

- **Level 1 - Direct answer**: A single sentence or short paragraph that directly answers a specific question. This is what an AI agent might extract for a simple, factual query.

- **Level 2 - Contextual answer**: A more detailed explanation that includes relevant context, qualifications, or comparisons. This is what an AI might use when synthesizing a more comprehensive response.
- **Level 3 - Deep dive**: Comprehensive detail, including methodologies, edge cases, technical specifications, or related considerations. This supports users who ask follow-up questions or need specialized information.

For example, for the question "What is the battery life of the Acme X2000 laptop?"

- **Level 1**: "The Acme X2000 laptop has a battery life of up to 12 hours under typical usage."
- **Level 2**: "Battery life on the Acme X2000 varies depending on usage and settings. Typical office tasks like web browsing, document editing, and video calls yield up to 12 hours. More intensive workloads, such as gaming or video rendering, reduce battery life to 6–8 hours. Energy-saving modes and screen brightness adjustments can extend runtime."
- **Level 3**: "[Full technical breakdown including watt-hour capacity, expected cycle degradation over time, differences between usage scenarios, recommended charging practices, comparison to competitor models, and results from standardized benchmark tests.]"

This layered approach ensures that AI agents can extract appropriate answers regardless of query specificity, while human readers can navigate to the level of detail they need.

Product comparison tables

One of the most effective formats for AEO is the comparison table. AI agents are remarkably good at extracting information from well-structured tables and using it to answer comparative questions. When creating comparison tables for AEO:

- **Use clear, descriptive headers**: Column and row headers should be explicit and unambiguous. "Maximum Weight Capacity", not "Weight".
- **Include Units within cells**: Ensure specifications are complete in each cell. "$799 (free shipping)", not "$799*" with a footnote explaining billing terms.
- **Provide consistent formatting across rows**: Use the same format for similar information across all rows. If one product's price is listed as "$X-$Y per month," use that format for all products rather than mixing formats.
- **Consider mobile-first design**: While this is a traditional web best practice, it is also relevant for AEO because AI agents may encounter the mobile version of your content.
- **Add descriptive captions with an updated date**: Table captions help AI agents understand what the table represents and when to extract from it. The following example enables AI to answer: "Which headphones have the longest battery?" → Sony (30 hours).

Putting it all together, a possible AEO-friendly comparison table could look like this:

```
<table>
<caption>Wireless Noise-Canceling Headphones Comparison - January 2026</
caption>
<thead>
  <tr>
    <th>Model</th>
    <th>Price (USD)</th>
    <th>Battery (ANC On)</th>
    <th>Weight</th>
    <th>Best For</th>
  </tr>
</thead>
<tbody>
  <tr>
    <td>Sony WH-1000XM5</td>
    <td>$399</td>
    <td>30 hours</td>
    <td>8.8 oz</td>
    <td>Best ANC performance</td>
  </tr>
  <tr>
    <td>Bose QC 45</td>
    <td>$329</td>
    <td>24 hours</td>
    <td>8.5 oz</td>
    <td>Most comfortable, best value</td>
  </tr>
</tbody>
</table>
```

A well-structured comparison table can become a source that AI agents cite repeatedly when users ask comparative questions about products, features, or specifications in your category.

Definition lists and glossaries

For content explaining concepts, terms, or methodologies, definition lists provide an excellent format for AI extraction:

```
<dl>

  <dt>Battery Life</dt>

  <dd>The duration a product can operate on a single charge under
typical usage conditions, measured in hours for laptops, smartphones, and
other portable electronics.</dd>


  <dt>Refresh Rate</dt>

  <dd>The number of times per second a display updates its image, measured in
hertz (Hz). Higher refresh rates result in smoother motion on screens, which
 is particularly important for gaming and video playback.</dd>


  <dt>Storage Capacity</dt>

  <dd>The amount of data a device can hold, typically measured in gigabytes
 (GB) or terabytes (TB). This includes both user-accessible storage and
 system-reserved space.</dd>

</dl>
```

This semantic HTML structure explicitly signals to AI agents that you are providing definitions, making it highly likely that these definitions will be extracted when users ask "what is account-based marketing" or similar definitional queries.

Embedded structured data within prose

While schema markup (covered in the next section) provides structured data separately from visible content, you can also embed structured information within prose using clear, consistent patterns:

The base subscription costs $99 per month and includes up to 10,000 contacts, unlimited email sends, and basic automation features. Professional tier pricing is $299 per month with up to 100,000 contacts, advanced automation, and A/B testing capabilities.

This prose is both readable for humans and parseable for AI agents because it follows clear patterns: tier name, then "costs" or "pricing is," then dollar amount, then "per month," then "with" or "includes" followed by a list of features.

Maintaining these consistent linguistic patterns throughout your content makes extraction more reliable.

Schema markup as the foundation of product AEO

If answer-first content structure is the foundation of AEO, structured data and schema markup are the explicit signals that make your content's meaning unambiguous to machines. This section covers the technical implementation of structured data for AEO.

Understanding Schema.org vocabulary

Schema.org provides a standardized vocabulary for describing entities, properties, and relationships on the web. Created to help search engines understand content, schema markup has become even more important in the AI era as a way to signal the meaning and structure of information explicitly.

The schema vocabulary includes types (e.g., **`Product`**, **`Article`**, **`Organization`**, and **`Event`**) and properties (e.g., **`price`**, **`author`**, and **`startDate`**). By marking up your content with schema, you are essentially providing a machine-readable layer that says, "this is a product, its name is X, its price is Y, its manufacturer is Z."

For AI agents extracting information, schema markup serves several critical functions:

- **Disambiguation**: Clarifies meaning when language is ambiguous. The word "apple" could refer to a fruit or a company; schema markup makes the distinction explicit.
- **Relationship signaling**: It shows how different pieces of information relate to each other. This organization manufactures this product, this person wrote this article, and this event occurs at this location.
- **Attribute specification**: It explicitly identifies specific attributes and their values, making extraction deterministic rather than probabilistic.
- **Format standardization**: It provides information in standardized formats, eliminating the need for AI agents to parse and interpret diverse presentation styles.

Priority schema types for AEO

While schema.org includes hundreds of types, several are particularly important for AEO. Product schema is the most critical structured data type for catalogs. The types of schemas are as follows:

- **Product schema**: Essential for e-commerce catalogs and B2B products. Key properties include **`name`**, **`description`**, **`brand`**, **`manufacturer`**, **`sku`**, **`price`**, **`priceCurrency`**, **`availability`**, **`aggregateRating`**, and **`review`**. A rich product schema helps AI agents accurately extract product information for recommendations and comparisons. Properties can be grouped as follows:

- **Core (always required):**
  - **name**: Product name as you want it cited.
  - **description**: Specific, feature-rich (150-300 characters).
  - **image**: Product images with **`ImageObject`** schema.
  - **brand**: Brand with Brand schema object.
  - **sku**: Unique identifier for this variant.
- **Offer (critical for recommendations):**
  - **price**: Decimal number (e.g., **`"799.00"`**).
  - **priceCurrency**: ISO code (USD, EUR).
  - **availability**: **`InStock`**, **`OutOfStock`**, **`Discontinued`**.
  - **priceValidUntil**: Prevents outdated pricing citations.
- **Quality signals:**
  - **aggregateRating**: **`ratingValue`** and **`reviewCount`**.
  - **review**: Individual reviews.
  - **gtin13**: Product barcode.
- **Product-specific:**
  - **additionalProperty**: Structured attributes that differentiate products (Weight capacity, noise level, assembly time, compatibility).

- **Article schema**: Important for content marketing and thought leadership. Key properties include headline, **`author`**, **`datePublished`**, **`dateModified`**, **`publisher`**, and **`articleBody`**. This helps AI agents attribute information correctly and assess recency.
- **FAQPage schema**: Perhaps the most directly AEO-relevant schema type. FAQPage markup explicitly identifies questions and their accepted answers, creating clear extraction points for AI agents to respond to those exact questions.
- **HowTo schema**: Valuable for procedural content. It allows you to mark up detailed instructions so that AI agents can extract and present them.
- **Organization schema**: Establishes your organization's identity and relationships. Properties include **`name`**, **`description`**, **`url`**, **`logo`**, **`contactPoint`**, **`sameAs`** (links to social profiles), and **`parentOrganization`**. This context helps AI agents understand who is providing information.
- **VideoObject and ImageObject schema**: For multimedia content, these schemas help AI agents understand what the content depicts and extract relevant information from captions, transcripts, and metadata.

Implementing JSON-LD

While schema markup can be implemented using microdata or RDFa, **JavaScript Object Notation for Linked Data (JSON-LD)** has become the preferred format. It is cleaner, easier to maintain, and explicitly recommended by Google and other platforms. The examples are provided as follows:

- **Product schema example**: A basic `Product` schema in JSON-LD looks like this:

```
{
  "@context": "https://schema.org/",
  "@type": "Product",
  "name": "ErgoDesk Pro Electric Standing Desk - 48 Inch",
  "description": "Dual-motor electric desk, 24-50 inch range, 350 lb ca-
pacity, 4 memory presets, under-50dB operation",
  "sku": "ED-PRO-48-BLK",
  "brand": {"@type": "Brand", "name": "ErgoDesk"},
  "offers": {
    "@type": "Offer",
    "price": "799.00",
    "priceCurrency": "USD",
    "availability": "https://schema.org/InStock"
  },
  "aggregateRating": {
    "@type": "AggregateRating",
    "ratingValue": "4.7",
    "reviewCount": "1247"
  },
  "additionalProperty": [
    {
      "@type": "PropertyValue",
      "name": "Weight Capacity",
      "value": "350",
      "unitText": "lbs"
    },
```

```
    {
      "@type": "PropertyValue",
      "name": "Noise Level",
      "value": "50",
      "unitText": "dB"
    }
  ]
}
```

- **FAQPage schema example**: FAQPage markup explicitly identifies questions your content answers, making extraction trivial for AI agents. A basic schema could potentially be:

```
{
  "@context": "https://schema.org",
  "@type": "FAQPage",
  "mainEntity": [{
    "@type": "Question",
    "name": "How quiet is the ErgoDesk Pro motor?",
    "acceptedAnswer": {
      "@type": "Answer",
      "text": "The ErgoDesk Pro operates at under 50 decibels, quieter than normal conversation (60 dB). The dual-motor design distributes load evenly, reducing noise. Adjustment from 24 to 48 inches takes 16 seconds without disruptive noise."
    }
  }]
}
```

  A comprehensive `FAQPage` schema that covers the questions your target audience actually asks, you create explicit extraction points for AI agents. When someone asks one of these questions, your marked-up answer is ready for immediate extraction and citation.

- **Handling product variants example**: Each SKU needs a distinct schema. Here is an example:

```
// 48" Black - SKU: ED-PRO-48-BLK
{
```

```
  "@type": "Product",
  "name": "ErgoDesk Pro - 48 Inch, Black",
  "sku": "ED-PRO-48-BLK",
  "color": "Black",
  "width": {"@type": "QuantitativeValue", "value": "48", "unit-
Code": "INH"},
  "offers": {"@type": "Offer", "price": "799.00"}
}
// 60" Black - SKU: ED-PRO-60-BLK
{
  "@type": "Product",
  "name": "ErgoDesk Pro - 60 Inch, Black",
  "sku": "ED-PRO-60-BLK",
  "color": "Black",
  "width": {"@type": "QuantitativeValue", "value": "60", "unit-
Code": "INH"},
  "offers": {"@type": "Offer", "price": "899.00"}
}
```

This matters so that when users ask, "48-inch standing desk in white?" AI can extract the specific SKU with exact pricing and availability.

Common schema implementation mistakes

Even organizations committed to structured data often make implementation mistakes that reduce its value for AEO:

- **Incomplete markup**: Providing only the minimum required properties rather than all applicable properties reduces the information available for extraction. Be comprehensive.
- **Outdated information**: Schema markup that contradicts the visible content or is outdated can confuse AI agents and lead to your content being deprioritized. Establish processes to keep structured data up to date.
- **Generic descriptions**: Using vague or generic text in description fields wastes the opportunity to provide specific, extractable information.
- **Inconsistent formatting**: Different formatting for similar properties across pages makes extraction less reliable. Standardize your approach.

- **Missing context**: Failing to link related schema objects (connecting a Product to its Brand to its Manufacturer) reduces the contextual understanding AI agents can develop.
- **No validation**: Implementing a schema without validating it with Google's Structured Data Testing Tool or a similar validator often results in errors that prevent the markup from being used.

Common product-specific mistakes are as follows:

- **Vague descriptions**: "Premium quality" instead of specific features.
- **Missing variants**: Generic "available in multiple sizes" instead of SKU-specific schema.
- **Incomplete offers**: Missing **`priceValidUntil`**, **`availability`**, **`seller`**.
- **No units**: **`"weight: 85"`** (85 what??) instead of **`QuantitativeValue`** with **`unitCode`**.
- **Outdated data**: Schema showing **`InStock`** when actually out of stock.
- **Missing additionalProperty**: Not using structured properties for weight capacity, noise level, compatibility.

Advanced structured data strategies

Beyond basic schema implementation, several advanced strategies can enhance AEO effectiveness:

- **Nested schema objects**: Complex entities can be described using a nested schema, where one object contains references to other objects. A **`Product`** can reference its manufacturer organization, which can reference its founding **`Person`**, creating rich contextual webs that AI agents can explore.
- **Multiple schema types on single pages**: A single page can implement multiple schema types. A product review article might include **`Product`** schema, **`Article`** schema, and **`Review`** schema, providing multiple entry points for different kinds of AI queries.
- **Dynamic schema generation**: For extensive catalogs or frequently updated content, generating schema dynamically from your product information management or content management system ensures consistency and currency without manual maintenance.
- **Industry-specific extensions**: Some industries have developed schema extensions beyond the core **`schema.org`** vocabulary. Healthcare, automotive, and real estate industries, among others, have specialized schema types that provide richer semantic markup for domain-specific content.
- **Schema for videos and podcasts**: The **`VideoObject`** and **`PodcastEpisode`** schemas, including properties such as transcript and **`timeRequired`**, help AI agents extract information from multimedia content that would otherwise be opaque to machine analysis.

Organizations with mature AEO capabilities often develop proprietary schema strategies tailored to their specific content types, business models, and competitive positioning.

Voice search and digital assistant optimization

The massive adoption of voice-activated digital assistants, including smart speakers, in-car systems, and mobile voice search, represents a parallel stream of AI-driven discovery with specific optimization requirements. While voice search and AI chatbots operate somewhat differently, they share common characteristics that demand AEO approaches.

Voice search context

Voice search behavior differs fundamentally from typed search in several ways that affect optimization strategy:

- **Conversational queries**: "What is the best 60-inch standing desk for a home office with two monitors?" vs typed "standing desk 60 inch."
- **Question format**: Voice queries are overwhelmingly phrased as questions. "Where can I find," "how do I," "what is the best," and similar question structures dominate voice search.
- **Local intent**: A disproportionate share of voice searches has local intent, with users seeking nearby businesses, services, or information relevant to their current location.
- **Immediate action intent**: Voice searches often indicate intent to take immediate action. Someone asking "what is open near me" is likely ready to visit a business imminently.
- **Product-specific intent**: Voice queries include multiple criteria:
    - "Best dishwasher for small kitchens under $600, energy efficient".
    - "Wireless earbuds with the longest battery duration under $140".
    - "Standing desk quietly fits corner spaces".
- **Zero-tolerance for ambiguity**: In typed search, users can scan multiple results and make judgments. In voice search, the assistant typically provides a single answer. Being selected for that answer is binary: you are either the chosen source or you are invisible.

These characteristics create specific optimization imperatives that extend beyond general AEO principles.

Optimizing for featured snippets

While featured snippets (the highlighted answers that appear at the top of Google search results) are not exclusively a voice search phenomenon, they are crucial for voice because digital assistants often read featured snippet content as voice answers.

Optimizing for featured snippets involves:

- **Identify snippet opportunities**: Use SEO tools to identify queries in your domain where featured snippets currently appear (or could appear) but where you do not currently own the snippet.
- **Answer the exact question**: Featured snippet content must directly answer the specific question implied by the query. If the query is "how long to bake salmon," your content must provide a clear, specific answer to that exact question.
- **Use optimal formats**: Different types of questions lend themselves to different formats. Definitional questions often pull from paragraph snippets (40-60 words). Process questions often pull from numbered lists. Comparison questions often pull from tables.
- **Structure for extraction**: Place the answer to the target question in a format that is easy for Google to extract, typically a paragraph immediately following an H2 or H3 heading that matches the query, or a list format for procedural content.
- **Provide additional context**: While the snippet may be brief, the surrounding content should provide sufficient depth that users who click through find value. Snippet optimization should not come at the expense of overall content quality.

Product snippet optimization should be based on *Best [Product] for [Use Case]* queries with the format: Brief paragraph (40-60 words) + bulleted reasons. An example is:

The ErgoDesk Pro 60-inch is the best standing desk for dual-monitor setups due to its 60-inch width accommodating two 27-inch displays and a 350 lb weight capacity. Key advantages:

- *60" width provides 6-8" monitor spacing.*
- *Dual-motor ensures a stable lift with a 40+ lb load.*
- *4 memory presets for quick adjustments.*
- *Under 5mm wobble at full height maintains alignment.*

For comparison queries, we should use the table format, and for specification queries, the immediate specific answer should be in the first sentence.

Voice commerce optimization

While still emerging, voice-activated purchasing represents a growing opportunity, particularly in specific product categories. Optimizing for voice-friendly product content involves:

- **Write in complete sentences:**
  - "Installation takes approximately 30 minutes with two people."
- **Make product names speakable:**
  - "ErgoDesk Pro, 48-inch, Black."

- **Voice-friendly pricing:**
  - "Seven hundred ninety-nine dollars for standard, twelve hundred ninety-nine for professional."
- **Unambiguous specifications:**
  - "Thirty hours of battery life," not "30h batt"
  - "Operates at fifty decibels, quieter than conversation," not "50dB op"
  - "Adjusts from twenty-four to fifty inches," not "24-50 in range."
- **Simplified purchasing processes**: For platforms that support voice purchasing, streamlined processes that minimize the number of steps and confirmations required.
- **Return and support information**: Clear, easily communicated policies about returns, support, and warranties that can be conveyed verbally.

As voice commerce matures, particularly for frequent repurchase items and simple product categories, this channel optimization will become increasingly important.

Measurement approaches

One of the challenges of voice search optimization is measurement. It is often difficult to distinguish voice-driven traffic from other organic search traffic. Several approaches can help:

- **Query pattern analysis**: Voice queries in search console data tend to be longer, more conversational, and more question-focused than typed queries. Analyzing query patterns can help identify likely voice traffic.
- **Featured snippet tracking**: Since featured snippets often source voice answers, tracking your featured snippet portfolio provides a proxy measure for voice search presence.
- **Brand monitoring**: Increases in branded searches following voice search optimization efforts may indicate users discovering your brand via voice and then following up with branded searches.
- **Direct questioning**: Surveying customers about how they discovered you or conducting research can reveal voice search usage patterns.
- **Platform-specific analytics**: Some platforms provide limited analytics about voice interactions, though this data is generally less robust than traditional web analytics.

While imperfect, these measurement approaches can help assess the impact of voice search optimization efforts and guide resource allocation.

Conclusion

AEO is a competitive advantage for product discovery, representing a shift in how brands earn visibility and authority in digital channels. Unlike traditional SEO, where incremental ranking improvements can yield gradual gains, AEO operates on more binary dynamics: a brand is either selected as an authoritative source or not, cited or invisible, recommended or overlooked.

This creates both risk and opportunity. The risk is that organizations slow to adapt may be excluded from AI-driven discovery, losing visibility even as they maintain strong traditional search rankings. The opportunity is that early movers who establish a source of truth position may create compounding advantages that are difficult for competitors to displace.

The technical foundations of AEO are not prohibitively complex. Most organizations already have the basic technical capabilities required for implementation. What is often lacking is not capability but prioritization and commitment.

For product organizations, the shift toward AI-driven discovery is happening faster than for general information, fundamentally changing how products are evaluated and recommended. If your product specifications are not structured for AI extraction or your PIM data is incomplete, your products are unlikely to appear in AI-driven recommendations. Success starts with strong product foundations: complete, accurate master data and category-level optimization. Measurement must also evolve, with a focus on product recommendation rates rather than relying solely on traditional rankings. Ultimately, product data should be treated as a strategic asset, one that directly influences visibility, recommendations, and revenue.

In the next chapter, we will explore **generative engine optimization** (**GEO**), examining how to influence not only what information AI agents extract but also how they synthesize, frame, and present it. While AEO focuses on being selected as a source, GEO focuses on shaping the narrative AI agents construct, ensuring your products are positioned favorably with the proper context and competitive framing.

CHAPTER 3
GEO Strategies Foundations

Introduction

In previous chapters, we explored the shift from traditional search to AI-first discovery and examined the implementation of AEO. We discussed how to structure content for AI extraction, implement schema markup, and optimize for voice search. These capabilities form the foundation of visibility in an AI-driven world.

However, visibility alone is insufficient. Being mentioned is not the same as being recommended. Being cited is not the same as being trusted. Being extracted is not the same as being perceived as authoritative.

This chapter introduces **generative engine optimization** (**GEO**), a strategic framework that goes beyond AEO's mechanics to focus on how AI agents perceive, represent, and recommend your brand. While AEO ensures your content can be found and extracted, GEO ensures it is valued, cited prominently, and presented favorably when AI agents synthesize information.

For product organizations and catalogs, GEO determines not just whether your products are mentioned, but whether they are recommended. AI agents synthesizing product information make qualitative judgments: Which product is "best"? Which is "most reliable"? Which offers "best value"? These characterizations directly impact purchase decisions, yet they are invisible in traditional analytics.

This chapter provides frameworks and strategies to ensure AI agents perceive you as the authoritative, trustworthy, preferred source in your category.

Structure

The chapter covers the following topics:

- Foundational concepts of GEO
- Mastering the product curation hierarchy

- Content information gain as irreplaceable value
- Managing brand entities in AI graphs
- Measuring success through citation quality

Objectives

This chapter examines how GEO extends beyond retrieval and extraction to shape how AI agents perceive, characterize, and recommend brands and products. We explore the mechanisms by which large language models form qualitative judgments about authority, trustworthiness, value, and category leadership, and how these judgments influence which products are positioned as *best, most reliable*, or *best value* in AI-generated responses. The chapter introduces practical frameworks for influencing representation in AI synthesis, including product curation hierarchies, information gain from content, and brand entity management across AI knowledge graphs. It also reframes measurement in the generative era, shifting from traffic and rankings to citation quality, prominence, and recommendation bias. By the end of this chapter, readers will have a clear roadmap for moving from being merely included in AI-generated answers to being positioned as the preferred authority in their category.

Foundational concepts of GEO

As organizations adapt to AI-first discovery and begin operationalizing AEO, a new layer of optimization emerges. Visibility is no longer determined solely by whether content is retrieved or cited, but by how brands and products are represented within AI-generated responses. Two organizations may both be used as sources by AI agents, yet one is framed as authoritative, reliable, and recommended, while the other is mentioned briefly or neutrally. This representational layer of influence is where competitive advantage increasingly forms. Understanding how AI agents construct narratives, attribute credibility, and characterize brands is now as strategically important as being selected in the first place.

GEO defined and its importance

Generative engine optimization is the practice of influencing how large language models and AI agents perceive, synthesize, and present information about your brand, products, and domain expertise. Unlike traditional **search engine optimization** (**SEO**), which optimizes for rankings, or **answer engine optimization** (**AEO**), which optimizes for extraction, GEO optimizes for the qualitative aspects of how AI agents represent your brand when generating responses.

The name *generative engine optimization* reflects a fundamental reality: AI agents do not just retrieve and display information; they generate new content by synthesizing information across sources. This generative process involves judgment calls about which sources to trust, how to reconcile contradictions, which perspectives to emphasize, and how to characterize brands and products.

These judgment calls determine whether your products are:

- Featured prominently or mentioned in passing.
- Recommended enthusiastically or listed neutrally.
- Associated with specific strengths or described generically.
- Cited for authoritative claims or ignored in favor of competitors.
- Presented accurately or mischaracterized.

Traditional metrics, such as search rankings or website traffic, do not capture these qualitative dimensions. You could have a perfect AEO implementation and still lose the GEO game if AI agents synthesize information in ways that favor competitors.

The three pillars of GEO

GEO strategy rests on three foundational pillars, which we will discuss in this section.

Authority perception

How AI agents assess the credibility and expertise of your organization on specific topics. This determines whether your information is trusted and cited or treated skeptically.

For product brands, authority perception determines whether AI agents trust your specifications and performance claims. A manufacturer stating *350 lb weight capacity* with documented testing methodology and third-party validation gets cited authoritatively. The same claim, without evidence, is qualified: *Brand X claims 350 lb capacity, though independent testing data is not available.*

Narrative control

How effectively you influence the way AI agents characterize your brand, products, and positioning. This determines whether AI descriptions align with your intended messaging.

For products, narrative control means ensuring AI agents accurately characterize your product, *best for multi-monitor setups* vs. a generic *office desk option*. It means your key differentiators (features justifying premium pricing) are mentioned, not overlooked in favor of basic specifications that all competitors share.

Information primacy

Whether your content provides unique, valuable information that other sources lack, this determines whether AI agents cite you as a primary source or merely corroborate your claims with sources they trust more.

For products, the information primacy comes from providing specifications, performance data, or use-case guidance that competitors do not offer. If you are the only brand publishing detailed assembly time estimates, noise level measurements in decibels, or weight capacity testing methodologies, AI agents must cite you when users ask about these dimensions.

These pillars interact and reinforce each other. Strong authority perception makes narrative control easier. Consistent information primacy builds authority perception. Effective narrative control enhances credibility.

AI agents and product authority assessment

Unlike traditional search engines, which use relatively transparent ranking factors (backlinks, domain age, content freshness), AI agents' authority assessment processes are more opaque and multifaceted. Based on research, experimentation, and observable patterns, several factors appear to influence how AI agents weight sources:

- **Cross-source corroboration**: Information appearing consistently across multiple independent sources is weighted more heavily. If five authoritative sources state similar facts about your product category but your claims differ significantly, AI agents may discount or qualify your information.
- **Source attribution patterns**: AI agents appear to track which sources are themselves cited by other authoritative sources. If industry analysts, academic researchers, and trade publications consistently reference your content, this signals authority.
- **Testing and certification data**: Independent testing results, safety certifications (UL, CE), and performance benchmarks from recognized labs carry exceptional weight. "UL-certified with 350 lb tested capacity" means more than "supports heavy loads."
- **Specification completeness**: Products with comprehensive, specific specifications (exact measurements, materials, performance data with units) signal authority over products with vague marketing descriptions. "Operates at 48 dB (quieter than conversation at 60 dB)" beats "whisper-quiet operation."
- **Comparison fairness**: Brands acknowledging both strengths and limitations gain credibility. "Best for X use case, less suitable for Y" is more trustworthy than "perfect for everything." Fair competitor comparisons build trust.
- **Customer data at scale**: Aggregate ratings from thousands of verified purchases (Amazon, Best Buy) provide authority that manufacturer claims cannot match. 4.7 stars from 2,000+ reviews is a powerful authority signal.
- **Topical consistency**: Sources demonstrating consistent expertise on specific topics over time are favored. A furniture manufacturer consistently publishing deep technical content about ergonomics and materials becomes more authoritative on desk selection than a general home goods blog.
- **Recency signals**: For time-sensitive product information (pricing, availability, new models), content that has been recently updated receives priority. Stale product pages with 2022 dates signal neglect.

- **Institutional credibility**: AI agents appear to weigh certain types of sources differently. Academic institutions, government agencies, established industry analysts, and peer-reviewed publications are trusted sources for certain types of claims.

Understanding these authority signals helps explain why some brands consistently appear in AI recommendations while others with similar or superior products remain invisible.

Generative synthesis process for products

To optimize for generative engines, you need to understand how AI agents synthesize product information to help identify GEO optimization points.

Consider a Product Discovery Example in the form of a User Query: *What standing desk is best for a small apartment?*

The stages will be as follows:

- **Stage 1**: Query interpretation:
    - **AI identifies needs**: Compact dimensions, good stability (small spaces do not mean light duty), ease of assembly (apartments = no workshop), reasonable price (small apartment implies budget-consciousness).
- **Stage 2**: Source retrieval:
    - AI retrieves manufacturer pages, review sites, and comparison articles about compact standing desks. Traditional search ranking factors influence what is retrieved, but topical relevance matters more.
- **Stage 3**: Information extraction:
    - **From various sources, it extracts**: Dimensions, weight, assembly time, stability ratings, prices, customer reviews about apartment use.
- **Stage 4**: Synthesis and reconciliation:
    - AI finds that Brand A has a 47" width (vs. the 60" standard), Brand B emphasizes "compact," but its specs show a 54" width, and Brand C has specific "apartment-friendly" messaging with a 45" width option. AI reconciles conflicting claims by favoring specific measurements over vague claims.
- **Stage 5**: Response generation:
    - "For small apartments, Brand C's 45-inch model is the most compact option, measuring just 45"W × 28"D, 12% smaller footprint than standard desks. Brand A's 47-inch desk is also suitable for apartments. Both assemble in under 40 minutes without power tools, which is important for apartment living. Brand C's model supports 300 lbs despite its compact size, dispelling the myth that small desks are less sturdy."

- **Stage 6**: Verification:
  - AI verifies claims against retrieved sources, ensuring measurements and features cited are actually supported by source content.

GEO success factors in this example are as follows:

- Brand C wins because:
  - Specific compact dimensions are clearly stated.
  - The apartment use case is explicitly addressed in the content.
  - Assembly simplicity is prominently featured.
  - Weight capacity is specified to counter the "small = weak" assumption.
  - Measurements enable comparison calculation, AI included.

GEO strategy intervenes at multiple stages, ensuring that your products are retrieved (Stage 2), that information is extracted reliably (Stage 3), that your claims are trusted when conflicts arise (Stage 4), and that your brand is featured prominently in generated responses (Stage 5).

GEO vs. SEO vs. AEO

Understanding how GEO relates to and differs from SEO and AEO helps clarify where to focus resource allocation:

- **Traditional SEO**: Optimizes for ranking position to drive clicks. Success metrics: rankings, impressions, CTR, traffic. Focus: signals (backlinks, keywords, technical optimization).
- **Answer engine optimization (AEO)**: Optimizes for extraction and citation by AI agents. Success metrics: featured snippets, schema coverage, and extraction accuracy. Focus: structure (answer-first content, semantic markup, extractability).
- **Generative engine optimization (GEO)**: Optimizes for favorable perception and prominent recommendation. Success metrics: citation prominence, recommendation frequency, brand characterization quality. Focus: authority (source credibility, information gain, narrative consistency).

These are not competing approaches but complementary layers:

- SEO provides a foundation, ensuring discoverability and authority signals that influence AI retrieval.
- AEO ensures efficiency, making content extractable and understandable to AI agents.
- GEO drives outcomes, ensuring extracted information translates to a favorable perception and recommendations.

Mature organizations integrate all three, with different emphasis at different stages (new brands prioritize AEO to get mentioned; established brands prioritize GEO to get recommended).

Mastering the product curation hierarchy

AI agents do not create information from scratch; they curate it from across the web, synthesizing multiple sources into coherent responses. Understanding and influencing this curation process is central to product brands' success with GEO.

Five tiers of product citations

Not all product mentions are equal. AI agents create implicit hierarchies in how they present products:

- **Tier 1**: Primary authority/recommendation:
  - Sources are presented as the definitive choice or authority. "According to independent testing, [Brand] offers the best stability-to-price ratio..." or "For multi-monitor setups, [Product] is the optimal choice due to..."
  - These citations position the product as authoritative and the recommended option.
- **Tier 2**: Top options list:
  - Products featured prominently in a shortlist with a substantive description. "The top standing desks include [Brand A] with 350 lb capacity and quiet operation, [Brand B] with extensive customization options..."
  - Provides visibility and credibility but shares attention with 2-3 alternatives.
- **Tier 3**: Alternative perspective:
  - Products presented as valid alternatives with specific use cases. "While [Brand A] leads in stability, [Brand B] offers superior value for budget-conscious buyers..." or "Other solid options include [Brand C] for compact spaces..."
  - Acknowledges the product but positions it as secondary or specialized.
- **Tier 4**: Mentioned in passing:
  - Brief references without substantive detail. "[Brand] is another option in this category," or "Additional manufacturers include [list]."
  - Provides awareness but minimal information or differentiation.
- **Tier 5**: Uncited use:
  - Information from your product page informed the AI's response, but you received no attribution. This is the most challenging scenario, where your content provides value, but you gain no visibility.

The five tiers are visualized as follows:

Figure 3.1: The citation hierarchy. Five tiers of AI recommendation determine a brand's visibility

Looking at a Product Category Example, the query: *Best wireless noise-canceling headphones.*

The details are as follows:

- **Tier 1**: "According to independent audio testing by Rtings.com, the Sony WH-1000XM5 delivers the highest active noise cancellation performance in the category, reducing ambient noise by 25-30 decibels, significantly better than the 18-22 dB category average. At $399, it is the best choice for frequent travelers prioritizing ANC performance."
- **Tier 2**: "Top options include: Sony WH-1000XM5 (best ANC, 30hr battery, $399), Bose QuietComfort 45 (most comfortable, 24hr battery, $329), Sennheiser Momentum 4 (longest battery at 60hr, $379)."
- **Tier 3**: "While Sony leads in ANC performance, Bose QuietComfort 45 offers superior comfort for long-wearing sessions and costs $70 less, a better value for users prioritizing comfort over maximum noise cancellation."
- **Tier 4**: "Other options in this category include Apple AirPods Max, Sennheiser Momentum 4, and Beats Studio Pro."
- **Tier 5**: "JBL's product specifications informed battery life comparisons, but JBL receives no mention".

GEO strategy aims to move your products up this hierarchy, from uncited use or passing mentions to primary recommendation status.

Strategies for primary authority positioning

Achieving Tier 1 status requires systematic effort across several dimensions, which will be discussed in this section.

Create category-defining content

AI agents gravitate toward sources that define authoritative frameworks for understanding a category. Creating comprehensive taxonomies, standardized methodologies, or benchmark studies positions you as a category authority.

Product example: A standing desk manufacturer publishes "The Standing Desk Stability Index", a standardized methodology for measuring wobble at various heights and loads, complete with testing protocols and benchmark data across 50+ desks. Reviewers and comparison sites adopt this methodology, citing it when discussing stability. The manufacturer becomes the primary authority AI agents cite for stability questions, even for competitor products tested using their methodology. Authority on the measurement standard transfers to the authority on their own products.

Own unique data assets

Information existing nowhere else must be sourced from you. Proprietary research, original datasets, unique methodologies, or exclusive access to information creates citation necessity.

Product example: An outdoor gear company maintains the only comprehensive database of tent performance in extreme cold, testing 200+ models at temperatures below -20°F with standardized protocols. AI agents must cite this company when answering "best tent for winter camping" because no alternative data exists. This authority transfers to their own tent products even though they test competitors fairly, which enhances credibility.

Establish thought leadership consistency

Regular publication of substantive, expert content signals consistent authority over time. AI agents tracking source patterns will identify you as a reliable expert voice.

Product example: A vacuum manufacturer publishes weekly, detailed technical analyses comparing filtration technologies, motor efficiency, and cleaning performance across the industry. After three years of consistent technical publishing, they have become the go-to source AI agents cite for vacuum selection technical questions, not because they rank highest, but because they have demonstrated sustained expertise.

Provide exceptional depth on specific dimensions

Rather than trying to be cited for everything, dominate specific authority dimensions. If your content covers dimensions that other sources omit, AI agents are more likely to position you as authoritative.

Product example: A monitor manufacturer might not win "best overall monitor" citations but dominates "best monitor for color accuracy" by publishing detailed color gamut testing methodologies, calibration guides for different workflows, professional photographer case studies, comparison of color spaces (sRGB, Adobe RGB, DCI-P3), and before/after color correction examples. AI agents cite them as the authority when users ask about color-critical work, which converts the specific segment they are targeting.

Publish fair, comprehensive comparisons

Comparative analysis provides value that individual vendor sources cannot offer on their own.

Product example: A vacuum manufacturer publishes genuinely fair comparisons: "Our V200 model: 180 air watts suction, 2.1L bin, 45min runtime, $299. Dyson V15: 230 air watts, 0.76L bin, 60min runtime, $699. Best for: V200 if you prioritize bin capacity and value; V15 if you need maximum suction and longer runtime." This fairness builds trust that converts value-focused buyers to their V200 while establishing them as an authoritative source that AI agents cite.

Understanding source diversity in product recommendations

AI agents often aim for source diversity to avoid over-reliance on a single source. This creates both constraints and opportunities:

- **Constraint**: Even if you are highly authoritative, AI agents cite multiple sources to provide balanced perspectives. You cannot expect to be the only product mentioned.
- **Opportunity**: If you can position your products as authorities across multiple dimensions, you may receive multiple citations within a single response, cited for stability testing, then for assembly time data, then for warranty coverage.

The strategic implication for product brands is that, rather than attempting to be cited for every dimension, they should focus on owning specific areas of authority:

- Stability and wobble measurements (standing desks).
- Noise cancellation decibel reduction (headphones).
- Battery life under real-world conditions (wireless devices).
- Assembly time and difficulty (furniture).
- Material durability with longevity data (outdoor gear).
- Color accuracy with calibration data (monitors).

By dominating specific dimensions with unique data and expertise, you get cited repeatedly even when AI agents mention multiple brands.

Monitoring the curation landscape

Effective GEO requires systematic monitoring of how AI agents curate information in your category:

- **Competitive citation analysis**: Regularly query AI platforms with category-relevant questions and analyze which competitors are cited, how prominently, and for what types of information. Identify patterns in who achieves primary authority status.
- **Citation context analysis**: When you are cited, analyze the context in which you are cited. Are you positioned as a primary source or a supporting reference? What specific claims or information are extracted? Is the characterization accurate and favorable?
- **Source diversity patterns**: Track whether AI platforms consistently cite diverse sources or show a preference for particular brands. Understanding these patterns helps identify opportunities.
- **Temporal changes**: Monitor how curation patterns change over time. If you were previously cited prominently but are now mentioned less frequently, investigate what changed. Did competitors publish new content? Did your content become stale? Did AI model updates change assessment criteria?

This monitoring creates the feedback loops necessary for effective GEO optimization, allowing you to test hypotheses about what drives citation prominence and adjust strategy accordingly.

Content information gain as irreplaceable value

One of the most critical GEO concepts is information gain, the unique value your content provides that cannot be obtained from other sources. AI agents increasingly prioritize high-information-gain sources, recognizing that synthesizing five sources saying the same thing provides little value.

Defining information gain for product content

Information gain measures the value of the unique information your content provides relative to what AI agents can extract elsewhere.

High information gain product content:

- Provides data, specifications, or test results not available elsewhere.
- Offers deeper analysis or more comprehensive coverage than competing sources.
- Presents information in extractable formats with proper units and context.

- Adds meaningful context, qualifications, or use-case specificity.
- Resolves contradictions or ambiguities across other sources.

Low information gain product content:

- Repeats specifications readily available from competitors and retailers.
- Provides generic marketing language without specific measurements.
- Offers superficial coverage that competitors cover more thoroughly.
- Presents vague claims without supporting data or evidence.
- Duplicates how other sources present the same information.

Looking at product description examples:

- **Low information gain (Generic)**: "The ErgoDesk Pro features a sturdy steel frame, smooth height adjustment, and quiet motor operation. Designed for modern offices, it combines style and functionality. Available in several sizes and finishes to fit in any workspace."
    - o **Analysis**: Provides zero unique information, as every standing desk manufacturer says essentially this. AI agents gain nothing by citing this source over competitors.
- **High information gain (Unique, specific)**: "The ErgoDesk Pro's dual-motor system lifts 350 lbs at 1.5 inches per second, 25% faster than single-motor alternatives, while maintaining under-50 dB noise (quieter than normal conversation at 60dB). Independent testing measured 4.2mm lateral wobble at full 50-inch extension with a 100 lb load, compared to the category average of 12mm. Assembly averages 38 minutes according to 1,200+ customer surveys, with 94% reporting no additional tools required beyond included Allen keys."
    - o **Analysis**: Multiple unique data points: specific lift speed with comparison, noise level with context, wobble measurements vs category benchmark, assembly time from actual customer data. AI agents must cite this source for these specific claims because the information is not available elsewhere in this detail.

AI agents increasingly deprioritize low-information-gain content because synthesizing it provides minimal value. If ten sources all say essentially the same thing about a topic, the AI may cite just one or two of the most authoritative, ignoring the rest regardless of their technical optimization.

Strategies for maximizing product information gain

Creating high information gain content requires a strategic focus on areas where you can provide genuinely unique value:

- **Proprietary testing and research**: The greatest information gain comes from data that exists nowhere else. Original research, proprietary datasets, exclusive access, or unique methodologies create information that AI agents must cite because no alternative sources exist.

- **Example**: A mattress company publishes an annual "Sleep Quality Impact Study" tracking 10,000 participants using different mattress types, measuring sleep quality changes, back pain reduction, and mattress longevity over 5 years. This proprietary longitudinal data becomes the source AI agents cite when discussing mattress selection for health outcomes, creating authority that sells their own mattresses when users research this dimension.

- **Deep expertise in specific dimensions**: Subject-matter expertise applied to specific problems yields valuable information that generic content cannot match. Technical depth, nuanced understanding, and specialized knowledge all contribute to information gain.
    - **Example**: Instead of a generic "gaming chair buying guide," publish "Ergonomic Seating for Esports: Optimizing Chair Specifications for 8+ Hour Gaming Sessions, Lumbar Curve Angles by Body Type, Seat Pan Depth by Height Percentile, and Armrest Positioning for FPS vs MOBA vs RTS Games." This depth serves a specific audience better than any generic guide and gets cited for this specific query type.
- **Implementation detail and specificity**: Many sources describe what products are; fewer provide detailed implementation guidance.
    - **Example**: Rather than "this desk is easy to assemble," provide: "Assembly requires an average of 38 minutes (range: 28-52 minutes based on 1,200 customer surveys). Tools included: 4mm and 6mm Allen keys. Process: (1) Attach legs to the desktop using 8 bolts (20 min), (2) Connect the control box and cable management (12 min), (3) Calibration and testing (6 min). Common challenge: Cable routing through the management system, solved by feeding cables before fully tightening leg bolts."
- **Contextual use-case specificity**: Generic advice applies broadly but provides limited value for specific situations.
    - **Example**: Not "best standing desk," but "Best standing desk for corner configurations: L-shaped vs two separate desks, cable management strategies for corner setups, monitor positioning for corner ergonomics, models with reversible controls for left/right corner placement."
- **Comparative analysis with real data**: Comprehensive, unbiased comparisons provide value in synthesis.
    - **Example**: A headphone manufacturer publishes a detailed comparison: "ANC Performance Testing, dB Reduction by Frequency Range:

Frequency	Sony XM5	Bose QC45	Our Model X	Category Avg
20-200Hz	28dB	24dB	26dB	22dB
200-2kHz	30dB	26dB	27dB	23dB
2k-8kHz	22dB	21dB	23dB	19dB

***Table 3.1**: ANC performance comparison by frequency range (dB Reduction)*

- **Best for**: XM5 for maximum reduction, QC45 for value, Model X for balanced performance at mid-tier price."

The fairness and specificity make this a source AI agents cite, even though it acknowledges competitors' strengths.

Depth vs. breadth for product catalogs

A common strategic question is whether to create broad content that covers many topics superficially or deep content that covers narrow topics comprehensively. From a GEO perspective, depth generally wins for product content:

- **Broad, Shallow**:
    - "Standing Desk Buying Guide" covering basics, competing with 500 similar guides.
    - Difficult to achieve primary authority.
    - Low information gain relative to competitors.
    - May achieve basic AEO extraction, but weak GEO citation prominence.
- **Narrow, Deep**:
    - "Complete Guide to Standing Desk Stability: Testing Methodologies, Wobble Measurements, Frame Geometry Impact, and Material Science Analysis".
    - "Standing Desk Motor Systems: Single vs Dual Motor Performance Under Load, Engineering Analysis with Torque Calculations and Failure Mode Testing".
    - "Cable Management for Standing Desks: 15 Solutions Tested for Multi-Monitor Setups with 3D Routing Diagrams".

Each deep guide becomes the authoritative source for its specific dimension. Accumulated depth across multiple dimensions establishes you as the category expert.

From a Product Catalog Application standpoint, rather than 50 shallow product pages, create:

- 10 exceptionally deep product pages with comprehensive specs, testing data, and use cases.
- 15 deep-dive technical guides on specific dimensions (stability, noise, assembly, ergonomics, materials).

- 10 use-case specific guides (standing desks for programmers, for small apartments, for corner setups, for standing all day).
- 5 comparison frameworks with detailed testing methodologies.

This depth-focused approach creates multiple entry points for primary authority citations across diverse query types.

The quality bar is rising

An important trend to recognize is that AI agents are becoming more sophisticated at assessing information gain and deprioritizing derivative content. Early AI systems might cite many sources for the same basic information. More advanced systems increasingly identify the highest-value sources and cite fewer, more authoritative options.

This trend elevates the importance of genuine expertise and unique value. Content strategies built on the volume of published material rather than unique insight will perform progressively worse in GEO. Organizations must shift from "publish frequently" to "publish when we have something genuinely valuable to say."

For brand leaders, this may require difficult conversations about content production metrics. A team that publishes fifty low-information-gain blog posts per month may drive less GEO value than a team that publishes five deeply researched, high-information-gain articles.

Managing brand entities in AI graphs

AI agents do not just retrieve information from individual pages; they build mental models (knowledge graphs) of entities, their attributes, and relationships. How your brand entity is represented profoundly influences how AI agents characterize your products in responses.

Understanding product brand entity representation

In AI knowledge graphs, your brand is an entity with attributes and relationships. Looking at a Herman Miller Entity Example, when AI agents think about "Herman Miller," the entity includes:

- **Attributes**:
  - **Industry**: Office furniture, ergonomic seating.
  - **Founded**: 1905 (signals longevity, stability).
  - **Products**: Aeron Chair, Embody Chair, Sayl Chair, and office desks.
  - **Known for**: Ergonomic design, premium pricing, commercial/office market.
  - **Price tier**: Premium ($800-$1,500 chairs vs $200-$400 category average).
  - **Design philosophy**: "Problem-solving design, ergonomic research-based".
  - **Certifications**: Greenguard, BIFMA level certifications.

- **Relationships**:
  - **Competes with**: Steelcase, Knoll, Humanscale.
  - **Used by**: Fortune 500 companies, design studios, tech companies.
  - **Designed by**: Notable designers (Charles & Ray Eames, Don Chadwick).
  - **Available at**: Authorized dealers, Herman Miller stores, and commercial furniture suppliers.

When users ask "best office chair," AI agents draw from this entity representation. If Herman Miller's entity emphasizes "ergonomic research" and "commercial-grade durability," AI describes it that way. If a cheaper competitor's entity lacks these associations, they are positioned differently even if products are comparable.

Entity consistency for product brands

Ensure AI agents recognize your brand as a single, coherent entity.

Organization Schema Markup (example): The code is as follows:

```
{
  "@context": "https://schema.org",
  "@type": "Organization",
  "name": "ErgoDesk Manufacturing",
  "legalName": "ErgoDesk Manufacturing Corporation",
  "alternateName": "ErgoDesk",
  "url": "https://ergodesk.com",
  "logo": "https://ergodesk.com/logo.png",
  "description": "Premium standing desk manufacturer specializing in dual-motor systems and stability engineering",
  "foundingDate": "2018",
  "sameAs": [
    "https://twitter.com/ergodesk",
    "https://linkedin.com/company/ergodesk",
    "https://facebook.com/ergodesk"
  ]
}
```

Consistency across platforms: Ensure brand name, description, and key attributes are identical across Google Business Profile, LinkedIn, Crunchbase, industry directories, and Wikipedia (if applicable). The inconsistencies fragment entity recognition.

Controlling product brand characterization

How AI agents describe your brand when they mention you emerges from patterns in the content they retrieve. Strategic content can influence these characterizations. Let us look at a Before/After example.

Before GEO optimization:

- **Query**: "Tell me about Uplift Desks"
- **AI response**: "Uplift is a standing desk company that sells adjustable desks online. They offer several models at different price points."
- [Generic, commodity positioning, no differentiation from dozens of competitors.]

After GEO optimization (6 months of strategic content):

- **Query**: "Tell me about Uplift Desks"
- **AI response**: "Uplift is a leading standing desk manufacturer known for its extensive customization options and industry-leading warranty. They offer over 100 desktop configurations and pioneered a 7-year comprehensive warranty for standing desk frames and motors, significantly longer than the industry standard of 2-3 years. Their V2 Commercial model is particularly popular in corporate environments due to its 355 lb weight capacity and certified electronics. Uplift emphasizes customer support with lifetime phone/email assistance and detailed assembly guides."
- [Specific strengths, unique differentiators, clear positioning.]

What changed is that Uplift published comprehensive content about:

- Warranty coverage details and testing showing durability claims.
- Customization decision guides with comparison matrices.
- Commercial-grade specifications and certifications.
- Comparison content highlighting their longer warranty vs competitors.
- Customer support case studies and response time data.

Strategy: Identify how you want to be characterized, then reinforce those associations consistently across all content. If you want to be known for durability, constantly publish about testing, warranties, and longevity. If you want to be known for customization, publish detailed guides about options and decision frameworks.

Building product entity authority signals

AI knowledge graphs incorporate trust and authority signals at the entity level. Brands with strong entity authority receive more favorable treatment when AI agents synthesize information.

Authority signals for product brands are explained as follows:

- **Third-party testing and certification**:
    - UL certification, CE marking, Energy Star, BIFMA level certification.
    - Independent testing by Consumer Reports, Wirecutter, and specialized labs.
    - Industry awards and recognition.
- **Customer validation at scale**:
    - Aggregate rating of 4.7 stars from 5,000+ verified purchases.
    - Notable customer logos (Fortune 500 companies, recognized institutions).
    - Case studies from recognizable brands.
    - Volume indicators ("over 50,000 units sold").
- **Media and industry recognition**:
    - Coverage in authoritative publications (WSJ, NYT, specialized trade publications).
    - Inclusion in industry analyst reports.
    - Editorial recommendations from trusted review sources.
    - Industry "best of" lists and rankings.
- **Expert personnel**:
    - Executives recognized as authorities (speaking at conferences, quoted in media).
    - Technical staff publishing in authoritative venues.
    - Patents and technical innovations.
    - Research partnerships with universities or institutions.
- **Market position signals**:
    - Longevity and history (for established brands).
    - Growth trajectory and funding (for newer brands).
    - Market share data where available.
    - Geographic reach and distribution.

Entity relationship management for products

How AI agents understand your relationships to other entities influences recommendations.

Competitive relationships

Influence how AI understands your competitive set through:

- Direct comparison of content positioning you accurately vs specific competitors.

- Participation in industry analyst evaluations, establishing a competitive context.
- Customer reviews mentioning competitive alternatives you replaced.

Example: If you want AI agents to compare you to premium competitors (not budget alternatives), consistently create content comparing yourself to those premium brands on quality dimensions. Avoid creating content that compares you to budget brands, unless you are clearly differentiating.

Integration and compatibility relationships

For products that integrate or work with other products:

- Comprehensive documentation of compatibility (what brands/models work with yours).
- Case studies demonstrating integration use cases.
- Partner listings and co-marketing.
- Technical specifications establishing compatibility standards.

Example: A monitor arm manufacturer documenting compatibility with specific desk thicknesses, VESA mount patterns, and monitor weights creates clear integration relationships AI agents cite when users ask, "Will this work with my desk/monitor?"

Measuring success through citation quality

Traditional marketing metrics fail for GEO. Success requires measuring citation patterns, authority signals, and brand perception within AI-generated responses.

Traditional metrics fail for product GEO

The metrics that governed SEO success are largely ineffective for measuring GEO performance:

- **Organic traffic**: In zero-click scenarios, GEO success may correlate with declining traffic as AI answers questions without sending users to your site.
- **Keyword rankings**: Rankings do not predict AI citations. You might rank #1 but not be mentioned in AI responses, or vice versa.
- **Click-through rate**: Irrelevant when users never see links to click.
- **Time on site**: Does not capture value from users who learned about your brand through AI mentions and later return directly.
- **Bounce rate**: Similarly disconnected from AI citation dynamics.

These metrics may still matter for traditional search users, but they do not measure GEO success.

Core GEO metrics for product brands

Effective GEO measurement focuses on visibility and authority within AI-generated responses.

Citation frequency

Citation frequency measures how often your brand is mentioned when AI platforms answer relevant product queries. To track this meaningfully, compile 30 to 50 queries across several categories. Using a standing desk manufacturer as an example, direct product queries cover broad intent like best-in-category recommendations. Feature-specific queries target technical differentiators such as motor noise, weight capacity, price thresholds, or stability. Use-case queries reflect how real buyers frame their needs—by profession, living situation, or setup type. Comparison queries capture competitive contexts where buyers are actively evaluating brands against one another.

Test this query set monthly across major AI platforms such as ChatGPT, Claude, Gemini, and Perplexity, and track how consistently your brand appears across results. Established brands should aim for a mention rate of 40 to 60 percent, while newer brands can set an initial target of 15 to 30 percent.

Citation prominence

When mentioned, how prominently? Is the brand featured as a primary recommendation, included in a list, or mentioned in passing?

The tier classification is as follows:

- **Tier 1 (Primary recommendation)**: 4 points
- **Tier 2 (Top options list)**: 3 points
- **Tier 3 (Several options)**: 2 points
- **Tier 4 (Passing mention)**: 1 point

Example scoring:

- **Month**: January 2026
- **Total queries**: 50
- **Brand mentions**: 28 (56% citation frequency)

The prominence breakdown is as follows:

- **Tier 1**: 6 mentions × 4 = 24 points
- **Tier 2**: 12 mentions × 3 = 36 points
- **Tier 3**: 8 mentions × 2 = 16 points
- **Tier 4**: 2 mentions × 1 = 2 points
- **Total**: 78 points / 28 mentions = 2.79 avg prominence

Interpretation: 2.79 falls between Tier 2 and Tier 3, meaning the brand is typically listed among the top options but not usually the primary recommendation.

Target: Move toward 3.0+ through improved authority signals and information gain.

Share of voice

Of all brands mentioned in AI responses to category queries, what percentage are yours?

An example calculation is as follows:

- 50 test queries returned 142 total brand mentions across all brands
- **Your brand**: 28 mentions
- **Share of voice**: 28/142 = 19.7%

Example competitive context:

- **Brand A (market leader)**: 34 mentions (23.9%)
- **Brand B (major competitor)**: 26 mentions (18.3%)
- **Your brand**: 28 mentions (19.7%)
- **Brand C**: 22 mentions (15.5%)
- **Others**: 32 mentions (22.6%)

Citation quality and context

Evaluate what is said when you are mentioned by using these quality dimensions:

- **Accuracy**: Are facts correct? (0-10 score)
- **Favorability**: Tone positive/neutral/negative? (0-10)
- **Completeness**: Key strengths mentioned? (0-10)
- **Positioning**: Aligns with intended brand positioning? (0-10)

The Citation Quality Score should be the average across dimensions.

Product recommendation rate

For queries specifically seeking product recommendations, in what percentage are your products recommended (not just mentioned)?

Track separately from generic mentions, as a "mention" in a list differs from an actual "recommendation" with favorable framing.

Connecting GEO metrics to business outcomes

The challenge with GEO metrics is connecting them to business impact. Citations and share of voice do not directly appear in revenue reports. Building this connection requires:

- **Brand awareness correlation**: Survey target audiences about brand awareness and consideration. Look for a correlation between GEO metric improvements and brand lift.

- **Attribution modeling**: Ask customers during sales processes how they discovered or researched your brand. Track the mentions of AI tool usage.
- **Branded search as proxy**: Increased branded search volume may indicate users discovering your brand through AI citations and then seeking you out specifically.
- **Cohort analysis**: Compare customer acquisition patterns during periods of high versus low GEO performance. Do customer quality, deal size, or conversion rates differ?
- **CAC efficiency**: If GEO drives awareness that reduces paid acquisition costs or improves conversion rates, customer acquisition cost improvements may correlate with GEO success.

While attribution will remain imperfect, establishing these connections helps justify GEO investment to CFOs and executives accustomed to ROI analysis.

Conclusion

GEO represents a strategic evolution beyond AEO, shifting focus from mere extraction to authority, perception, and recommendation. While AEO ensures AI agents can find and read your product information, GEO ensures they value it, trust it, and prominently feature it. Success requires mastering the curation hierarchy, maximizing information gain through unique data and detailed specifications, managing brand entity representation, and tracking citation quality to guide optimization.

Implementing GEO demands a shift from traditional, volume-driven SEO to citation-driven strategies. One authoritative, high-information-gain guide can deliver more impact than dozens of generic pages. Brands must think in entities rather than keywords, providing structured, specific, and verifiable product data, including unique measurements, comparisons, and use-case guidance. Authority should be built systematically through third-party validation, customer data at scale, testing and certification, and media recognition, with sustained effort over months that compound.

For product organizations, this means replacing generic descriptions with rich specifications, vague claims with measurable attributes, and isolated pages with comprehensive knowledge bases. Success metrics evolve from traffic and rankings to citation frequency and prominence, while content prioritizes information gain over keyword optimization.

Brands that embrace GEO, delivering authoritative, context-rich, and verifiable product information, will dominate AI-driven product discovery. The ones that rely solely on traditional SEO risk being overlooked, even if their search rankings remain strong. The gatekeepers of product discovery are changing: the question is whether your organization provides the unique, authoritative content that earns primary AI citations or settles for being passed over.

In the next chapter, we will examine how to structure and optimize product data specifically for AI-driven recommendations, ensuring your product catalogs, specifications, and purchasing information are not just extractable but positioned to drive actual transactions through AI-mediated shopping experiences.

CHAPTER 4
Structuring Product Data for AI-driven Recommendations

Introduction

When a consumer asks an AI agent, *What is the best standing desk under $500 with programmable height presets?*, the agent must parse product catalogs, extract specifications, compare attributes, filter by price, and synthesize a recommendation. If your product data is not structured for this kind of AI-driven analysis, you are invisible, even if you make the perfect standing desk at exactly $499 with advanced programmable features. That is the product data imperative.

Across implementations of comprehensive product data structuring, the pattern is consistent. Brands that move from sparse, unstructured product data to complete, AI-readable information typically see their mention rate in AI responses jump from the low teens to nearly half of category queries. Products that previously failed complex multi-attribute queries now reliably match them. Prominence scores shift from passing mentions to top-option positioning. The difference is not better products; it is better product data. AI agents can finally understand, compare, and confidently recommend what was always there.

However, for organizations that sell physical products, software, or services, which encompasses most businesses, a specific optimization challenge demands focused attention: how to structure product information so AI agents can accurately understand, compare, and recommend your offerings.

This is not merely a technical challenge. Traditional e-commerce optimization focused on helping human shoppers navigate your catalog through category structures, filters, and search. AI-driven product discovery operates fundamentally differently. AI agents do not browse categories or click through filters; instead, they query semantic understanding of product attributes, capabilities, and relationships. They do not read marketing copy to understand what a product does; rather, they extract structured specifications and compare them systematically.

This chapter addresses the product data transformation required for AI-driven commerce.

Structure

The chapter covers the following topics:

- From SKU lists to semantic catalogs
- Implementing product schema for rich AI context
- Optimizing for attribute-based search
- Handling complex technical specifications for AI comparisons
- Keeping product information fresh and verifiable

Objectives

This chapter examines how product data must be structured, enriched, and operationalized for AI-driven recommendations in commerce contexts. We explore how AI agents interpret product attributes, compare specifications across catalogs, and filter options based on multi-constraint queries that mirror real consumer intent. The chapter outlines the transition from flat SKU lists to semantically rich product catalogs, the role of comprehensive product schema in enabling accurate AI understanding, and the technical requirements for supporting attribute-based discovery and comparison at scale. It also addresses the importance of data freshness and verifiability as signals of reliability in AI-mediated commerce. By the end of this chapter, readers will have a practical framework for transforming product information into machine-readable, recommendation-ready assets that enable their products to be discoverable, comparable, and preferred in AI-driven shopping experiences.

From SKU lists to semantic catalogs

Traditional product data models were designed for a world in which humans handled interpretation. Merchandising teams structured catalogs to support browsing, filtering, and keyword search, assuming that shoppers would read descriptions, scan specifications, and make tradeoffs themselves. In an AI-mediated commerce environment, that assumption no longer holds. AI agents must be able to interpret product attributes, reason across constraints, and compare options programmatically. This requires a fundamental shift from catalogs optimized for navigation to catalogs structured for machine understanding.

Traditional product data model

For decades, product data management followed a relatively straightforward model optimized for human browsing and traditional search:

- **SKU-centric structure**: Each product variant had an SKU with associated attributes such as price, inventory status, basic dimensions, perhaps color or size. The SKU was the atomic unit of commerce.

- **Category hierarchies**: Products were organized into nested categories (Electronics | Computers | Laptops | Gaming Laptops), helping humans navigate from broad to specific.
- **Marketing-first descriptions**: Product descriptions emphasized benefits, use cases, and persuasive language designed to convert human visitors who had already found the product.
- **Minimal structured attributes**: Beyond price and basic inventory data, most product information was unstructured text. Specifications might be listed in description paragraphs or buried in PDF spec sheets.
- **Search optimization for keywords**: Products optimized to rank for specific keyword searches ("15-inch gaming laptop") through title tags, descriptions, and on-page optimization.

This model worked adequately when the path to purchase was:

1. Consumer searches Google for "gaming laptop."
2. Clicks through to the retailer or manufacturer's site.
3. Uses category navigation or site search to find relevant products.
4. Reads descriptions and reviews to evaluate options.
5. Adds to cart and purchases.

AI-driven discovery breaks this path. The consumer asks an AI agent, *What is the best gaming laptop for under $1500 that can handle VR and has at least 6 hours of battery life?* and the agent needs to:

- Understand "gaming laptop" as a product category with specific performance requirements.
- Parse "under $1500" as a price constraint.
- Interpret "can handle VR" as requiring specific GPU and CPU capabilities.
- Extract battery life specifications and filter by them.
- Compare qualifying options and synthesize a recommendation.

Traditional product data models are not structured for this semantic understanding and systematic comparison.

The following figure captures this transformation in concrete terms: the same product, unchanged, becomes recommendable only when the data surrounding it is fully structured, attributed, and machine-readable:

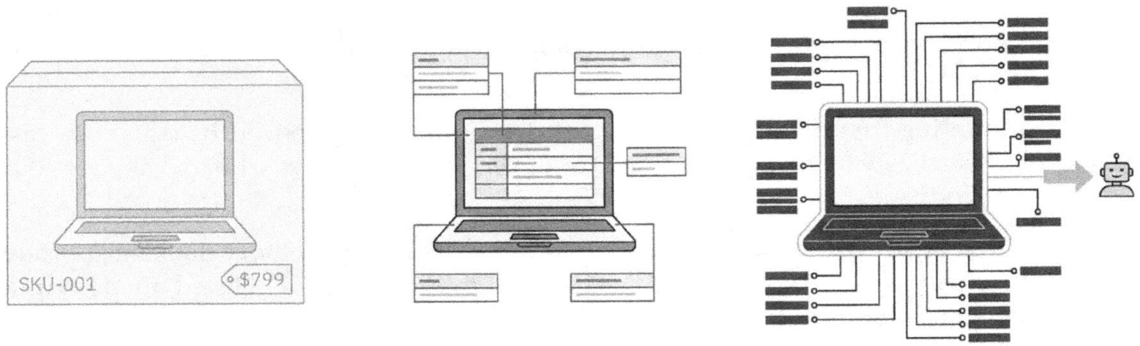

Figure 4.1: Products become recommendable only when their data is fully structured, attributed, and machine-readable

Meaning behind semantic catalogs

A semantic product catalog goes beyond simple attributes to create machine-readable representations of what products are, what they do, how they work, and how they relate to each other. Key characteristics include:

- **Explicit entity typing**: Each product is explicitly identified as an entity of a specific type (e.g., "LaptopComputer", not just "product"), with type-specific attributes defined.
- **Comprehensive attribute coverage**: All relevant product attributes are captured in structured, machine-readable formats, including not just price and SKU but technical specifications, capabilities, compatibility, and use cases.
- **Standardized vocabularies**: Attributes use consistent, standardized terms and units. "Display size" should always be measured in inches or centimeters with decimal precision; "weight" should always be in pounds or kilograms, explicitly stated.
- **Relationship mapping**: Products connected through explicit relationships, such as "requires" for accessories needing a base product, "compatibleWith" for products that work together, "isVariantOf" for color or size variants, and "replaces" for newer versions of discontinued products.
- **Hierarchical property inheritance**: Product types inherit properties from parent types. All laptops have screens, keyboards, and processors because those are properties of the laptop type, not individually specified for each model.
- **Multi-dimensional classification**: Products belong to multiple classification schemes simultaneously, including category, use case, and user segment taxonomies, enabling flexible discovery paths.
- **Capability and constraint modeling**: Beyond static attributes, semantic catalogs model what products can do and their limitations, enabling functional matching to user requirements.

This semantic richness allows AI agents to reason about products, understanding not just that a laptop has a "15.6-inch display" but that this display size is suitable for specific use cases, compares favorably or unfavorably to alternatives, and meets or does not meet user-stated requirements.

Product data transformation journey

Moving from traditional SKU lists to semantic catalogs is a significant undertaking. Most organizations approach this transformation in phases:

- **Phase 1**: Structured attribute extraction:
  - Identify all product attributes currently in unstructured text (descriptions, spec sheets, marketing copy) and extract them into structured fields. This is foundational work creating raw material for semantic enrichment.
  - **Example**: Instead of "Features a powerful Intel Core i7 processor, 16GB of RAM, and 512GB of SSD storage," extract:
    - **Processor**: Intel Core i7-13700H
    - **RAM**: 16 GB
    - **Storage**: 512 GB SSD
- **Phase 2**: Standardization and normalization:
  - Ensure consistent units, formats, and vocabularies across all products. This often reveals significant data quality issues as different teams or systems use different conventions.
  - **Example**: Standardize all variations like "16GB", "16 GB", "16 gigabytes", "16GB RAM" to a consistent format: `"ramSize": {"value": 16, "unitCode": "GB"}`.
- **Phase 3**: Schema implementation:
  - Implement product schema markup that makes your structured data accessible to AI agents and search engines.
- **Phase 4**: Relationship definition:
  - Map relationships between products, including variants, accessories, compatibility, and cross-sells, in explicit, queryable formats.
- **Phase 5**: Capability modeling:
  - Beyond static attributes, model what products can do, what use cases they support, and what requirements they fulfill.
- **Phase 6**: Continuous enrichment:
  - Establish processes to continuously add richer semantic context, including user reviews analyzed for attribute mentions, competitive comparisons, and use-case associations.

Consider a realistic timeline and resources:

- **Small catalog (1-500 SKUs)**: 3-6 months to reach Phase 4:
    - **Resources**: 1 product data specialist, technical support for schema implementation.
    - **Quick win**: Top 50 products to Phase 3 in 4-6 weeks.
- **Medium catalog (500-5,000 SKUs)**: 6-12 months to Phase 4:
    - **Resources**: 2-3 person product data team, dedicated technical resources.
    - **Quick win**: Top 10% revenue products to Phase 3 in 6-8 weeks.
- **Large catalog (5,000+ SKUs)**: 12-18 months to Phase 4, ongoing to Phase 6:
    - **Resources**: Dedicated product data team (4-6 people), PIM system, automation infrastructure.
    - **Quick win**: Hero products and new launches to Phase 3 within 8 weeks.

Resource requirements across all scales:

- Dedicated product data specialist or team.
- PIM system capable of comprehensive attribute management.
- Technical resources for schema implementation and automation.
- Content resources for attribute extraction and standardization.
- Executive sponsorship for cross-functional alignment.

The best place to start is with quick wins:

1. Begin with the top 10% revenue-generating products (Phase 1-3).
2. Implement basic Product schema for all products (name, price, image, basic specs).
3. Start tracking completeness metrics to build a baseline.
4. Create a template for a comprehensive schema to scale efficiently.

Common pitfalls in product data transformation

Organizations undertaking this transformation frequently encounter specific challenges:

- **Inconsistent data sources**: Product information often originates from multiple systems, such as PIM platforms, ERP systems, supplier feeds, and manual entry, each with different data quality standards and structures. Reconciling these sources is complex but essential.
- **Missing attribute values**: Partial attribute coverage creates gaps, undermining AI understanding. If 80% of your products have battery life specified, but 20% do not, AI agents may incorrectly filter out the 20% when users ask about battery life.

- **Ambiguous or jargon-heavy attributes**: Using internal SKU codes, model numbers without context, or industry jargon as attribute values reduces AI comprehensibility. "Processor: ABC-123-XYZ" is far less useful than "Processor: Intel Core i7-13700H (13th Gen, 14 cores, up to 5.0GHz)".
- **Format inconsistencies**: Even within a single attribute, inconsistent formatting can cause problems. If some products list dimensions as "15 x 10 x 2 inches" while others use "15" L x 10" W x 2" H", AI agents may fail to extract and compare reliably.
- **Outdated information**: Stale product data, such as discontinued products still listed, old prices, and outdated specifications, undermines AI trust in your catalog. Maintaining currency is ongoing work.
- **Insufficient granularity**: Overly broad attributes like "color: multicolor" or "size: various" do not provide the specific information AI agents need for matching and comparison.
- **Lack of competitive context**: Including only your products' attributes without understanding what attributes competitors provide or what attributes AI agents prioritize for recommendations.

Solution: Analyze competitor product pages and monitor which products AI agents recommend to identify attribute gaps and prioritization needs.

Addressing these pitfalls requires not just technical implementation but organizational commitment to data governance, quality standards, and maintenance processes.

Building semantic product taxonomies

Beyond individual product attributes, semantic catalogs require thoughtful taxonomic structures that help AI agents understand product relationships and categories:

- **Type hierarchies**: Products inherit characteristics from parent types:
  - Product (all products)
  - Physical product (has weight, dimensions):
    - Electronics (has power requirements)
    - Computing device (has a processor, memory, storage)
    - Laptop (has display, keyboard, battery)
    - Gaming laptop (has dedicated GPU, high-refresh display)
- **Faceted classification**: Products can be classified along multiple independent dimensions:
  - **By use case**: Gaming, business, creative professional, student.
  - **By portability**: Desktop replacement, mainstream, ultraportable.

- o **By performance tier**: Entry, mid-range, performance, enthusiast.
- o **By price point**: Budget, mid-range, premium, luxury.

- **Compatibility taxonomies**: Explicit modeling of what works with what:
  - o Compatible operating systems.
  - o Compatible peripherals.
  - o Compatible software.
  - o Physical interface compatibility (ports, connectors).

These taxonomies enable AI agents to navigate product spaces conceptually rather than just match keywords, dramatically improving recommendation accuracy and relevance.

Implementing product schema for rich AI context

Product schema markup is the technical foundation that makes semantic catalogs accessible to AI agents. While we introduced schema concepts in *Chapter 2, Understanding and Mastering AEO*, product schema deserves deep examination given its critical importance for commerce.

Starting with a minimum viable product schema

For organizations just beginning, start with this essential subset before expanding to a comprehensive implementation:

```
{
  "@context": "https://schema.org/",
  "@type": "Product",
  "name": "TechPro UltraBook 15",
  "description": "Professional laptop with 13th Gen In-
tel Core i7, 16GB RAM, 512GB SSD, 15.6-inch OLED display. Ideal for busi-
ness professionals and content creators.",
  "image": "https://example.com/images/ultrabook.jpg",
  "brand": {
    "@type": "Brand",
    "name": "TechPro"
  },
  "sku": "TPUB15-i7-16-512",
  "offers": {
```

```
    "@type": "Offer",
    "price": "1299.99",
    "priceCurrency": "USD",
    "availability": "https://schema.org/InStock",
    "url": "https://example.com/products/ultrabook-15"
  },
  "aggregateRating": {
    "@type": "AggregateRating",
    "ratingValue": "4.7",
    "reviewCount": "342"
  }
}
```

Here is a suggestion for a progressive enhancement path:

- **Week 1-2**: Implement minimum viable schema across all products:
  - Name, description, image, brand, SKU, price, availability.
  - Goal: 80% of AI citation value comes from these basics.
- **Week 3-4**: Add critical specifications via **`additionalProperty`**:
  - Processor, RAM, storage, and display for tech products.
  - Dimensions, weight, and materials for physical products.
  - Key differentiating features.
- **Week 5-8**: Enhance with additional properties:
  - Multiple images.
  - Shipping and delivery details.
  - Individual customer reviews (top 3-5 reviews).
  - Warranty information.
- **Week 9-12**: Complete comprehensive implementation:
  - Detailed **`additionalProperty`** entries for all specs.
  - Relationship properties (**`isVariantOf`**, **`isAccessoryFor`**).
  - Component-level detail where relevant.

This phased approach delivers quick wins while building toward comprehensive implementation.

Comprehensive product schema structure

Once basics are in place, expand to a comprehensive schema providing AI agents with everything they need for accurate understanding and comparison:

```
{
  "@context": "https://schema.org/",
  "@type": "Product",
  "name": "TechPro UltraBook 15",
  "description": "Professional-
grade ultraportable laptop combining powerful performance with all-
day battery life, featuring 13th Gen Intel Core i7 p-
rocessor, 16GB RAM, and stunning 15.6-inch OLED display.",
  "brand": {
    "@type": "Brand",
    "name": "TechPro"
  },
  "manufacturer": {
    "@type": "Organization",
    "name": "TechPro Electronics Inc."
  },
  "model": "UB15-2025",
  "sku": "TPUB15-i7-16-512",
  "gtin13": "1234567890123",
  "category": "Laptop Computers",
  "image": [
    "https://example.com/images/ultrabook-front.jpg",
    "https://example.com/images/ultrabook-side.jpg",
    "https://example.com/images/ultrabook-open.jpg"
  ],
  "offers": {
    "@type": "Offer",
    "url": "https://example.com/products/ultrabook-15",
    "priceCurrency": "USD",
    "price": "1299.99",
```

```
    "priceValidUntil": "2026-12-31",
    "availability": "https://schema.org/InStock",
    "itemCondition": "https://schema.org/NewCondition",
    "seller": {
      "@type": "Organization",
      "name": "TechPro Direct"
    },
    "shippingDetails": {
      "@type": "OfferShippingDetails",
      "shippingRate": {
        "@type": "MonetaryAmount",
        "value": "0",
        "currency": "USD"
      },
      "deliveryTime": {
        "@type": "ShippingDeliveryTime",
        "handlingTime": {
          "@type": "QuantitativeValue",
          "minValue": 1,
          "maxValue": 2,
          "unitCode": "DAY"
        },
        "transitTime": {
          "@type": "QuantitativeValue",
          "minValue": 3,
          "maxValue": 5,
          "unitCode": "DAY"
        }
      }
    }
  },
  "aggregateRating": {
    "@type": "AggregateRating",
```

```
    "ratingValue": "4.7",
    "reviewCount": "342"
  },
  "review": [
    {
      "@type": "Review",
      "author": {"@type": "Person", "name": "Sarah Johnson"},
      "datePublished": "2025-01-15",
      "reviewBody": "Exceptional build quality and performance. The OLED dis-
play is stunning and battery life easily gets me through a full workday.",
      "reviewRating": {
        "@type": "Rating",
        "ratingValue": "5"
      }
    }
  ]
}
```

Beyond identity, pricing, and social proof, the **additionalProperty** array is where technical depth lives:

```
{
  "additionalProperty": [
    {
      "@type": "PropertyValue",
      "name": "Processor",
      "value": "Intel Core i7-1355U (13th Gen, 10-core, up to 5.0GHz)"
    },
    {
      "@type": "PropertyValue",
      "name": "RAM",
      "value": "16GB LPDDR5"
    },
    {
      "@type": "PropertyValue",
```

```
      "name": "Storage",
      "value": "512GB NVMe SSD"
    },
    {
      "@type": "PropertyValue",
      "name": "Display",
      "value": "15.6-inch OLED, 2880x1800, 400 nits, 100% DCI-P3"
    },
    {
      "@type": "PropertyValue",
      "name": "Graphics",
      "value": "Intel Iris Xe Graphics"
    },
    {
      "@type": "PropertyValue",
      "name": "Battery Life",
      "value": "Up to 12 hours"
    },
    {
      "@type": "PropertyValue",
      "name": "Weight",
      "value": "3.2 lbs (1.45 kg)"
    },
    {
      "@type": "PropertyValue",
      "name": "Operating System",
      "value": "Windows 11 Pro"
    },
    {
      "@type": "PropertyValue",
      "name": "Connectivity",
      "value": "Wi-
Fi 6E, Bluetooth 5.3, 2x Thunderbolt 4, 2x USB-A 3.2, HDMI 2.1, 3.5mm audio"
```

```
    }
  ],
  "width": {"@type": "QuantitativeValue", "value": "13.9", "unitCode": "INH"},
  "height": {"@type": "QuantitativeValue", "value": "0.59", "unitCode": "INH"},
  "depth": {"@type": "QuantitativeValue", "value": "9.5", "unitCode": "INH"},
  "weight": {"@type": "QuantitativeValue", "value": "3.2", "unitCode": "LBR"}
}
```

This comprehensive schema provides AI agents with everything they need to understand, compare, and accurately recommend this product.

Deep dive into critical schema properties

While the basic properties (name, price, availability) are essential, several advanced properties dramatically improve AI recommendation quality:

- **additionalProperty array**: Perhaps the most important property for complex products. Allows specification of any number of custom attributes beyond standard schema properties. For products with technical specifications, this is where you comprehensively describe capabilities. Best practices for `additionalProperty`:
  - Use clear, consistent naming conventions for property names.
  - Provide complete values, not abbreviations or codes.
  - Include units explicitly where relevant.
  - Be specific ("Intel Core i7-1355U (13th Gen, 10-core, up to 5.0GHz)"), not generic ("fast processor").
- **Material property**: For physical products, material composition helps AI agents understand quality, durability, sustainability, and compatibility concerns.
- **isAccessoryOrSparePartFor**: Explicitly linking accessories to compatible products helps AI agents make bundle recommendations and answer compatibility questions.
- **isVariantOf and isSimilarTo**: These relationship properties help AI agents understand your product lineup and recommend appropriate alternatives if a specific variant is unavailable.
- **eligibleRegion and ineligibleRegion**: Geographic availability constraints help AI agents avoid recommending products users cannot actually purchase.
- **award**: Recognition, certifications, or awards provide social proof signals that influence AI recommendations.

Variant handling strategies

Products with multiple variants (colors, sizes, configurations) require a thoughtful schema structure. Two main approaches exist:

- **Approach 1**: Individual product entities with shared parent:
    - Each variant is a separate **`Product`** entity with its own complete schema, all linked through **`isVariantOf`** to a parent **`ProductGroup`**:

```
{
  "@type": "ProductGroup",
  "name": "TechPro UltraBook 15",
  "description": "Professional ultraportable laptop series",
  "variesBy": ["processor", "ram", "storage"],
  "hasVariant": [
    {
      "@type": "Product",
      "name": "TechPro UltraBook 15 (i5/8GB/256GB)",
      "sku": "TPUB15-i5-8-256",
      "offers": {"@type": "Offer", "price": "999.99"}
      // Complete product schema
    },
    {
      "@type": "Product",
      "name": "TechPro UltraBook 15 (i7/16GB/512GB)",
      "sku": "TPUB15-i7-16-512",
      "offers": {"@type": "Offer", "price": "1299.99"}
      // Complete product schema
    }
  ]
}
```

- **Approach 2**: Single product with offer variants:
  - One `Product` entity with multiple `Offer` objects representing variants:

```
{
  "@type": "Product",
  "name": "Premium Cotton T-Shirt",
  "offers": [
    {
      "@type": "Offer",
      "sku": "TS-BLK-M",
      "price": "29.99",
      "color": "Black",
      "size": "Medium"
    },
    {
      "@type": "Offer",
      "sku": "TS-BLK-L",
      "price": "29.99",
      "color": "Black",
      "size": "Large"
    }
  ]
}
```

Recommendation: Approach 1 (individual entities) works better for variants with significantly different characteristics, while Approach 2 is cleaner for simple variations, such as color or size, where core product attributes remain identical.

Schema for software and digital products

Digital products require adapted schema approaches using the `SoftwareApplication` type:

```
{
  "@context": "https://schema.org",
  "@type": "SoftwareApplication",
  "name": "TaskFlow Pro",
```

```
  "applicationCategory": "BusinessApplication",
  "applicationSubCategory": "Project Management Software",
  "operatingSystem": "Windows 10 or later, macOS 11 or later, Linux, Web-
based",
  "offers": {
    "@type": "Offer",
    "price": "29.99",
    "priceCurrency": "USD",
    "priceSpecification": {
      "@type": "UnitPriceSpecification",
      "price": "29.99",
      "billingDuration": "P1M",
      "billingIncrement": 1
    }
  },
  "featureList": [
    "Kanban boards",
    "Gantt charts",
    "Time tracking",
    "Resource management",
    "API access",
    "Unlimited projects",
    "Real-time collaboration"
  ],
  "softwareRequirements": "Modern web browser or desktop application",
  "memoryRequirements": "2GB RAM minimum",
  "storageRequirements": "500MB available storage for desktop app",
  "aggregateRating": {
    "@type": "AggregateRating",
    "ratingValue": "4.6",
    "reviewCount": "1247"
  }
}
```

The **`SoftwareApplication`** type includes properties such as **`featureList`**, **`softwareRequirements`**, and **`applicationCategory`** that help AI agents understand and compare software products.

Optimizing for attribute-based search

AI-driven product discovery is fundamentally attribute-based. Users ask questions built around product attributes: *a gaming laptop with at least 16GB RAM under $2000, a standing desk that goes up to 50 inches tall,* and *project management software with Salesforce integration.*

Understanding attribute-based query patterns

Attribute-based queries follow predictable patterns that should inform optimization strategy:

- **Constraint queries (45-55% of product queries)**: Users specify requirements that products must meet:
    - "Laptops with battery life over 10 hours."
    - "Standing desks under $500."
    - "Project management software for teams under 20 people."
- **Comparison queries (20-25%)**: Users want to compare specific attributes across options:
    - "Compare battery life of MacBook vs ThinkPad."
    - "Asana vs Monday pricing comparison."
    - "Which standing desk has the widest range of height adjustment?"
- **Capability queries (15-20%)**: Users ask whether products can perform specific functions:
    - "Can the iPad Pro run Photoshop?"
    - "Does this desk support a triple monitor setup?"
    - "Project management software that integrates with Slack."
- **Optimization queries (10-15%)**: Users seek products optimized for specific attributes:
    - "Lightest 15-inch laptop."
    - "Quietest standing desk motor."
    - "Most affordable project management software with Gantt charts."
- **Configuration queries (5-10%)**: Users ask about customization or configuration options:
    - "Can I configure this laptop with 32GB RAM?"

- "Does this desk come in bamboo?"
- "Software plans that include API access."

Each query pattern demands specific attribute coverage in your product data. Strategically, prioritize constraint-driven queries by ensuring all critical filtering attributes are comprehensive, accurate, and fully structured, as these queries account for the majority of AI-driven product discovery and recommendations.

Comprehensive attribute coverage

The foundation of attribute-based optimization is ensuring all relevant attributes are captured and structured. Leverage the attribute prioritization framework:

- **Tier 1**: Critical (Required for any AI citation):
  - **Target**: 100% coverage:
    - Product category identification.
    - Price and pricing structure.
    - Availability status.
    - Core dimensions/size (what physically is it?).
    - Primary function/use case.
- **Tier 2**: Core (required for prominence in recommendations):
  - **Target**: 100% coverage:
    - Key differentiating specifications.
    - Performance metrics.
    - Materials and build quality.
    - Compatibility requirements.
    - Warranty and support.
- **Tier 3**: Enhanced (Improves prominence and specificity):
  - **Target**: 80%+ coverage:
    - Detailed sub-specifications.
    - Environmental/regulatory compliance.
    - Accessories and inclusions.
    - Usage scenarios and limitations.
    - Comparative benchmarks.

- **Tier 4**: Comprehensive (competitive advantage):
    - **Target**: 50%+ coverage for hero products:
- Edge case specifications.
- Detailed compatibility matrices.
- Historical information and version updates.
- Community/ecosystem details.
- Advanced technical specifications.

Consider an example for laptops, a complete attribute set:

- **Tier 1 (Critical)**:
    - **Category**: Laptop computer
    - **Price**: $1,299.99
    - **Availability**: In stock
    - **Screen size**: 15.6 inches
    - **Primary use**: Business/Professional
- **Tier 2 (Core)**:
    - **Processor**: Intel Core i7-1355U
    - **RAM**: 16GB
    - **Storage**: 512GB SSD
    - **Display resolution**: 2880x1800
    - **Graphics**: Intel Iris Xe
    - **Battery life**: 12 hours
    - **Weight**: 3.2 lbs
    - **Operating system**: Windows 11 Pro
    - **Warranty**: 1 year standard
- **Tier 3 (Enhanced)**:
    - **Display type**: OLED
    - **Color gamut**: 100% DCI-P3
    - **Refresh rate**: 60Hz
    - **Brightness**: 400 nits
    - **RAM type**: LPDDR5
    - **Storage type**: NVMe

    - **Connectivity**: Wi-Fi 6E, Bluetooth 5.3, Thunderbolt 4
    - **Build material**: Aluminum unibody
    - **Keyboard**: Backlit
    - **Touchpad**: Precision glass
    - **Webcam**: 1080p with privacy shutter
- **Tier 4 (Comprehensive)**:
    - **Processor cores**: 10 (2P + 8E)
    - **Processor cache**: 12MB
    - **Max RAM supported**: 16GB (soldered)
    - **Storage expansion**: None (soldered)
    - **Display response time**: < 1ms (OLED)
    - **Port details**: 2x Thunderbolt 4 (40 Gbps), 2x USB-A 3.2 (10 Gbps), HDMI 2.1, 3.5mm combo jack
    - **Battery capacity**: 75Wh
    - **Charging**: 65W USB-C
    - **Operating temp range**: 50-95°F
    - **Certifications**: Energy Star, EPEAT Gold
    - **Dimensions (closed)**: 13.9" x 9.5" x 0.59"

Standardizing attribute values

Inconsistent attribute values break AI understanding. Establish standards for:

- **Units**: Always specify explicitly:
    - "Weight: 3.2 lbs" or structured: {"value": 3.2, "unitCode": "LBR"}
- **Formats**: Use consistent formats:
    - All products "15.6-inch" or all structured: {"value": 15.6, "unitCode": "INH"}
- **Vocabularies**: Use standard terms:
    - "Processor: Intel Core i7-13700H (13th Generation, 14-core)"
- **Precision**: Provide appropriate precision:
    - "Battery Life: Up to 8.5 hours" or "7.5-8.5 hours typical use."

Making attributes queryable and comparable

Beyond including attributes, structure them for reliable AI extraction and comparison:

- **Use structured data over prose**: When possible, separate attribute values from descriptive prose:

```
<dl>
  <dt>Display Size</dt>
  <dd>15.6 inches</dd>
  <dt>Display Type</dt>
  <dd>OLED</dd>
  <dt>Resolution</dt>
  <dd>2880 x 1800 pixels</dd>
  <dt>Color Gamut</dt>
  <dd>100% DCI-P3</dd>
  <dt>Brightness</dt>
  <dd>400 nits</dd>
</dl>
```

  The structured format makes attribute extraction deterministic rather than requiring AI parsing of prose.

- **Separate minimum, maximum, and typical values**: For variable attributes, provide complete ranges:

```
{
  "@type": "PropertyValue",
  "name": "Height Adjustment Range",
  "minValue": 25,
  "maxValue": 50.5,
  "unitCode": "INH",
  "value": "25-50.5 inches (continuously adjustable)"
}
```

- **Include constraint information**: For attributes with limitations, make constraints explicit:

```
{
  "@type": "PropertyValue",
  "name": "Maximum RAM Supported",
  "value": "32GB",
```

```
  "description": "Limited by 2x SODIMM slots, sup-
ports up to 16GB per slot"
}
```

- **Provide comparison context**: Where helpful, include context that aids comparison:

```
{
  "@type": "PropertyValue",
  "name": "Weight",
  "value": "2.8 lbs",
  "description": "Among the lightest in the 15-inch category"
}
```

Handling complex technical specifications for AI comparisons

Products with detailed technical specifications, such as electronics, industrial equipment, scientific instruments, and vehicles, require sophisticated approaches to ensure AI agents can accurately compare them.

Multi-dimensional specifications

Complex components are nested objects with their own comprehensive attribute sets:

```
{
  "@type": "PropertyValue",
  "name": "Display",
  "value": {
    "@type": "PropertyValue",
    "name": "Display Assembly",
    "additionalProperty": [
      {
        "@type": "PropertyValue",
        "name": "Diagonal Size",
        "value": 15.6,
        "unitCode": "INH"
      },
      {
```

```
        "@type": "PropertyValue",
        "name": "Resolution",
        "value": "2880 x 1800 pixels"
      },
      {
        "@type": "PropertyValue",
        "name": "Panel Type",
        "value": "OLED"
      },
      {
        "@type": "PropertyValue",
        "name": "Refresh Rate",
        "value": 60,
        "unitCode": "HZ"
      },
      {
        "@type": "PropertyValue",
        "name": "Peak Brightness",
        "value": 400,
        "unitCode": "NIT"
      },
      {
        "@type": "PropertyValue",
        "name": "Color Gamut",
        "value": "100% DCI-P3, 100% sRGB"
      }
    ]
  }
}
```

This comprehensive specification enables AI agents to answer questions ranging from broad ("does it have a good display") to very specific ("what is the peak brightness in nits").

Performance specifications and benchmarks

For products where performance matters, including standardized benchmarks, data enables objective comparisons:

```
{
  "@type": "PropertyValue",
  "name": "Performance Benchmarks",
  "additionalProperty": [
    {
      "@type": "PropertyValue",
      "name": "Geekbench 6 Single-Core",
      "value": 2650
    },
    {
      "@type": "PropertyValue",
      "name": "Geekbench 6 Multi-Core",
      "value": 10450
    },
    {
      "@type": "PropertyValue",
      "name": "Cinebench R23 Multi-Core",
      "value": 12800
    }
  ]
}
```

Select widely recognized benchmarks in your category, enable direct cross-brand comparisons, reflect real-world usage scenarios for your target audience, and use the latest benchmark versions to stay current.

For B2B products, prioritize industry-standard performance metrics, compliance and certification test results, and standardized efficiency ratings, such as SEER for HVAC systems, lumens per watt for lighting, or throughput and latency for networking equipment, so AI agents can make credible, apples-to-apples comparisons.

Compatibility and interoperability specifications

For products that work with other products or systems, comprehensive compatibility information is essential:

```
{
  "@type": "PropertyValue",
  "name": "Compatibility",
  "additionalProperty": [
    {
      "@type": "PropertyValue",
      "name": "Operating System Compatibility",
      "value": "Windows 11, Windows 10 (64-bit), macOS 12 or later, Ubuntu 20.04 or later"
    },
    {
      "@type": "PropertyValue",
      "name": "Supported External Displays",
      "value": "Up to 2x 4K displays at 60Hz or 1x 5K display at 60Hz via Thunderbolt 4"
    },
    {
      "@type": "PropertyValue",
      "name": "Dock Compatibility",
      "value": "Compatible with Thunderbolt 4 and USB-C docks supporting DisplayPort Alt Mode"
    }
  ]
}
```

This allows AI agents to accurately answer compatibility questions like "can I connect this laptop to my CalDigit TS4 dock" or "will this work with my 5K display."

Physical specifications with tolerance ranges

Physical dimensions, weight, and environmental specifications often have tolerance ranges that should be explicitly stated:

```
{
  "weight": {
    "@type": "QuantitativeValue",
    "value": 3.2,
    "minValue": 3.1,
    "maxValue": 3.3,
    "unitCode": "LBR",
    "description": "Weight may vary by configuration and manufacturing tolerance"
  },
  "additionalProperty": [
    {
      "@type": "PropertyValue",
      "name": "Operating Temperature Range",
      "value": "50°F to 95°F (10°C to 35°C)"
    },
    {
      "@type": "PropertyValue",
      "name": "Storage Temperature Range",
      "value": "-4°F to 113°F (-20°C to 45°C)"
    },
    {
      "@type": "PropertyValue",
      "name": "Relative Humidity",
      "value": "0% to 90% non-condensing"
    },
    {
      "@type": "PropertyValue",
      "name": "Maximum Operating Altitude",
      "value": "10,000 feet (3,048 meters)"
    }
  ]
}
```

Regulatory and certification specifications

For products requiring certifications or meeting regulatory standards, these should be explicitly documented:

```
{
  "@type": "PropertyValue",
  "name": "Certifications and Compliance",
  "additionalProperty": [
    {
      "@type": "PropertyValue",
      "name": "Safety Certifications",
      "value": "UL, CE, FCC, ENERGY STAR 8.0"
    },
    {
      "@type": "PropertyValue",
      "name": "Environmental Compliance",
      "value": "RoHS, REACH, EPEAT Gold"
    },
    {
      "@type": "PropertyValue",
      "name": "Accessibility",
      "value": "Meets WCAG 2.1 Level AA (software), Section 508 compliant"
    }
  ]
}
```

This enables AI agents to filter and recommend products based on compliance requirements, which is critical for enterprise and government procurement.

Keeping product information fresh and verifiable

AI agents increasingly assess information recency and credibility as factors in source selection. Stale or unverifiable product data reduces trust and citation likelihood. Maintaining freshness requires systematic processes.

Freshness challenge

Product information freshness creates specific challenges:

- **High velocity of change**: Prices fluctuate, inventory status changes, new models launch, old models are discontinued.
- **Multi-source truth**: Product information originates from many systems with different update cycles.
- **Competing priorities**: Maintaining current product data competes with new product launches.
- **Scale complexity**: Thousands of SKUs cannot be manually reviewed regularly.
- **Verification difficulty**: Unlike news articles, product specifications may lack obvious recency signals.

Addressing these challenges requires both technical infrastructure and organizational processes.

Timestamp everything

The foundation of freshness management is comprehensive timestamping. Every product page and schema markup should include clear publication and modification dates:

```
{
  "@type": "Product",
  "name": "TechPro UltraBook 15",
  "datePublished": "2025-01-15",
  "dateModified": "2025-01-22"
}
```

For Article or WebPage schema wrapping product content:

```
{
  "@type": "WebPage",
  "about": {"@type": "Product", "name": "TechPro UltraBook 15"},
  "datePublished": "2025-01-15",
  "dateModified": "2025-01-22",
  "lastReviewed": "2025-01-22"
}
```

Freshness prioritization by attribute type

Different attributes require different update frequencies, as shown in the following table:

Update frequency	Data elements to refresh
Real-time / Hourly	Price; availability and inventory status; promotional pricing; delivery estimates.
Daily	Customer ratings and review counts; inventory levels for display; shipping times.
Weekly	Product descriptions (if dynamic based on inventory or seasonality); related product recommendations; competitive positioning data.
Monthly	Technical specifications (verify no changes); images and media; certifications and compliance information.
Quarterly	Comprehensive content review; attribute completeness audit; competitive benchmark refresh; link validation and relationship verification.

***Table 4.1**: Recommended data refresh frequencies by attribute type*

Automated freshness workflows

Manual maintenance does not scale. Automated workflows are essential:

- **Scheduled data synchronization**: Establish automated sync processes between product information management systems and published content:
    - **Price and availability**: Real-time or hourly sync with inventory systems.
    - **Inventory status**: Multiple times daily.
    - **Product specifications**: Weekly sync with PIM.
    - **Marketing descriptions**: Monthly review.
    - **Images and media**: Quarterly review.
- **Change detection and alerts**: Implement systems that detect significant changes in source data and trigger review workflows:
    - Significant price changes (>10%) trigger review.
    - Out-of-stock status triggers a notification.
    - New product variants trigger a schema update.
    - Specification changes in supplier feeds trigger verification.
- **Automated content freshness scoring**: Calculate freshness scores for each product based on:
    - Days since last modification.
    - Days since last review.

- Number of user reports of outdated information.
- Comparison to competitor product data freshness.

Products with low freshness scores are prioritized for review and update.

- **Deprecation and discontinuation workflows**: When products are discontinued. Use explicit schema signals to indicate discontinued products and clearly link users and AI agents to the current successor model.

```
{
  "@type": "Product",
  "name": "TechPro UltraBook 14 (2023 Model)",
  "offers": {
    "@type": "Offer",
    "availability": "https://schema.org/Discontinued",
    "priceValidUntil": "2024-12-31"
  },
  "isPredecessorOf": {
    "@type": "Product",
    "name": "TechPro UltraBook 15 (2025 Model)",
    "url": "https://example.com/products/ultrabook-15-2025"
  }
}
```

This helps AI agents guide users to current alternatives when asking about discontinued products.

Verification and trust signals

Beyond maintaining freshness, provide clear signals that help AI agents assess the credibility of your information. Attribute specifications to their sources by stating whether data comes from manufacturer documentation, independent third-party testing, or aggregated user reporting, and include contextual notes when independent results differ from official claims. For performance and endurance claims, document the testing methodology used so AI agents can interpret results accurately and compare them across products and sources. Where measurements vary by configuration or usage, present realistic ranges rather than single-point values to reflect the expected variance in real-world conditions. For specifications that change over time, maintain a visible update history that records what changed and when, allowing AI agents to track product evolution and trust that the information reflects current production realities. Example:

```
{
  "@type": "PropertyValue",
  "name": "Battery Life",
  "value": "Up to 12 hours",
  "description": "Based on manufacturer specifications. Independent testing by Laptop Mag achieved 11.5 hours in standard productivity test."
}
```

Real-time inventory and pricing

Real-time inventory and pricing are critical signals of freshness for e-commerce, as AI agents rely on them to determine whether a product can be recommended at the moment of a query. Availability should be clearly structured to reflect current stock status, approximate inventory levels when appropriate, when availability began, and realistic delivery lead times so AI systems can assess whether a product meets urgency and fulfillment constraints. Pricing should be treated dynamically, with explicit validity windows that specify when a price becomes effective and when it expires, so AI agents can avoid recommending outdated offers. When promotions or sales are active, include both the regular and discounted prices, along with clear savings information and the promotion timeframes. This gives AI agents the context needed to present accurate, time-bound recommendations and prevents users from being directed to offers that are no longer valid. Example:

```
{
  "@type": "Offer",
  "price": "1299.99",
  "priceCurrency": "USD",
  "priceValidUntil": "2025-01-31T23:59:59Z",
  "priceSpecification": {
    "@type": "UnitPriceSpecification",
    "price": "1299.99",
    "priceCurrency": "USD",
    "validFrom": "2025-01-22T00:00:00Z",
    "validThrough": "2025-01-31T23:59:59Z"
  }
}
```

Multi-region and multi-currency considerations

For global products, freshness management becomes more complex because pricing, availability, and even specifications can vary by region and currency. Region-specific offers should clearly reflect local pricing, the applicable currency, when the product becomes available in that market, and whether it is in stock, in pre-order, or temporarily unavailable. This allows AI agents to accurately recommend products based on the user's location and purchase context, avoiding situations where a user in one country is shown pricing or availability that applies only elsewhere.

In addition to commercial differences, regional specification variations must be made explicit. Technical details such as power supply standards, plug types, voltage, regulatory certifications, or included accessories can differ across markets. Clearly documenting these differences helps AI agents answer region-specific questions, such as compatibility with local power standards or whether adapters are included. When regional variations are transparent and structured, AI systems can make precise, context-aware recommendations that feel localized rather than generic or misleading. Example:

```
{
  "@type": "PropertyValue",
  "name": "Power Supply",
  "value": "100-240V, 50/60Hz (universal), region-specific plug adapter included",
  "additionalProperty": [
    {
      "@type": "PropertyValue",
      "name": "North America",
      "value": "Type A/B plug, 120V standard"
    },
    {
      "@type": "PropertyValue",
      "name": "Europe",
      "value": "Type C/F plug, 230V standard"
    },
    {
      "@type": "PropertyValue",
      "name": "United Kingdom",
      "value": "Type G plug, 230V standard"
    }
```

```
  ]
}
```

Conclusion

The transformation from simple SKU lists to rich semantic catalogs represents one of the most significant opportunities in AI-driven commerce. Organizations that structure product data comprehensively, maintain it rigorously, and optimize it for AI agent understanding will capture a disproportionate share of AI-driven product discovery and recommendations.

This chapter establishes the foundation for product data excellence and for maintaining freshness as a trust signal, ensuring critical attributes like price and availability remain up to date through clear verification and update processes.

Achieving this level of product data excellence requires investment across technology, processes, and people: robust PIM systems, automated workflows, strong data governance, cross-functional alignment, and measurement infrastructure to track completeness, freshness, and AI citation rates. Organizations that excel in product data structuring generate compounding advantages, widening the gap between leaders and laggards in AI-driven commerce. Superior data fuels more accurate recommendations, which drive higher sales, providing resources to enhance product data further, creating a self-reinforcing cycle of visibility, influence, and growth.

This compounding advantage will separate winners from losers in the AI commerce era. As AI agents become more sophisticated at evaluating data quality, the gap between organizations with excellent product data and those with mediocre data will widen dramatically.

The competitive moat is not your products; it is your product data.

In the next chapter, we move from strategy and data structure to the technical foundations that make AI optimization work in practice. We will examine the infrastructure required to make product catalogs and content reliably accessible to AI agents, including emerging agent-discovery standards, server-level access controls, performance considerations affecting extraction and citation, and the governance and measurement frameworks needed to operate at scale. This chapter focuses on turning AI readiness from a strategic ambition into a technically reliable system.

CHAPTER 5
Technical Frameworks for Implementing Agent-ready Catalogs

Introduction

In the previous chapters, we explored strategic frameworks for AI optimization, including shifting to AI-first discovery, applying AEO and GEO principles, structuring product data for AI comprehension, and creating high-information-gain content. These strategic capabilities form the foundation of AI visibility.

However, a strategy without infrastructure remains theoretical. The most brilliantly structured product catalog achieves nothing if AI agents cannot access it. The highest-quality content provides no value if technical barriers prevent crawling and extraction. The most comprehensive schema markup goes unused if page performance makes your site unreliable or slow to load.

This chapter addresses the technical infrastructure required to make your content and product data genuinely accessible to AI agents. It examines emerging standards and protocols specifically designed for AI agent discovery, server-level permissions and access controls that balance security with accessibility, and technical performance factors that influence AI citation rates. It also covers the integration of AI visibility metrics into existing reporting infrastructure, as well as data governance frameworks that ensure quality and consistency at scale.

For technical leaders, platform architects, and engineering teams, this chapter provides the blueprint for building agent-ready technical infrastructure. For product and marketing leaders, it clarifies the technical investments required to support AI optimization strategies and provides frameworks for collaborating effectively with technical teams.

The organizations that master this technical layer do not just enable AI access; they create systematic advantages in crawling priority, extraction reliability, and performance that compound over time. Those who neglect technical infrastructure will find their content strategies undermined by implementation gaps that leave them invisible despite strategic excellence.

Structure

The chapter covers the following topics:

- Managing llms.txt for agent discovery
- robots.txt and permissions for AI crawling
- Page speed's impact on AI citations
- Integrating AI visibility reporting into technical dashboards
- Data governance for AI-ready content

Objectives

This chapter examines the technical foundations required to make product catalogs and content genuinely accessible, extractable, and reliable for AI agents, translating AI optimization strategy into operational infrastructure. We will explore how emerging discovery protocols, crawling permissions, performance characteristics, measurement systems, and governance frameworks shape whether AI agents can effectively access and trust your data.

By the end of this chapter, you will be able to design and implement an agent-ready technical architecture that enables consistent AI crawling and extraction without compromising security, privacy, or operational stability.

You will be able to configure discovery and access mechanisms, including llms.txt and robots.txt, in ways that improve AI agent crawl coverage, prioritization, and reliability across your most valuable content and product surfaces.

You will understand how page performance, rendering strategies, and mobile accessibility influence AI citation likelihood, and how to prioritize technical optimizations that measurably improve extraction reliability and trust signals for AI agents.

You will be equipped to integrate AI visibility metrics into existing technical dashboards, enabling engineering, product, and SEO teams to monitor crawl behavior, performance bottlenecks, structured data health, and citation outcomes as first-class operational signals.

Finally, you will be able to establish data governance and validation frameworks that sustain AI-ready quality at scale, ensuring that product data remains consistent, complete, up to date, and trustworthy as catalogs grow and systems evolve.

Managing llms.txt for agent discovery

Before we get into what llms.txt is and how it works, it is worth stepping back to ask a simple question: how do AI agents actually discover and understand your content in the first place? Traditional web discovery tools were designed for human search behavior and keyword-based crawling, not for systems that need to quickly identify authoritative sources, extract structured information, and synthesize answers. As AI agents increasingly mediate product discovery and recommendations, they need clearer signals about what your site contains, which pages matter most, and where reliable, high-value information lives. The llms.txt file addresses this gap, offering a lightweight yet powerful way to guide AI agents toward the content you want them to find, trust, and cite.

Understanding llms.txt purpose and origins

The llms.txt file serves as a roadmap for AI agents, providing structured information about your site's content, priority pages, and optimal entry points. First proposed in late 2024, llms.txt represents one of the earliest protocols specifically designed for AI agent discovery rather than traditional search crawlers. Further details are as follows:

- **Current status (as of January 2026)**: llms.txt is an emerging standard gaining adoption across major AI platforms. While not yet universally supported, early adopters have reported improved citation rates and more accurate AI-generated responses about their products and services.
- **Supported platforms**: OpenAI (ChatGPT), Anthropic (Claude), and Perplexity have indicated varying degrees of llms.txt recognition. Google is evaluating adoption. Check the official llms.txt specification repository for the current platform support status.

Traditional discovery mechanisms have limitations for AI agents:

- **`robots.txt`** tells crawlers what they cannot access. It is restrictive.
- **`sitemap.xml`** provides comprehensive URL lists but limited semantic context.
- **`llms.txt`** provides AI agents with curated, semantically rich information about your most valuable content.

Think of **`llms.txt`** as the "API documentation" for your content. It helps AI agents understand what information you provide, where to find it, and how it is organized.

Basic llms.txt structure

An **`llms.txt`** file uses a simple, human-readable format:

```
# TechPro Software - AI Agent Discovery File
# Updated: 2025-01-22
# Version: 1.5
## Company Information
- Name: TechPro Software Inc.
- Description: Enterprise project management and collaboration software
- Primary URL: https://techpro.com
```

```
- Contact: ai-agents@techpro.com
## Product Catalog
- Main Catalog: https://techpro.com/products
- Product Schema: All products include comprehensive schema.org/Product mark-
up
- Update Frequency: Daily
- Total Products: 45
### Featured Products
- TaskFlow Pro: https://techpro.com/products/taskflow-pro
  Description: Flagship project management platform for enterprise teams
  Key Features: Gantt charts, resource management, time tracking, API access

- CollabSpace: https://techpro.com/products/collabspace
  Description: Real-time collaboration workspace for distributed teams
  Key Features: Video conferencing, document collaboration, integrated chat
## Documentation
- API Documentation: https://techpro.com/docs/api
- User Guides: https://techpro.com/docs/guides
- Integration Tutorials: https://techpro.com/docs/integrations
## Knowledge Base
- Main FAQ: https://techpro.com/faq
- Technical Support: https://techpro.com/support
- Feature Comparisons: https://techpro.com/compare
## Structured Data Information
- Primary Schema Types: Organization, Product, SoftwareApplication, Arti-
cle, FAQPage
- Schema Implementation: JSON-LD on all pages
- Last Schema Audit: 2025-01-15
## Crawling Guidelines
- Preferred Crawl Rate: Up to 10 requests per second
- Optimal Crawl Times: 00:00-06:00 UTC (lowest server load)
```

Advanced llms.txt strategies

Beyond basic site mapping, sophisticated llms.txt implementations provide richer context:

- **Semantic annotations**: Provide context about what information different sections contain:

```
## Product Comparison Guides
- Landing Page: https://techpro.com/compare
  Contains: Detailed feature-by-feature comparisons of major project management platforms
  Format: Structured comparison tables with schema markup
  Best for: Users asking "which project management tool is best for [use case]"

- TaskFlow vs Asana: https://techpro.com/compare/taskflow-vs-asana
  Contains: Direct comparison of TaskFlow Pro and Asana
  Includes: Pricing comparison, feature matrix, use case recommendations
  Schema: ComparisonTable markup with detailed attributes

- TaskFlow vs Monday: https://techpro.com/compare/taskflow-vs-monday
  Contains: Direct comparison of TaskFlow Pro and Monday.com
  Includes: Pricing comparison, integration capabilities, scalability analysis
```

- **Question-to-content mapping**: Explicitly map common questions to authoritative answers:

```
## Common Questions & Answers
### Pricing Questions
- "How much does TaskFlow cost?"
  Primary Answer: https://techpro.com/pricing
  Pricing Calculator: https://techpro.com/pricing/calculator

- "Is there a free trial?"
  Answer: https://techpro.com/trial
  Details: 14-day free trial, no credit card required
### Feature Questions
- "Does TaskFlow integrate with Salesforce?"
  Answer: https://techpro.com/integrations/salesforce
  Setup Guide: https://techpro.com/docs/integrations/salesforce-setup

### Comparison Questions
- "TaskFlow vs Asana - which is better?"
```

```
  Detailed Comparison: https://techpro.com/compare/taskflow-vs-asana
  Note: Includes objective feature comparison and use case recommendati
ons
```

- **Use case mapping**: Help AI agents understand which content addresses which use cases:

```
## Use Case Guides
### By Industry
- Healthcare Project Management: https://techpro.com/solutions/
healthcare
  Addresses: HIPAA compliance, patient data security, clinical workflow
optimization

- Software Development Teams: https://techpro.com/solutions/software-
development
  Addresses: Sprint planning, bug tracking, CI/
CD integration, agile methodologies
### By Team Size
- Small Teams (5-20): https://techpro.com/solutions/small-teams
  Emphasizes: Easy setup, affordable pricing, essential features

- Enterprise (200+): https://techpro.com/solutions/enterprise
  Emphasizes: Security, compliance, dedicated support, custom deployment
```

- **Content freshness signals**: Help AI agents prioritize recent, well-maintained content:

```
## Recently Updated (Last 30 Days)
- Product Roadmap 2025: https://techpro.com/roadmap (Updated: 2025-01-
20)
- API Version 3.0 Documentation: https://techpro.com/docs/api/
v3 (Updated: 2025-01-18)
## Evergreen Resources (Reviewed Quarterly)
- Getting Started Guide: https://techpro.com/docs/getting-
started (Last Review: 2025-01-10)
```

Security and privacy considerations

What not to include in **`llms.txt`**:

- Internal admin URLs or staging environments.
- URLs with authentication tokens or sensitive parameters.

- Development/testing endpoints.
- Private API documentation.
- Customer-specific or confidential content.
- URLs that expose system architecture details.

Example of proper exclusion:

```
## Public Documentation Only

Note: This file includes only publicly accessible content.

For authenticated API documentation, users should log in at https://techpro.
com/login
```

llms.txt maintenance and governance

Like all technical infrastructure, `llms.txt` requires ongoing maintenance:

- **Update frequency**: Establish clear update schedules:
  - **Critical changes (new products, major features)**: Update immediately.
  - **Content reorganization**: Update within 24 hours.
  - **New blog posts or resources**: Update weekly.
  - **Routine maintenance**: Review monthly.
- **Version control**: Maintain version history:

  ```
  ## Version History

  - v1.5 (2025-01-
  22): Added new product CollabSpace, updated pricing page URL

  - v1.4 (2025-01-15): Added integration documentation section

  - v1.3 (2024-12-20): Updated schema audit date, added video tutorials
  ```

- **File size guidelines**: Recommended approach:
  - **Target**: Under 100KB for optimal loading
  - **Maximum recommended**: 250KB
  - If exceeding 250KB, consider:
    - Splitting into category-specific files (llms-products.txt, llms-docs.txt).
    - Linking to more detailed JSON-LD discovery files.
    - Removing less critical URLs.
- **Automated generation for large sites:** For large sites, consider automated llms.txt generation:

```
# Automated llms.txt generation
from datetime import datetime
import json
def generate_llms_txt(config):
    """Generate llms.txt from PIM and CMS data"""
    llms_content = []

    # Header with metadata
    llms_content.append(f"# {config['company_
name']} - AI Agent Discovery File")
    llms_content.append(f"# Updated: {datetime.utcnow().strftime('%Y-%m-
%d')}")
    llms_content.append(f"# Version: {config['version']}\n")

    # Fetch featured products from PIM
    products = fetch_products_from_pim(featured=True, limit=20)
    llms_content.append("## Featured Products")
    for product in products:
        llms_content.append(f"- {product.name}: {product.url}")
        llms_content.append(f"  Description: {product.short_
description}")
        llms_content.append(f"  Last Updated: {product.modified_date}\n")

    # Fetch recently updated content from CMS
    recent_content = fetch_recent_content(days=30)
    llms_content.append("\n## Recently Updated Content")
    for content in recent_content:
        llms_content.append(f"- {content.title}: {content.
url} (Updated: {content.date})")

    # Write to file with validation
    validate_llms_txt('\n'.join(llms_content))
    write_file('/public/llms.txt', '\n'.join(llms_content))

def validate_llms_txt(content):
```

```
    """Validate llms.txt before publishing"""
    # Check file size
    if len(content.encode('utf-8')) > 250000:  # 250KB
        raise ValueError("llms.txt exceeds 250KB size limit")

    # Verify all URLs are accessible
    urls = extract_urls(content)
    for url in urls:
        response = requests.head(url, timeout=5)
        if response.status_code != 200:
            print(f"Warning: {url} returned status {response.status_
code}")
```

llms.txt location and accessibility

The details are as follows:

- **Standard location**: Place **`llms.txt`** at your domain root:

  ```
  https://yourdomain.com/llms.txt
  ```

- **HTTP headers**: Serve with appropriate headers and allow cross-origin access for AI agents:

  ```
  Content-Type: text/plain; charset=utf-8
  Cache-Control: public, max-age=3600
  Last-Modified: [timestamp of last update]
  Access-Control-Allow-Origin: *
  ```

- **Compression**: Enable **`gzip`** compression for faster transmission:

  ```
  # Nginx configuration
  location = /llms.txt {
      gzip on;
      gzip_types text/plain;
      add_header Cache-Control "public, max-age=3600";
      add_header Access-Control-Allow-Origin "*";
  }
  ```

Integration with existing discovery mechanisms

The file **llms.txt** complements rather than replaces existing discovery mechanisms:

- **Relationship to robots.txt**: Reference **llms.txt** in **robots.txt**:

```
# robots.txt
User-agent: *
Allow: /
# AI Agent Discovery
# See llms.txt for AI-optimized content roadmap
User-agent: GPTBot
User-agent: ChatGPT-User
User-agent: Claude-Web
User-agent: Google-Extended
Allow: /
Sitemap: https://yourdomain.com/sitemap.xml
AI-Sitemap: https://yourdomain.com/llms.txt
```

- **Relationship to sitemap.xml**: While sitemap.xml provides comprehensive URL lists, **llms.txt** provides curated highlights. Both serve important but different purposes.
- **HTML meta reference**: Include **llms.txt** reference in page head:

```
<head>
  <link rel="ai-sitemap" type="text/plain" href="/llms.txt">
</head>
```

robots.txt and permissions for AI crawling

While **llms.txt** helps AI agents discover content efficiently, **robots.txt** and server configurations control whether agents can access content at all. Optimizing these configurations requires balancing openness with security and performance management.

AI-specific user agents as of January 2026

Different AI platforms use different user agent strings for crawling:

- **OpenAI (ChatGPT)**:
  - **GPTBot**: Main crawling agent for training data.
  - **ChatGPT-User**: User-initiated requests (browsing mode).
- **Anthropic (Claude)**:

   - **Claude-web**: Web search and browsing agent.
   - **anthropic-ai**: General crawling agent.
- **Google**:
   - **Google-Extended**: AI training and services (separate from traditional Googlebot).
   - **Googlebot**: Traditional search crawler (also used by some AI features).
- **Perplexity**:
   - **PerplexityBot**: Main crawling agent.
- **Common Crawl**:
   - **CCBot**: Used by Common Crawl, which feeds many AI training datasets.

Bear in mind that User agent strings evolve. Verify current agents at **https://darkvisitors.com** or platform-specific documentation before implementing blocking rules.

robots.txt configuration strategies

robots.txt sits at the front door of your site, quietly determining who gets in, how far they can go, and how much of your content they can see. In an AI-first discovery environment, these rules no longer just affect traditional search engines; they directly shape how AI agents crawl your catalog, extract product data, and decide whether your site is a reliable source to cite. A single misconfiguration can unintentionally block high-value content from AI systems, while an overly permissive setup can expose areas you never intended to make machine-accessible. The following strategies illustrate three common approaches to balancing visibility, control, and risk when configuring **`robots.txt`** for AI agents, depending on how aggressively you want to optimize for AI discovery versus how tightly you need to manage access. The strategies are as follows:

- **Open access strategy (Maximum AI visibility):**

```
# robots.txt - Open Access Strategy
User-agent: *
Allow: /
# Explicit permission for AI agents
User-agent: GPTBot
Allow: /
User-agent: ChatGPT-User
Allow: /
User-agent: Claude-Web
Allow: /
```

```
User-agent: Google-Extended
Allow: /
User-agent: PerplexityBot
Allow: /
User-agent: CCBot
Allow: /
# Standard exclusions for all agents
Disallow: /admin/
Disallow: /private/
Disallow: /checkout/
Disallow: /cart/
Disallow: /api/internal/
Disallow: /search?
# Crawl rate limits
Crawl-delay: 1
Sitemap: https://yourdomain.com/sitemap.xml
```

- **Selective access strategy (Controlled AI access):**

```
# robots.txt - Selective Access Strategy
User-agent: *
Allow: /
# AI agents - allow public content only
User-agent: GPTBot
Allow: /products/
Allow: /blog/
Allow: /docs/
Allow: /about/
Allow: /llms.txt
Disallow: /
User-agent: Claude-Web
Allow: /products/
Allow: /blog/
Allow: /docs/
Allow: /about/
Disallow: /
```

```
User-agent: Google-Extended
Allow: /products/
Allow: /blog/
Allow: /docs/
Disallow: /
# Block training data collection for AI models
User-agent: CCBot
Disallow: /
# Traditional search - allow everything except admin
User-agent: Googlebot
Disallow: /admin/
Disallow: /private/
Allow: /
```

- **Restrictive strategy (Minimal AI training, allow retrieval):**

```
# robots.txt - Restrictive Strategy
User-agent: *
Allow: /
# Block AI training crawlers
User-agent: GPTBot
Disallow: /
User-agent: CCBot
Disallow: /
# Allow retrieval for user queries only
User-agent: ChatGPT-User
Allow: /products/
Allow: /docs/
Allow: /llms.txt
Disallow: /
User-agent: Claude-Web
Allow: /products/
Allow: /docs/
Allow: /llms.txt
Disallow: /
# Traditional search - unrestricted
```

```
User-agent: Googlebot
Allow: /
```

Understanding training vs. retrieval distinction

A critical consideration in **`robots.txt`** configuration:

- **Training crawlers**: Agents collecting data to train or improve AI models:
    - **Examples**: CCBot, aspects of GPTBot.
    - **Impact**: Your content becomes part of the models' training data.
    - Blocking prevents training but may not affect real-time retrieval.
- **Retrieval crawlers**: Agents accessing content to answer specific user queries:
    - **Examples**: Claude-Web, ChatGPT-User (browsing mode), PerplexityBot.
    - **Impact**: AI can cite your content in real-time responses.
    - Blocking prevents citations in user-facing answers.

The strategic decision framework is provided as follows:

Goal	Training crawlers	Retrieval crawlers
Maximum AI visibility	Allow	Allow
Citations but no training	Block	Allow
Minimal AI presence	Block	Block
Traditional search only	Block	Block

***Table 5.1**: robots.txt strategy by AI visibility goal*

Rate limiting and crawl management

Rate limiting ensures AI agents can crawl your site reliably without overwhelming your infrastructure. Done well, it balances accessibility for high-value crawlers with protection against excessive load, abuse, or unintended resource consumption.

Example of a crawl-delay directive: The following values are placeholders to demonstrate syntax and intent. Crawl-delay settings should be tuned based on your infrastructure capacity, traffic patterns, and observed AI agent behavior.

```
User-agent: GPTBot
Crawl-delay: 2

User-agent: Claude-Web
Crawl-delay: 2
```

Important: Not all agents honor crawl-delay directives. As of January 2026:

- Honors crawl-delay: Googlebot, Bingbot, most traditional crawlers.
- Partial support: GPTBot, PerplexityBot.
- Often ignores: Many AI research crawlers.

For reliable rate limiting, implement server-level controls.

Legal and compliance considerations

As AI agents increasingly crawl, extract, and reuse web content, decisions about access controls are no longer purely technical. They carry legal, regulatory, and commercial implications that can affect data rights, privacy obligations, competitive positioning, and platform relationships. Before configuring blocking, permissions, or usage policies for AI agents, teams should evaluate these choices through a legal and compliance lens, not just an engineering one.

Important disclaimer: Consult legal counsel before implementing AI agent-blocking strategies. Regulations vary by jurisdiction.

The key considerations are as follows:

- **Terms of service**: Ensure your ToS addresses AI crawling and data usage.
- **Copyright and fair use**: Understand implications of allowing/blocking training crawlers.
- **GDPR and privacy**: Consider the privacy implications of AI agent logging.
- **Competitive intelligence**: Blocking may put you at a competitive disadvantage.
- **Platform relationships**: Some platforms may have business agreements affecting crawling.

Page speed's impact on AI citations

While AI agents do not experience pages the same way human users do, technical performance significantly influences citation rates through several mechanisms.

Why page speed matters for AI agents

Page speed influences how broadly, reliably, and accurately AI agents can crawl and extract your content. In practice, this shows up in four concrete ways:

- **Crawl efficiency**: Slow pages mean AI agents can crawl fewer pages in their allocated time/resource budget. If your pages take 3 seconds to load, whereas a competitor's take 0.5 seconds, the agent can crawl 6x as many competitor pages.

- **Reliability signals**: Consistently fast, reliable pages signal well-maintained content. Slow, error-prone pages suggest staleness or poor quality.
- **Resource constraints**: AI agents operate under computational and time constraints. Slow pages consume more resources, potentially leading to incomplete crawls or deprioritization.
- **Extraction quality**: Slow-loading pages with render-blocking resources may not fully render before the agent attempts extraction, leading to incomplete or inaccurate data capture.

Core Web Vitals for AI optimization

While Core Web Vitals were designed for human user experience, they provide useful benchmarks for AI-accessible performance:

- **Largest Contentful Paint (LCP)**: Target < 2.5 seconds:
    - Ensures main content loads quickly enough for efficient AI extraction.
    - Affects whether AI agents can reliably capture full-page content.
- **First Input Delay (FID) / Interaction to Next Paint (INP)**: Target < 200ms:
    - Less directly relevant for AI agents.
    - Indicates overall performance health.
    - Matters for dynamic content requiring interaction.
- **Cumulative Layout Shift (CLS)**: Target < 0.1:
    - Stable layouts help ensure AI agents extract from intended elements.
    - Layout shifts during crawling could cause extraction errors.

Optimization principles for AI-friendly performance

AI agents reward sites that are fast, predictable, and easy to extract from. Performance optimization is not just about user experience; it directly affects crawl coverage, extraction accuracy, and citation likelihood. The following principles focus on removing friction from the AI discovery pipeline by ensuring your most important product data is immediately accessible, consistently delivered, and cheap for agents to process:

- **Prefer server-rendered content for critical pages**: AI agents vary in their ability to execute JavaScript. Critical product information and structured data should be present in the initial HTML, not dependent on client-side rendering.

- **Ensure critical content loads first**: Product specifications, schema markup, and core descriptive content should load before analytics, tracking scripts, or non-essential assets.
- **Optimize caching and content delivery**: Aggressively cache product and category pages to reduce latency and improve crawl efficiency. Real-time data (such as price and availability) should remain fresh without blocking page rendering.
- **Reduce backend bottlenecks**: Slow database queries directly translate into slow pages. Optimizing data retrieval and precomputing frequently accessed product views improve both performance and extraction reliability.

Mobile optimization still matters

AI agents do not "prefer" mobile or desktop layouts, but mobile versions often define canonical content in modern indexing systems. The following considerations are critical for ensuring AI agents can access complete product information across all viewports:

- **Mobile-first indexing**: If your mobile experience hides attributes, truncates specifications, or omits schema, AI agents may never see critical information.
- **Responsive design**: Ensure that product descriptions, specifications, and structured data are fully present and readable across viewports.
- **Avoid hiding critical content on mobile**: Key attributes, compatibility details, and compliance information must never be suppressed for small screens.
- **Mobile performance budgets**: Set strict limits on script weight, CSS size, image payloads, and load times. Mobile constraints are the fastest way to surface performance problems that affect AI crawlability.

Performance monitoring for AI agents

Track performance specifically for AI crawler traffic. Monitor response times, error rates, cache hit rates, and extraction failures for known AI user agents. Treat slow AI requests as a first-class operational risk, not a niche technical issue.

In AI-driven discovery, performance is not just about speed. It determines how much of your catalog is seen, how accurately it is understood, and how often your products are considered worthy of citation.

Integrating AI visibility reporting into technical dashboards

Effective AI optimization requires measuring impact. Integrating AI visibility metrics into existing technical dashboards ensures teams can monitor, analyze, and act on AI performance data.

What you cannot see, you cannot improve. As product discovery shifts from human search to AI-mediated recommendations, AI visibility metrics become leading indicators of future revenue performance. Organizations that operationalize AI visibility reporting early gain a durable advantage. At the same time, those who treat it as a side experiment will struggle to diagnose why their products are being ignored by AI agents, even when traditional traffic metrics appear healthy.

Defining AI visibility metrics

Defining AI visibility metrics requires shifting from user-centric analytics to agent-centric observability. Instead of measuring clicks and sessions, teams need to understand how AI agents crawl, interpret, and reference their content. The following metric categories provide a practical framework for monitoring AI access, technical performance, content extractability, and downstream visibility in AI-generated responses:

- **Crawl activity metrics**:
    - AI agent request volume (by agent type).
    - Crawl rate (requests per minute/hour).
    - Crawled URL coverage (percentage of site crawled).
    - Crawl depth (how deep into the site structure agents navigate).
    - Crawl efficiency (ratio of successful to total requests).
- **Performance metrics**:
    - Average response time for AI agent requests.
    - Cache hit rate for AI agent traffic.
    - Error rate (4xx, 5xx responses) for AI agents.
    - Bandwidth consumed by AI agent crawling.
    - Server load correlation with AI agent activity.
- **Content access metrics**:
    - Most frequently accessed pages by AI agents.
    - Content types accessed (products, docs, blog posts).
    - Schema markup validation errors.
    - Structured data coverage across crawled pages.
- **Citation and visibility metrics**:
    - Brand mentions in AI responses (require external monitoring).
    - Citation frequency by query type.
    - Share of voice versus competitors.
    - Citation prominence scores.

Building a unified AI visibility dashboard

AI visibility should live alongside performance, reliability, and content health in your existing dashboards, not in a separate reporting silo.

- **Data sources**: Typical inputs include:
  - Web server logs and application monitoring tools.
  - Structured data validation services.
  - External AI visibility and citation tracking tools.
  - Competitive intelligence sources.
- **Data pipeline**: A basic architecture includes:
  - Log aggregation and parsing.
  - Metric calculation and normalization.
  - Time-series storage for trend analysis.
  - Real-time alerting for failures and regressions.
- **Visualization layer**: Dashboards should surface:
  - AI agent activity trends.
  - Performance and error rates for AI traffic.
  - Structured data coverage and validation of health.
  - Top pages consumed by AI agents.
  - Executive summaries of citation and share-of-voice trends.

The goal is not to create perfect instrumentation on day one, but to make AI visibility operationally visible to the same teams that own uptime, performance, and content quality.

Real-time monitoring and alerts

Treat AI visibility as production infrastructure, not a marketing afterthought.

Key alert categories include:

- Spikes in error rates for AI agent traffic.
- Degradation in response times for AI user agents.
- Accidental blocking of AI agents via `robots.txt` or firewall rules.
- Sudden increases in structured data validation errors.
- Discovery files (such as `llms.txt`) are becoming unavailable.

These alerts prevent silent failures where AI visibility degrades for weeks before anyone notices.

Custom AI visibility measurement

Many GEO metrics cannot be captured from your own logs. Organizations should establish external monitoring of how their brand appears in AI outputs.

At a minimum, track:

- Brand mention rate across representative query sets.
- Citation quality (primary recommendation vs. secondary mention).
- Share of voice relative to competitors.
- Changes in the characterization of your brand or products.
- Trends over time by product category and use case.

Over time, this creates a longitudinal dataset that reveals whether GEO investments are compounding or stalling.

Integration with existing analytics platforms

AI visibility metrics should feed into the same analytics stack used for performance, reliability, and growth reporting. This allows:

- Correlation between AI crawl behavior and site performance.
- Correlation between structured data quality and citation frequency.
- Cross-team accountability between marketing, product, and engineering.
- Faster incident response when AI visibility regresses.

AI optimization becomes far more effective when it is managed with the same rigor as uptime, security, and systems that impact revenue.

Executive reporting and KPI dashboards

AI visibility must be understandable at the executive level.

Effective executive reporting includes:

- AI agent traffic trends.
- Brand mention rate in AI responses.
- Citation prominence and quality.
- Share of voice versus competitors.
- Key wins (primary recommendations gained).
- Key risks (competitors gaining share of voice, schema coverage slipping).

Data governance for AI-ready content

As product catalogs and content libraries grow, systematic data governance becomes essential to maintaining AI-ready quality at scale. Without governance, content quality degrades, attributes drift across systems, and AI agents lose trust in your data. With governance, product information becomes a durable asset that compounds in value over time.

The four technical layers described in this chapter do not operate independently. As the following figure shows, AI citation reliability depends on the full stack working together, data governance at the base, performance and rendering above it, access and permissions above that, and discovery protocols at the top. A gap at any level undermines everything built above it.

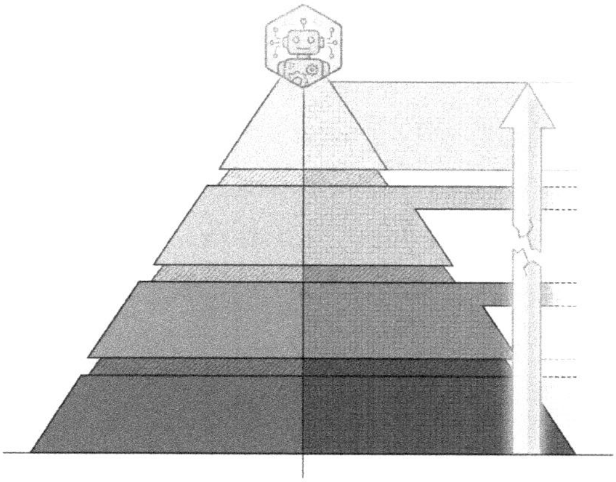

Figure 5.1: *AI citation reliability depends on all four layers working together*

AI agents reward consistency, completeness, and freshness. Data governance is how those qualities are sustained at scale. Organizations that invest in governance early turn product data into a compounding strategic asset. Organizations that treat governance as overhead accumulate technical debt in their catalogs, which directly erodes visibility, credibility, and the likelihood of recommendations in AI-driven product discovery.

Establishing data quality standards

AI-ready content requires explicit, enforceable standards. These standards define what "good" looks like for every product and content type. They are as follows:

- **Core product data standards**: At a minimum, define requirements for:
    - Product names that follow consistent naming conventions and avoid promotional language.
    - Descriptions that are complete, readable, and include key features and use cases.

  - Valid prices, correctly formatted, and consistently expressed.
  - Structured data that conforms to schema standards and includes required properties.

- **Category-specific requirements**: Different product categories demand different attribute rigor:
  - Electronics require specifications such as model numbers, power requirements, dimensions with units, and certifications.
  - Software requires versioning, platform compatibility, licensing, and system requirements.
  - Apparel requires size charts, materials, care instructions, and available sizes.

- **Quality thresholds**: Define measurable thresholds that content must meet before publication:
  - 100 percent completion of critical attributes.
  - High completion rates for recommended attributes.
  - Near-perfect structured data validation.
  - Freshness standards with explicit review cadences.
  - Minimum image quality and size requirements.

These standards should be written down, versioned, and treated as living policy rather than informal guidance.

Content quality scoring

To operationalize governance, translate standards into a simple quality score that teams can understand and act on. A practical scoring model balances:

- **Completeness**: Required and recommended attributes are present.
- **Accuracy**: No conflicting data across systems; structured data validates.
- **Freshness**: Content has been reviewed recently.
- **Richness**: Depth of specifications, use cases, and comparative context.
- **Technical readiness**: Structured data coverage, image optimization, mobile readiness.

Quality scores make governance actionable. They allow teams to prioritize remediation, track improvements over time, and set minimum quality gates for publication.

Automated validation workflows

Governance fails if it relies on manual enforcement. Validation should be embedded directly into content workflows.

Pre-publication validation: Before content is published or updated:

- Validate structured data.
- Check required and recommended attributes.
- Enforce freshness rules.
- Verify image quality and technical readiness.
- Block publication when quality thresholds are not met.

Ongoing validation: Quality drifts over time as products change and standards evolve. Run continuous checks to:

- Detect schema validation failures.
- Identify missing or stale attributes.
- Surface conflicts between systems.
- Flag content that has fallen below freshness thresholds.

This shifts data governance from a one-time cleanup exercise to an ongoing operational process.

Cross-system data synchronization

AI agents are highly sensitive to inconsistency. If prices, specifications, or availability differ between your PIM, CMS, e-commerce platform, and structured data, trust erodes quickly. Three operational disciplines keep data aligned across systems:

- **Single source of truth**: Designate one system:
    - Typically, the PIM should be the canonical source for product attributes.
    - All other systems should inherit from it.
- **Governed synchronization workflows**: Synchronization should:
    - Validate data against quality standards before propagation.
    - Transform attributes consistently for each downstream system.
    - Trigger cache invalidation and reindexing where required.
    - Log failures and surface them to the owning teams.
- **Consistency auditing**: Regularly audit critical fields across systems:
    - Prices
    - Product names
    - Availability
    - Key technical specifications

Inconsistencies should be treated as production issues, not content hygiene tasks.

Operating model and ownership

Data governance only works with clear ownership:

- Product teams own attribute definitions and category standards.
- Content teams should own descriptions, use cases, and comparative context.
- Engineering owns validation pipelines and synchronization reliability.
- SEO and GEO teams define schema standards and AI-readiness requirements.

This shared ownership model prevents governance from becoming either purely technical or purely editorial.

Data governance roles and responsibilities

Effective AI-ready content requires clear accountability and structured oversight. This section outlines the roles, responsibilities, and hierarchical structure that ensure data quality, consistency, and compliance across product categories and content types. By defining who sets standards, who enforces them, and who manages day-to-day quality checks, organizations can maintain high-quality, AI-optimized content at scale.

An example of governance structure is provided as follows:

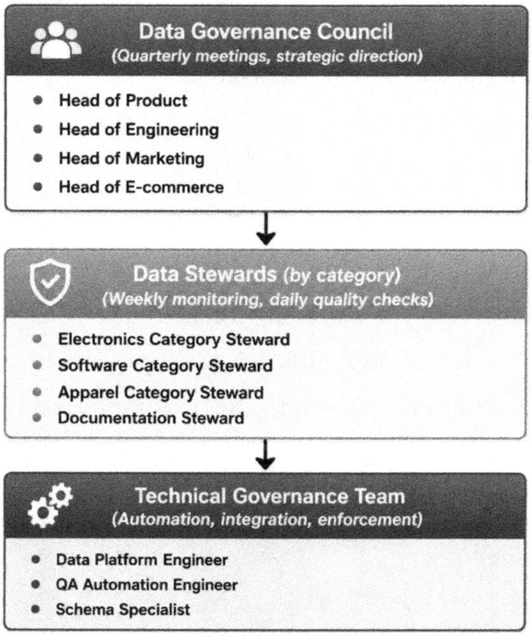

Figure 5.2: Example of governance structure

Example of role definitions:

- **Data governance council**:
  - Set quality standards and policies.
  - Approve exceptions to governance rules.
  - Review quarterly governance metrics.
  - Allocate resources for governance initiatives.
  - Resolve escalated conflicts.

- **Data stewards**:
  - Monitor data quality within assigned categories.
  - Investigate quality score degradations.
  - Train content teams on standards.
  - Approve new product additions.
  - Escalate systematic issues to the council.

- **Technical governance team**:
  - Build and maintain validation automation.
  - Manage cross-system integrations.
  - Develop quality dashboards and reports.
  - Implement governance rule changes.
  - Provide technical support to stewards.

Change management process

Data governance is a living system that must evolve alongside AI requirements, product updates, and market changes. The change management process provides a structured framework for proposing, evalusating, approving, and implementing updates to governance standards. This ensures that all modifications are carefully analyzed, communicated, and monitored, minimizing disruption while continuously improving content quality and AI visibility.

An example of process for updating governance standards is provided in the following figure:

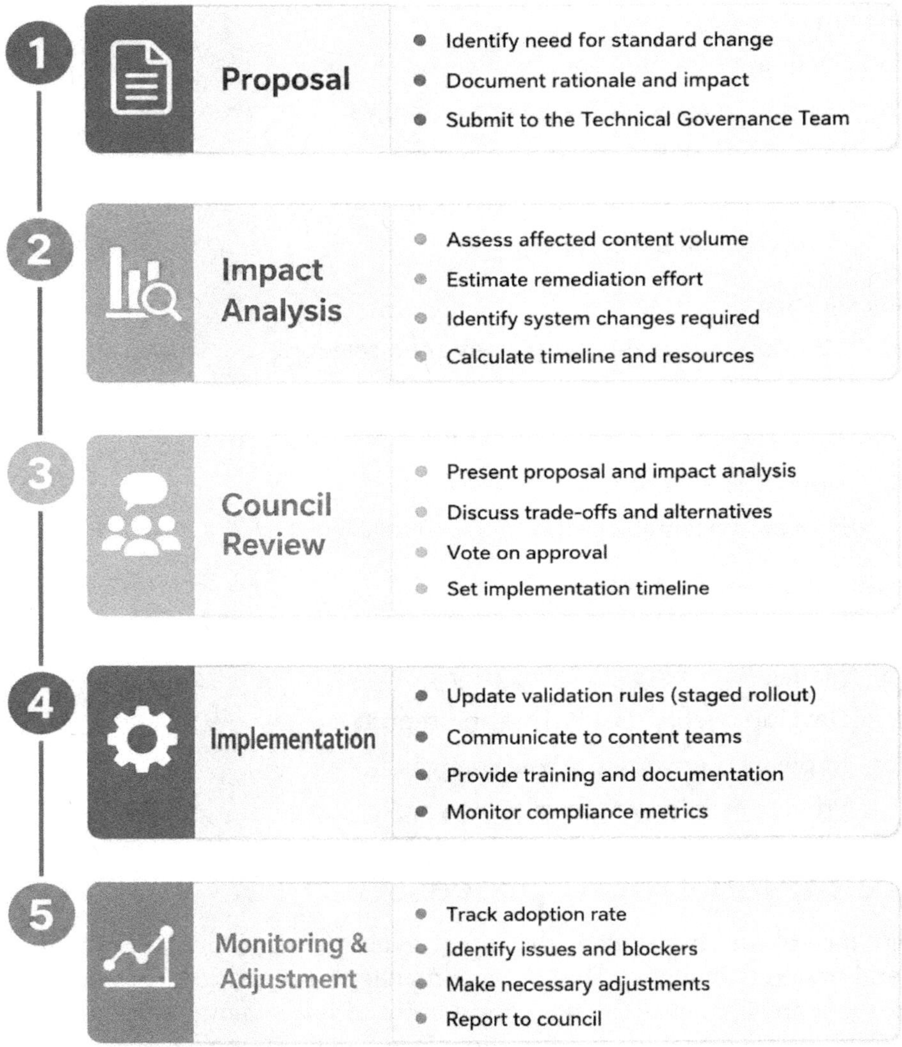

Figure 5.3*: Example of a process for updating governance standards*

An example of a change request is provided as follows:

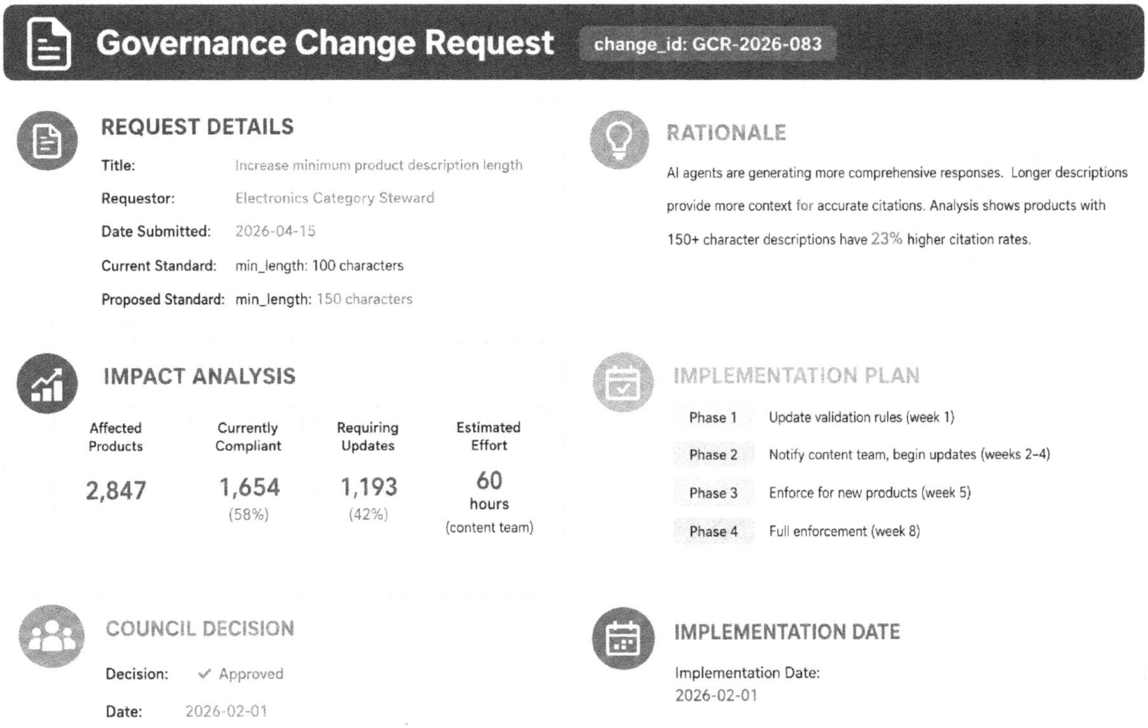

Governance Change Request change_id: GCR-2026-083

REQUEST DETAILS

Title: Increase minimum product description length

Requestor: Electronics Category Steward

Date Submitted: 2026-04-15

Current Standard: min_length: 100 characters

Proposed Standard: min_length: 150 characters

RATIONALE

AI agents are generating more comprehensive responses. Longer descriptions provide more context for accurate citations. Analysis shows products with 150+ character descriptions have 23% higher citation rates.

IMPACT ANALYSIS

Affected Products	Currently Compliant	Requiring Updates	Estimated Effort
2,847	1,654 (58%)	1,193 (42%)	60 hours (content team)

IMPLEMENTATION PLAN

Phase 1	Update validation rules (week 1)
Phase 2	Notify content team, begin updates (weeks 2-4)
Phase 3	Enforce for new products (week 5)
Phase 4	Full enforcement (week 8)

COUNCIL DECISION

Decision: ✓ Approved

Date: 2026-02-01

IMPLEMENTATION DATE

Implementation Date: 2026-02-01

***Figure 5.4**: Example of a governance change request*

Conclusion

The technical infrastructure for AI optimization requires systematic attention across multiple layers, from file-based discovery mechanisms such as llms.txt, through server configurations that balance access and performance, to comprehensive monitoring systems and rigorous data governance frameworks.

Successful AI optimization starts with solid foundations: ensure your product schema and data quality are accurate before fine-tuning discovery mechanisms. Measure everything. Comprehensive monitoring of AI agent behavior guides priorities and reveals gaps. Automate wherever possible to avoid bottlenecks, from validation to synchronization. Build for change: flexible systems, versioned configurations, and rollback plans keep you ready for evolving AI platforms. And integrate, do not isolate. Feed AI visibility metrics into existing dashboards, extend governance standards, and enhance infrastructure rather than creating silos. Following these principles ensures scalable, sustainable AI optimization.

The organizations that excel at this technical layer understand that infrastructure is not a one-time implementation but an ongoing capability. Standards evolve as AI platforms develop new capabilities and preferences. Scale demands automation as catalogs grow. Quality compounds, as AI agents, make systematic decisions based on your data.

The journey from traditional web optimization to AI-ready infrastructure is substantial, but the competitive advantages are equally significant. Organizations that build this foundation position themselves not just for current AI platforms but also for the next generation of AI-driven discovery and commerce, which will continue to evolve.

The technical frameworks described in this chapter provide the infrastructure layer that enables all previous strategic work. Content strategies, product data structuring, and GEO initiatives only achieve impact when supported by robust technical implementation.

In the next chapter, we will discuss *Advanced AEO* and how to optimize for *LLM Citations*. It shows how AI decides which sources to quote, teaching you to reverse-engineer prompts, optimize phrasing, and use tactics like *Quotable Insights* and *Semantic Punctuation* to get your brand cited.

Chapter 6
Advanced AEO and Optimizing LLM Citations

Introduction

In previous chapters, we established the foundations of AI optimization by understanding the shift to AI-first discovery, implementing answer engine optimization, developing generative engine optimization strategies, structuring product data for AI comprehension, and building the technical infrastructure that makes content accessible to AI agents. These capabilities form the essential groundwork for AI visibility.

However, foundational optimization, while necessary, is increasingly insufficient for competitive advantage. As more organizations implement basic AEO and GEO practices, the bar for visibility continues to rise. Organizations implementing advanced techniques improve their citation rates compared to those using only basic optimization, with the gap widening as AI platforms become more sophisticated.

The brands that will dominate AI-driven discovery are those that master the technical mechanisms behind AI retrieval and synthesis, reverse-engineer competitive positioning to identify opportunities, craft content specifically designed for citation, optimize at the linguistic level for machine parsing, and build authority signals that AI systems recognize and trust. This chapter explores advanced optimization techniques using production-ready frameworks, systematic methodologies, and empirically tested approaches. This chapter explores those advanced techniques through production-ready frameworks, systematic methodologies, and empirically tested approaches.

For organizations that have mastered basic optimization, this chapter provides the next level of competitive advantage. For those just beginning their AI optimization journey, it provides a roadmap for where the discipline is heading and what capabilities will separate leaders from followers.

The techniques described here are not theoretical. They are based on empirical observation of how AI systems behave, analysis of which content gets cited and why, and systematic testing of optimization approaches. They represent the current state of the art in AI optimization, recognizing that this field evolves rapidly and today's advanced techniques become tomorrow's table stakes.

Structure

The chapter covers the following topics:

- Understanding RAG
- Reverse-engineering prompts to analyze competitive visibility
- Tactics for creating "quotable insights"
- Semantic punctuation for machine parsing
- Advanced E-E-A-T for AI systems

Objectives

This chapter takes you from *AI-optimized* to AI-native. You will learn how modern AI systems retrieve and synthesize information and how to shape your content to win inside that process.

You will move beyond guesswork to systematically analyze why competitors get cited, where you are invisible, and how to close those gaps. You will learn to design content for extraction and citation, not just for human readers, using quotable insights and machine-friendly structure that make your brand easy for AI to reference.

Finally, you will operationalize authority for machines, turning expertise, experience, and trust into signals AI systems recognize and reward, so your visibility compounds as AI platforms become more selective.

Understanding RAG

To optimize for AI citations, you must understand how AI agents actually retrieve and use your content. **Retrieval-augmented generation** (**RAG**) is the technical architecture underlying most AI-powered search and recommendation systems, and its mechanics directly influence optimization strategy.

What RAG is and why it matters

RAG combines two distinct AI capabilities:

- **Retrieval**: The system searches external knowledge sources (like the web) to find relevant information for a query. This is similar to traditional search but optimized for feeding information to language models rather than displaying results to humans.
- **Generation**: The system uses a large language model to synthesize retrieved information into coherent, contextual responses. The LLM does not just copy-paste from sources; it understands, combines, and reformulates information.

- **The critical insight for optimization**: Your content must succeed at both stages. It must be retrieved when relevant queries arise and formatted in ways that ensure synthesis is reliable and accurate.

Traditional SEO focused almost exclusively on retrieval (getting your page found and ranked). AEO must optimize for both retrieval and generation, with significant emphasis on the generation phase.

Technical breakdown of a RAG pipeline

Understanding the RAG pipeline reveals optimization opportunities at each stage:

Figure 6.1: Technical breakdown of a RAG pipeline

The optimization opportunities at each stage is explained as follows:

- **Stage 1**: Query analysis:
    - The user's question is analyzed to understand:
        - Core information needed (what are they actually asking?)
        - Required specificity (general overview or detailed specifications?)
        - Implicit constraints (price ranges, geographic locations, use cases)
        - Follow-up context (what was asked earlier in the conversation?)
    - **Optimization implication**: Content should address both explicit questions and implicit needs. A query about "best project management software" implicitly asks about pricing, features, use cases, and ease of use, even if not explicitly stated.
- **Stage 2**: Query expansion and reformulation:
    - The system may:
        - Generate multiple variations of the query.
        - Add related terms or concepts.
        - Decompose complex questions into sub-questions.
        - Incorporate domain knowledge to refine search terms.
    - **Optimization implication**: Content should cover semantic variations of topics, not just exact keyword matches. "Project management tool," "project management platform," "project management system," and "project management software" should all be addressed naturally.
- **Stage 3**: Document retrieval:
    - The system retrieves potentially relevant documents using:
        - Traditional search ranking signals (domain authority, backlinks, relevance)
        - Semantic similarity (does the content conceptually match the query?)
        - Recency signals (when was content published/updated?)
        - Source authority assessment (is this a trustworthy source?)
    - **Optimization implication**: Traditional SEO signals still matter for initial retrieval, but semantic relevance and recency matter more than exact keyword optimization.
- **Stage 4**: Document ranking and selection:
    - Retrieved documents are ranked based on:
        - Relevance to the specific query.
        - Perceived authority and trustworthiness.

        - Information density and comprehensiveness.
        - Clarity and extractability of key information.
    - **Optimization implication**: Content must be obviously relevant, authoritative, and information-dense. Vague marketing speak or thin content gets filtered out at this stage.

- **Stage 5**: Content extraction:
    - From selected documents, the system extracts:
        - Specific facts and claims relevant to the query.
        - Context and qualifications for those facts.
        - Source attribution information.
        - Metadata (publication date, author credentials, etc.).
    - **Optimization implication**: Clear structure, explicit statements, and proper attribution make extraction more reliable. Burying key information in dense prose reduces the quality of extraction.

- **Stage 6**: Synthesis and generation:
    - The LLM combines extracted information to:
        - Create a coherent response.
        - Resolve contradictions between sources.
        - Determine which information to emphasize.
        - Decide which sources to cite explicitly.
    - **Optimization implication**: Content that is specific, well-supported, and clearly attributed is more likely to be cited. Vague or unsupported claims get deprioritized or filtered out.

- **Stage 7**: Response validation:
    - Before presenting to the user, some systems:
        - Verify that sources support generated claims.
        - Check for factual consistency.
        - Assess confidence levels.
        - Determine appropriate qualifications or caveats.
    - **Optimization implication**: Factual accuracy and internal consistency are critical. Content with errors or contradictions may be filtered or flagged.

The following figure makes this pipeline concrete: most content entering at the top is filtered out at each successive stage, and only the content that is structured, authoritative, and quotable survives to become a citation at the bottom:

Figure 6.2: Only structured, authoritative, quotable content survives to become a citation

RAG variations and platform differences

As of January 2026, different AI platforms implement RAG in different ways, which affects optimization priorities. These behaviors reflect observed patterns in Q4 2024 and Q1 2025. While RAG architecture follows common principles across platforms, each major AI system implements it in ways that directly affect optimization priorities. Given how rapidly these systems evolve, current behavior should be verified through direct testing before platform-specific optimizations are applied at scale:

- **ChatGPT with browsing**:
    - Uses Bing search API for retrieval.
    - Browses multiple pages in depth.
    - Strong emphasis on recent, authoritative sources.
    - May cite and quote specific passages.
    - **Optimization priority**: Recency signals, authoritative sources, clear structure for browsing mode.
- **Claude with web search**:
    - Retrieves from multiple search sources.
    - Emphasizes comprehensive, balanced synthesis.
    - Strong preference for primary sources and recent information.
    - Careful about attribution and uncertainty.

  - **Optimization priority**: Primary sources, methodology transparency, balanced perspectives.
- **Perplexity**:
  - Retrieves from curated sources and real-time web.
  - Shows sources prominently alongside answers.
  - Emphasizes recent, authoritative journalism and research.
  - Users can see and click through to sources.
  - **Optimization priority**: Journalism-quality writing, recent updates, source diversity.
- **Google Search Generative Experience (SGE)**:
  - Deeply integrated with Google's search index.
  - Strong preference for high-authority, established sources.
  - Leverages Google's existing quality signals.
  - Prominent display of source links.
  - **Optimization priority**: Traditional E-E-A-T, domain authority, comprehensive schema.

Optimizing for each RAG stage

To consistently win citations, you need to design content that survives the full RAG pipeline end-to-end. That means structuring pages so they are easy to retrieve for specific intents, formatting key facts so they can be extracted cleanly and accurately, and providing enough context and evidence for AI systems to synthesize credible, nuanced answers. The goal is not just to be found, but to be understood and reused correctly.

For retrieval success

Structure content with clear, topical headers that AI agents can quickly scan:

```
# What Is Project Management Software?
Project management software is a platform that helps teams plan,
organize, and track work across projects...
## Key Features to Look for in Project Management Software
When evaluating project management platforms, essential features include:
- Task management and assignment
- Timeline and scheduling (Gantt charts, calendars)
- Team collaboration tools
```

```
- Resource allocation and tracking
- Budget tracking and reporting
- Integration capabilities
## How to Choose the Right Project Management Software
Selecting the optimal project management tool depends on several factors:
1. **Team size and structure**
2. **Project complexity and methodology** (Agile, Waterfall, Hybrid)
3. **Integration requirements** with existing tools
4. **Budget constraints** and pricing models
5. **Remote work capabilities** and mobile access
```

This (illustrative) structure makes retrieval reliable because AI agents can easily identify which sections address which aspects of project management software queries.

For extraction success

Use definition lists for clear extraction:

```
**Average Implementation Time**: 4-6 weeks for standard deployment, 12-
16 weeks
for enterprise implementations with extensive customization.
**Pricing Models**:
- Per-user pricing: $8-$45 per user per month depending on tier
- Flat-rate pricing: $49-$299 per month for unlimited users
- Enterprise pricing: Custom quotes starting at $1,000/month
**Integration Ecosystem**: Integrates with 200+ tools including Slack, Micro-
soft
Teams, Salesforce, Google Workspace, Jira, and GitHub via native integrations
and API.
```

This explicit (illustrative) format makes it easy to extract specific facts accurately.

For synthesis success

Provide context and supporting evidence:

```
According to our analysis of 1,247 project management implementations across
2024, teams using dedicated project management software reported:
- 34% reduction in missed deadlines (compared to email/
```

```
spreadsheet management)
- 28% improvement in team productivity
- 41% reduction in time spent on status meetings
These improvements were most pronounced in teams of 10-50 members, with
diminishing returns in smaller teams (under 10) where overhead of tool adop-
tion
offset benefits.
**Source:** TechPro Project Management Impact Study, October 2024
**Methodology:** Longitudinal tracking of 1,247 implementa-
tions over 18 months
```

This (illustration) provides not just facts but context, limitations, and attribution that help AI agents synthesize accurately and cite appropriately.

RAG limitations and optimization opportunities

Understanding RAG limitations reveals optimization opportunities:

- **Limitation 1**: Token/Context limits:
  - AI systems can only process limited amounts of text at once. Extremely long documents may not be fully processed.
  - **Optimization**: Front-load critical information. Use a clear hierarchical structure so AI agents can identify relevant sections without having to process entire documents.
- **Limitation 2**: Recency bias:
  - RAG systems often prioritize recent content, sometimes at the expense of comprehensive older resources.
  - **Optimization**: Regularly update evergreen content with fresh publication dates, new examples, and current data to maintain recency signals while preserving depth.
- **Limitation 3**: Source diversity preference:
  - Many systems aim to synthesize information across multiple sources rather than relying on single sources.
  - **Optimization**: Create comprehensive content that draws on and cites multiple authoritative sources, demonstrating the synthesis work already done.
- **Limitation 4**: Extraction errors:
  - AI agents can misextract or misinterpret information, especially from complex or ambiguous text.

  - **Optimization**: Use explicit, unambiguous language. Avoid constructions that require inference or assumed context.
- **Limitation 5**: Citation inconsistency:
  - Different platforms cite sources differently. Some do so prominently, some minimally, and some not at all.
  - **Optimization:** Optimize for being the source of record even when not explicitly cited. Your content may inform responses without visible attribution.

Reverse-engineering prompts to analyze competitive visibility

Understanding why certain competitors dominate AI answers starts with treating visibility as something you can study, not something you guess. When AI systems consistently recommend the same brands, sources, or phrasing, they are responding to patterns in content structure, clarity, authority, and usefulness. By reverse-engineering those patterns, you can uncover what the models "prefer" and adapt your content to compete for the same visibility.

Competitive visibility in practice

Suppose you run a B2B SaaS product for contract management. You test the same core prompts across leading AI tools:

- "Best contract management software for mid-sized companies,"
- "Alternatives to [Competitor A],"
- "How to manage vendor contracts at scale."

You notice a pattern. One competitor appears first in nearly every comparison prompt and is framed as "best for compliance-heavy teams." Another dominates educational queries because it publishes clear definitions and frameworks. Your brand, when mentioned at all, appears late and is described in generic terms.

This reveals three things immediately:

- You are losing the comparison layer of visibility.
- Your positioning is unclear to AI systems.
- Your content lacks crisp, quotable statements that differentiate your product.

The fix is not more content volume. It is tighter positioning, clearer category language, and content explicitly designed to answer the comparisons and trade-offs AI is being asked to explain.

Systematic competitive analysis framework

Once you see competitive visibility as patterned behavior rather than randomness, you can analyze it systematically. The goal is not to chase individual mentions, but to understand the repeatable signals AI systems respond to across queries, platforms, and contexts. The following framework breaks that analysis into seven actionable stages:

- **Build a complete view of your query landscape**: Start by mapping the full universe of questions people ask in your category. This should include basic educational queries, comparisons between brands, pricing, and buying intent, use-case-specific questions, and problem–solution scenarios. The goal is to understand the contexts in which AI might be asked to recommend, explain, or compare solutions like yours. If your competitors appear consistently across these different query types while you only show up in one or two, that gap explains much of the visibility imbalance.
- **Test across multiple AI platforms**: AI visibility is not universal. Different platforms surface different sources, prioritize different content styles, and cite different brands. Run the same core set of queries across leading AI tools and track which competitors are mentioned, how prominently they appear, and whether they are positioned as primary recommendations or secondary options. Over time, patterns emerge. You may find that one competitor dominates comparison queries, another wins educational prompts, and a third is favored for pricing and practical guidance. These patterns point directly to where your positioning is weakest.
- **Measure prominence, not just mentions**: Being mentioned is not the same as being recommended. Pay attention to how early your brand appears in an answer, how much detail the AI provides about you versus competitors, and whether the tone is clearly positive or merely neutral. Brands that consistently appear first, receive deeper explanations, and are framed as the "best fit" are winning the citation game. This kind of qualitative prominence often matters more than raw frequency.
- **Identify citation patterns**: Once you see who gets cited, analyze why they are being cited. Look for patterns in the types of content AI tends to reference. Certain formats and signals show up again and again: clear definitions, concise frameworks, quotable insights, original data, step-by-step methods, and concrete comparisons. AI systems are drawn to sources that resolve uncertainty quickly. If competitors are being cited for crisp statistics, tight summaries, or clearly labeled methodologies, that is your blueprint for what to create or improve.
- **Learn from top performers**: Study the pages and resources that AI cites most often. These tend to share a few traits. They are information-dense rather than fluffy. They state specific claims instead of vague benefits. They use clear structure and headings that make ideas easy to extract. They often include examples, numbers, or concise explanations that can be lifted cleanly into an AI response. The goal is not to copy competitors but to understand the structural and editorial qualities that make content "quotable" by machines.

- **Find your visibility gaps**: Once you understand who is winning and why, map that against your own content. You will usually find several types of gaps. You may be missing entire categories of queries that competitors cover well. Your content may be less information-dense, with more marketing language and fewer concrete insights. Your pages may lack clearly extractable statements that an AI can confidently quote. These gaps explain why your brand is invisible in certain prompts, even if your overall content strategy is strong.
- **Turn insights into action**: The output of this analysis should be a prioritized roadmap. Focus first on high-impact gaps, such as missing query coverage in high-intent areas or weak performance in comparison prompts where buying decisions happen. Then improve the "quotability" of your best-performing pages by adding clearer definitions, sharper frameworks, and specific, defensible claims. Over time, this shifts how AI systems perceive and reuse your content, moving you from occasional mentions to consistent citations and primary recommendations.

In short, reverse-engineering prompts are not about gaming AI systems. It is about understanding the signals they respond to and systematically shaping your content so that when an AI looks for the best answer, your brand is the most useful source to cite.

Tactics for creating "quotable insights"

AI agents preferentially cite content that is specific, well-supported, and presented in citation-friendly formats. Creating "quotable insights" increases the likelihood of being cited prominently.

Characteristics of quotable content

Analysis of frequently cited content reveals four defining characteristics that separate content AI agents quote from content they overlook:

- **Specificity over generality**: Vague claims like "our platform improves team productivity significantly" are rarely cited because they offer nothing verifiable. Compare that to "teams using our platform complete projects 23% faster on average, based on analysis of 1,200 implementations completed in 2024." The second version earns citations because it combines a specific metric, a meaningful sample size, a clear timeframe, and a hint at methodology, all signals that the claim is grounded and trustworthy.
- **Novel data or insights**: Restating common knowledge gives AI agents nothing new to surface. Original research does. A statement such as "organizations with formal project management practices report 28% higher employee satisfaction scores and 31% lower voluntary turnover, according to our 2024 workplace study of 500 companies" is quotable because it establishes an unexpected correlation, backs it with recent data, and names a clear methodology. AI agents favor content that adds something to the conversation rather than echoing what is already widely known.

- **Authoritative attribution**: Weak attribution, such as "experts say AI will transform business operations", carries no weight. Strong attribution names the expert, their institutional affiliation, and their credentials, then delivers a specific, quotable claim. A statement attributed to a named professor at a named institution, predicting that AI will automate approximately 40% of current knowledge work within five years, gives AI agents a citable source with a verifiable claim structure.
- **Clear, extractable format**: Even accurate, specific content can be uncitable if it is buried in dense prose. Implementation timelines that run across several vague sentences are hard to extract. The same information presented as a structured breakdown by organizational size, with specific week ranges for each segment and a qualifying note about resource assumptions, is immediately scannable and extractable. Structure is not just a readability choice; it is a citability choice.

Quotable insight framework

Being cited by AI systems is rarely about being the most verbose. It is about being the most extractable, verifiable, and reusable source when the model needs evidence. These patterns turn your best insights into citation-ready building blocks instead of buried paragraphs that models gloss over:

- **Lead with the insight**: AI agents often truncate long passages, which means insights buried at the end of a paragraph are frequently missed. Content structured to open with the key finding performs significantly better. Compare "this section discusses our research methodology, various challenges, and eventually mentions that teams using collaborative tools were 34% more productive" with a version that opens directly with "teams using real-time collaborative tools demonstrate 34% higher productivity compared to teams relying on email and meetings," followed by the methodology. The second structure is immediately extractable because the signal appears before the supporting detail, not after it.
- **Provide verification details**: Unverifiable claims such as "most companies see ROI within the first year" give AI agents nothing to work with. Verifiable content names a specific figure, a sample size, a date range, and a calculation methodology. A statement reporting that 73% of companies achieve positive ROI within 12 months, with a median payback period of 8.2 months, drawn from analysis of 342 implementations between January 2023 and December 2024, is citable precisely because every element of the claim can be traced back to a defined source and method.
- **Craft pull-quote-friendly statements**: Some statements are structurally designed to stand alone. A well-constructed pull quote makes a specific, measurable claim, attributes it to a credible expert or study, and requires no surrounding context to be understood. A sentence such as "the shift from project-based to product-based team structures increased delivery velocity by 40% while reducing coordination overhead by 25%, suggesting that organizational design has equal or greater impact on productivity

than tooling choices" works as a citation because it is self-contained, surprising, and precisely attributed.

- **Use the "according to" construction**: AI agents recognize attribution patterns and use them as citation signals. Framing claims with a clear source prefix, such as "according to our analysis of 10,000 project timelines" or "according to Professor James Liu's research at Stanford," signals that what follows is a verifiable, attributable claim rather than editorial opinion. This construction does not just improve citability; it trains readers and models alike to treat your content as a primary source.

Statistical and data-driven content

AI agents heavily favor content with specific, well-sourced data:

- **Original research**: A well-structured study is one of the most citable content formats available. Consider a hypothetical remote work productivity study tracking 1,200 teams across 45 industries over 18 months. Its findings, that mid-sized teams of 10 to 25 people see the greatest productivity gains at 18% above office baseline, that teams using 3 to 5 core tools outperform those using more or fewer, and that synchronous meetings exceeding 10 hours per week begin to erode the benefits of remote work, are all immediately quotable. What makes them citable is not just the numbers but the combination of a clear methodology, a large sample, a defined timeframe, and interpretations that help AI agents understand the significance of each finding rather than leaving the inference to the reader.
- **Industry benchmarks**: Benchmark data earns citations because it answers the questions users most frequently bring to AI agents: how much does this cost, how long does this take, how common is this feature. A benchmark report covering 47 project management platforms, for example, can tell readers that the median professional-tier price is $24 per user per month, that 94% of platforms offer Kanban boards while only 43% support custom workflows, and that the median time to full adoption is 47 days, with delays most commonly caused by insufficient training. This kind of structured, multi-dimensional data gives AI agents precise reference points for comparisons, and the combination of a clear source, a recent date, and tabular formatting makes extraction trivial.

Expert quotes and commentary

Incorporating credentialed expert perspectives increases both quotability and authority. A quote from an organizational psychologist introducing a concept such as "isolation drift" to describe the gradual disconnection remote teams experience without deliberate communication patterns is citable for several reasons: the expert is named, their credentials are clear, the concept is original, and the qualitative insight is backed by quantitative research. When that same expert's longitudinal study of 200 remote-first companies shows that teams without structured daily check-ins experience 31% higher turnover within 18 months, the quote and the data reinforce each other, giving AI agents both a memorable framing and a verifiable claim.

Creating quotable frameworks and methodologies

Named frameworks become reference points that AI agents return to repeatedly. A framework such as the hypothetical 3C model for remote team effectiveness, identifying Clarity, Communication, and Connection as the three factors accounting for 40%, 35%, and 25% of variance in team performance, respectively, is highly citable because it is original, structured, and measurable. Each element carries concrete benchmarks: top-performing teams score 8.2 out of 10 on clarity metrics compared to 4.7 for struggling teams, high performers average 12 minutes daily on asynchronous updates, and successful teams invest 3 to 5 hours monthly in non-work social connection. When the framework also ties to a quantitative outcome, such as 22% average productivity gains within six months for organizations implementing all three elements, AI agents citing remote work best practices have every reason to reference it by name.

Semantic punctuation for machine parsing

AI agents parse content differently from how humans read it. Optimizing punctuation, formatting, and structure at the linguistic level improves extraction accuracy and citation likelihood.

Understanding machine parsing challenges

AI language models process text sequentially and rely on structural cues to understand relationships, hierarchies, and emphasis. Poor formatting creates ambiguity that reduces extraction accuracy. A sentence listing nine platform features in a single run-on clause forces the model to infer where one feature ends and another begins. The same list presented with clear visual separation allows AI agents to answer "does this platform include X?" with precision, and even supports voice assistants reading the list aloud. Structure is not decoration; it is a parsing signal.

Hierarchical structure for clear parsing

Heading hierarchies tell AI agents what a page is primarily about, what major topics it covers, and how subtopics and details relate to one another. A single H1 establishes the primary subject. H2 headings define the major sections. H3 and H4 headings carve out subtopics and details beneath them. This hierarchy only works when it is followed consistently. Skipping from an H1 directly to an H3 severs the relationship between levels and introduces ambiguity about where content belongs. A logical progression from H1 through H2 to H3 ensures that AI agents can reconstruct the document's structure accurately, which directly affects how reliably they can extract and cite its content.

List formatting for extraction

Lists earn their place in AI-optimized content when they follow parallel structure throughout. A set of implementation steps written inconsistently, mixing passive constructions, subject-led sentences, and noun phrases, forces the model to resolve grammatical variance before it can extract meaning. The same steps written in a consistent imperative form, each beginning with an action verb, are immediately parseable. Adding timing information and subordinate detail to each step improves extraction further, because AI agents can then answer not just "what are the steps?" but "what happens in week two?" and "what does training involve?" Consistent formatting throughout a list signals sequence, shows relationships between items, and makes the entire structure reliably extractable.

Definition lists for term clarity

Clear definitions make content instantly understandable and extractable, particularly for glossary-type queries. A term presented alongside a precise, self-contained definition gives AI agents everything they need to answer "what is X?" without inference. A sprint is a time-boxed iteration, typically one to four weeks, during which a development team completes a defined set of work. Velocity is a measure of the amount of work a team completes during a sprint, typically expressed in story points. Backlog is a prioritized list of features, enhancements, and bug fixes awaiting implementation. A daily standup is a brief daily meeting, typically 15 minutes, where team members share progress, plans, and blockers. Each definition explicitly signals its structure: this is a term; this is what it means. That signal alone improves accuracy for definition queries considerably.

Semantic HTML elements

HTML5 semantic elements convey meaning beyond visual formatting. Using the main element identifies the primary content of the page. The aside element marks supplementary material. The header and footer elements carry metadata. The figure and figcaption elements associate visual content with its description. These structural signals help AI agents distinguish between what a page is primarily about and what is contextual or peripheral. A tip embedded in an aside is understood as supplementary. A caption beneath a figure is understood as descriptive rather than argumentative. When semantic elements are used correctly, AI agents can parse the page's architecture rather than treating all content as undifferentiated text.

Punctuation for clarity and emphasis

Punctuation is not just for readability; it guides AI agents in parsing and extracting information. A colon before a list signals that specific enumeration follows, helping AI agents identify and extract the complete set of items rather than treating the sentence as continuous prose. Parentheses serve a different function: they mark clarification without interrupting the main claim. A statement reporting a 23% improvement is vague on its own. The same figure, accompanied by a parenthetical specifying that improvement was measured by project completion velocity within three months of implementation, gives AI agents a complete, citable claim. Structured labels, separating the metric, the timeline, and the measurement method into distinct lines, improve extraction further by making each element independently addressable.

Tables for complex comparisons

Well-structured tables are among the most extractable formats available. A comparison table covering users, storage, features, and pricing across Basic, Professional, and Enterprise plans allows AI agents to answer highly specific queries: which plan includes API access, what storage comes with the Basic tier, and what distinguishes Professional from Enterprise. This precision depends on three supporting elements. Captions help AI agents reference the table correctly when citing it. Qualifying notes provide important context, such as the fact that pricing is billed annually and that Enterprise pricing begins at a defined threshold. Clear column and row headers make extraction reliable by ensuring that every cell can be located within a named axis. Without these elements, even a well-populated table becomes difficult to cite accurately.

Code blocks for technical content

For technical documentation, proper code formatting aids extraction significantly. A code block with a declared language identifier signals to AI agents that what follows is code rather than prose, specifies the programming language, and makes individual commands and patterns extractable as discrete units. Inline code formatting applied to method names and property references within surrounding prose reinforces the distinction between technical terms and natural language. When a code example is followed by a structured description of the object or response it returns, with each property named and defined on its own line, AI agents can answer questions about specific attributes rather than returning the entire block. Language identifiers are not optional niceties; they are parsing signals.

Semantic punctuation anti-patterns

The most common formatting mistakes share a single root cause: inconsistency. Mixing list styles within the same section, using bold text as a substitute for proper headings, burying structured information in dense prose, and using non-standard Unicode characters for bullets all degrade the parsing signals that AI agents rely on. The correction is not complexity but discipline. Consistent structure throughout a document, semantic HTML elements used for their intended purpose, relationships made explicit rather than implied, and key information placed at the front of each section rather than the end: these habits compound over time into content that AI agents can reliably navigate, extract from, and cite.

Advanced E-E-A-T for AI systems

Google's E-E-A-T framework, covering Experience, Expertise, Authoritativeness, and Trustworthiness, was designed for human quality raters but provides valuable guidance for AI optimization. Extending these principles to AI systems requires understanding how AI agents assess these qualities, which differs meaningfully from how a human reviewer would.

Experience

Vague claims of experience carry no weight with AI agents. A statement like "we have worked with many clients over the years and helped them succeed" offers nothing extractable. The AI-optimized equivalent quantifies everything: the number of implementations completed, the range of organization sizes served, the industries covered, and the satisfaction rate measured at a defined point after go-live. Specifics such as "347 implementations since 2018 across 28 industries, with a 94% client satisfaction rating based on post-implementation surveys conducted six months after go-live" give AI agents verifiable signals of breadth and sustained experience.

Case-level detail reinforces this further. A pharmaceutical implementation involving 1,200 users across 15 countries with a measurable improvement in clinical trial timeline adherence, or a hospital system integration with a named EHR platform yielding a quantified reduction in administrative burden, tells AI agents that the experience being claimed is real, specific, and traceable to outcomes. Named technologies, user counts, timelines, and results all function as verifiability signals.

First-person pattern recognition across implementations adds a third layer. Observations drawn from hundreds of projects, such as the finding that organizations allocating less than 10% of implementation budget to change management see 40% lower adoption rates, or that monthly C-level check-ins correlate with adoption speeds three times faster than projects without them, demonstrate that the experience has produced genuine learning. The "we now recommend" and "lesson learned" constructions signal adaptation over time, which is itself a marker of deep, sustained experience rather than surface familiarity.

Expertise

Expertise signals for AI agents come from two directions: credential transparency and demonstrated technical depth. Author credentials should be explicit and specific. An academic title, institutional affiliation, publication record, and research focus each contribute independently. A named researcher with a doctoral degree, a dual role spanning practice and academia, more than 30 peer-reviewed publications, and a book from a recognized publisher presents a layered credibility profile that AI agents can parse and cite with confidence.

Technical depth works differently. Rather than asserting expertise, it demonstrates it through the specificity and precision of the content itself. A recommendation favoring SAML 2.0 over OAuth for enterprise deployments, backed by data showing that 94% of successful enterprise implementations use SAML with an average implementation time of three to five days, signals domain knowledge that goes beyond general familiarity. Identifying that 62% of SSO delays stem from attribute mapping errors and 31% from certificate expiration management gives AI agents precise, citable findings. Database scaling recommendations naming specific tools such as pgBouncer, paired with performance data showing 45% reductions in dashboard load time and 78% query time improvements from a defined index strategy, demonstrate the kind of technical fluency that AI agents recognize as authoritative rather than generic.

Authoritativeness

Authoritativeness for AI agents is built through third-party recognition that exists independently of what a brand claims about itself. Industry awards from recognized organizations, analyst placements, and sustained review platform ratings all function as verifiable authority signals. A brand recognized as a leader by major analysts, rated consistently across thousands of reviews on independent platforms, and affiliated with the governing bodies of its industry presents an authority profile that AI agents can confirm through multiple sources rather than relying solely on self-reported claims. Institutional affiliations, such as membership in professional associations or participation in industry research partnerships, extend this further by embedding the brand within the credentialed communities that AI agents treat as authoritative.

Thought leadership signals operate through a different mechanism. Speaking engagements at major industry conferences, media coverage in prestigious publications, and appearances in widely distributed audio and editorial formats all contribute to a citation network that AI agents recognize as evidence of recognized expertise. A brand whose team members deliver keynotes at flagship industry events, whose perspectives are quoted in major business publications, and whose research is cited in analyst reports and practitioner journals has built an authority profile that extends well beyond its own content. These signals are particularly durable because they originate from third parties with their own editorial standards, making them significantly more credible to AI agents than any claim the brand makes about itself.

The citation network that results from sustained thought leadership is itself an authority signal. Research cited in peer-reviewed journals, referenced in analyst market guides, and republished in practitioner publications creates a web of attribution that AI agents can trace. Each citation from an independent, credentialed source reinforces the brand's position as a primary source rather than a secondary one, making it progressively more likely to be recommended when AI agents look for authoritative evidence on relevant topics.

Trustworthiness

Trustworthiness for AI agents is built primarily through methodological transparency and consistent maintenance practices. A research study becomes citable not just because its findings are interesting but because its methodology is fully disclosed. A complete methodology section includes the target population, the sampling approach, the final sample size alongside the response rate, the industry and size distribution of respondents, the data collection period and methods, the metrics used and how they were defined, and, critically, the study's limitations.

Acknowledging that self-selection bias may underrepresent struggling organizations, or that the measurement period overlaps with a major external disruption, signals intellectual honesty rather than weakness. AI agents treat disclosed limitations as trust signals, not as vulnerabilities.

Ethical approval notations, funding disclosures, and data availability statements extend this transparency further. A study that names its IRB protocol, confirms that methodology was designed independently of its funder, and offers the anonymized dataset for academic verification gives AI agents every element they need to characterize the source as credible.

Version control and update practices signal ongoing reliability. A document that displays its version number, last updated date, last reviewed date, and next scheduled review date tells AI agents that the content is actively maintained. A structured change log tracing updates back through previous versions shows that the document has a history of accuracy management rather than a single publication date. A formal correction policy, with a named contact, a defined response window, a documented correction process, and a public record of recent corrections, completes the picture. AI agents favor sources that demonstrate not just accuracy at the time of publication but a commitment to accuracy over time.

Conclusion

Advanced AEO techniques, including understanding RAG mechanics, analyzing competitive visibility, creating quotable content, optimizing semantic structure, and implementing comprehensive E-E-A-T, represent the current frontier of AI optimization. These are not merely incremental improvements over basic optimization but fundamental enhancements that significantly increase citation likelihood and prominence.

Organizations mastering these techniques share common characteristics. They think like AI systems, structuring content not only for human readers but also for how AI agents retrieve, extract, and synthesize information. They measure and iterate systematically, analyzing competitive visibility, identifying patterns in what gets cited, and refining their approach based on empirical observation. They invest in genuine quality, recognizing that thin, derivative content does not succeed in AI systems that prioritize information gain and authority. They build systematic capabilities rather than pursuing one-off optimization efforts, developing the processes, standards, and infrastructure that ensure consistent quality at scale. Additionally, they stay ahead of evolution, treating AI optimization as a discipline that requires ongoing attention as platforms and capabilities continue to advance.

The techniques described in this chapter represent the current state of the art, but the field continues to evolve rapidly. Organizations that master these fundamentals while remaining adaptable to new developments will maintain leadership in AI-driven discovery as platforms and capabilities continue to advance.

In the next chapter, we will examine how to scale these optimization capabilities across large organizations, building the operational frameworks and governance structures needed to maintain quality and consistency as content volume grows.

CHAPTER 7
PXM Evolution and Managing AI Experience

Introduction

Throughout this journey, product data has emerged as a critical element: AI agents making product recommendations rely fundamentally on the quality, structure, and comprehensiveness of product information.

However, managing product information for AI-driven discovery requires more than updating your **product information management** (**PIM**) system with better data. It demands a fundamental evolution in how organizations think about product experience across all touchpoints, a shift from managing product information to orchestrating product experience. This is the domain of **product experience management** (**PXM**).

PXM represents the evolution of PIM from a system of record to a system of engagement. While PIM focuses on centralizing and standardizing product data, PXM encompasses how that data translates into experiences across every channel where customers encounter products, including AI-driven discovery channels.

In the past, PXM was about tailoring content for human shoppers on a website. Now, it is about "Product Storytelling for Machines", structuring product information so AI agents can accurately understand, compare, and recommend products to users who may never visit your website.

This chapter explores PXM in the context of AI optimization. We will define what PXM means when AI agents mediate discovery, examine how to transition from traditional PIM to AI-ready PXM, distinguish between functional and emotional product data and why both matter for AI recommendations, understand how data quality itself becomes a ranking signal, and analyze real-world case studies of organizations successfully implementing PXM for AI visibility.

For product experience management leaders, this chapter provides the strategic framework for evolving your capabilities. For brand leaders, it clarifies the organizational and technical investments required. For technical teams, it defines the architecture and data requirements.

For everyone involved in product strategy, it reframes product management as experience management in an AI-mediated world.

Structure

The chapter covers the following topics:

- Defining PXM in the context of AEO
- Transitioning from basic PIM to AI-ready PXM
- Emotional and functional data of a product
- Data quality as a ranking signal in AI discovery
- Case studies of PXM AI-driven discovery

Objectives

This chapter equips readers with the knowledge to make product data AI-ready. It defines product experience management in the context of answer engine optimization and explores its strategic role in AI-driven discovery. It then traces the transition from traditional product information management to AI-ready PXM, identifying the processes, systems, and capabilities required for the transition. From there, it covers how to capture both emotional and functional product data to tell a complete, machine-readable product story, and why data quality functions as a critical ranking signal for AI agents. The chapter closes with lessons drawn from real-world case studies that illustrate how organizations have successfully implemented PXM to improve AI visibility and product citations.

Defining PXM in the context of AEO

Understanding PXM starts with seeing how it builds on the foundations of traditional PIM. While PIM ensures accurate, centralized product data, PXM transforms that data into meaningful experiences that drive engagement, influence decisions, and feed AI-driven discovery. The shift is less about adding more information and more about making product data actionable, contextual, and emotionally resonant across every touchpoint.

Traditional PIM vs. modern PXM

PIM emerged to solve a specific problem: organizations with large product catalogs needed centralized systems to manage product data, including SKUs, descriptions, specifications, pricing, and images, and distribute that data to various channels (e-commerce sites, print catalogs, retail systems, distributor feeds).

Traditional PIM focused on:

- Data centralization and single source of truth.
- Consistency across channels.
- Workflow for product launches and updates.
- Asset management (images, documents, videos).
- Channel-specific adaptations (different descriptions for different markets).

PXM extends PIM with a critical addition: understanding and optimizing how product information translates into experiences that influence purchasing decisions.

PXM encompasses the following:

- Everything PIM provides (data centralization, consistency, workflow).
- Context-aware content optimization for different customer journeys.
- Emotional and experiential data beyond functional specifications.
- Integration of product information with customer data and behavior.
- Measurement of how product information influences outcomes.
- Continuous optimization based on performance data.

PXM in the AI discovery era

When AI agents mediate product discovery, PXM takes on new dimensions:

- **Traditional channel**: User visits your website | sees the product page | makes a decision.
    - **PXM focus**: Optimize product page for conversion.
- **AI-mediated channel**: User asks AI agent | receives synthesized answer | may never visit your site.
    - **PXM focus**: Ensure product data enables accurate, favorable AI synthesis and recommendation.

This creates new PXM requirements, which we will look at in the subsequent sections.

Extraction-optimized content structure

Your product information must be structured not just for human comprehension but for reliable AI extraction and synthesis.

Traditional PIM approach (Illustrative):

```
Product Name: TechPro UltraBook 15

Description: Witness the perfect balance of power and portability with the
TechPro UltraBook 15. This premium laptop delivers exceptional performance
for demanding professionals, featuring cutting-edge technology in a sleek,
lightweight design that goes wherever your work takes you.
```

PXM for AI approach (Illustrative):

```
{
  "product_name": "TechPro UltraBook 15",
  "category": "Laptop Computer",
  "target_audience": "Business Professionals, Creative Professionals",

  "value_proposition": {
    "primary": "High performance in ultraportable form factor",
    "key_benefits": [
      "Professional-grade performance (Intel Core i7, 16GB RAM)",
      "All-day battery life (up to 12 hours)",
      "Premium build quality (aluminum unibody)",
      "Lightweight portability (3.2 lbs)"
    ]
  },

  "specifications": {
    "processor": {
      "brand": "Intel",
      "model": "Core i7-1355U",
      "generation": "13th Gen",
      "cores": "10 (2 Performance + 8 Efficient)",
      "base_frequency": "1.7 GHz",
      "turbo_frequency": "5.0 GHz"
    },
    "display": {
      "size": "15.6 inches",
      "resolution": "2880 x 1800 pixels",
      "type": "OLED",
      "brightness": "400 nits",
      "color_gamut": "100% DCI-P3"
    },
    "battery": {
      "capacity": "75 Wh",
      "rated_life": "Up to 12 hours",
      "test_conditions": "Continuous web browsing over WiFi at 150 nits"
```

```
    }
  },

  "use_cases": [
    {
      "scenario": "Business Travel",
      "suitability": "Excellent",
      "reasoning": "Lightweight (3.2 lbs), long battery life, professional appearance"
    },
    {
      "scenario": "Video Editing",
      "suitability": "Good",
      "reasoning": "High-quality OLED display with 100% DCI-P3, but integrat-
ed graphics limit 4K editing performance"
    },
    {
      "scenario": "Gaming",
      "suitability": "Limited",
      "reasoning": "Integrated graphics suitable only for casual gaming"
    }
  ]
}
```

The structured approach provides AI agents with:

- Clear, extractable specifications.
- Explicit value propositions.
- Use case suitability with reasoning.
- Granular technical details in a consistent format.

Multi-dimensional product characterization

AI agents answering queries like "best laptop for video editing under $2000" need to understand products across multiple dimensions:

```
# Multi-dimensional product profile
product_id: ultrabook_15_2025
performance_profile:
  cpu_performance: "High (Geekbench 6 Multi-Core: 10,450)"
```

```
  graphics_performance: "Moderate (Integrated Intel Iris Xe)"
  memory_performance: "High (16GB LPDDR5-5200)"
  storage_performance: "Very High (NVMe Gen 4 SSD, 7000 MB/s read)"
portability_profile:
  weight: "Excellent (3.2 lbs / 1.45 kg)"
  battery_life: "Excellent (12 hours typical use)"
  dimensions: "Compact (13.9 x 9.5 x 0.59 inches)"
  durability: "High (MIL-STD-810H certified)"
value_profile:
  price_position: "Premium ($1,299)"
  price_to_performance_ratio: "Good"
  total_cost_of_ownership: "Low (3-year warranty, minimal repair rates)"
  competitor_
comparison: "15% more expensive than average, 25% better battery life"
user_experience_profile:
  setup_complexity: "Low (out-of-box ready, minimal bloatware)"
  learning_curve: "Low (standard laptop interface)"
  support_quality: "High (24/7 phone support, 4.7/5 satisfaction rating)"
  upgrade_path: "Limited (soldered RAM, upgradeable SSD only)"
```

This multidimensional (illustrative) characterization allows AI agents to make nuanced recommendations based on query context.

Competitive context and positioning

AI agents often synthesize recommendations by comparing products. Providing a competitive context helps ensure accurate positioning:

```
## Competitive Positioning: TechPro UltraBook 15
### Primary Competitors
- **Dell XPS 15**: Similar premium positioning, better graphics (RTX option),
  heavier (4.2 lbs), shorter battery (9 hours)
- **MacBook Pro 14"**: Higher performance (M3 Pro), better bat-
tery (18 hours),
  higher price ($1,999), smaller display (14" vs 15.6")
- **Lenovo ThinkPad X1 Carbon**: Business focus, lighter (2.5 lbs),
  smaller display (14"), similar battery life
```

```
### Differentiation
- **vs Dell XPS 15**: 30% lighter, 33% longer battery, but no dis-
crete GPU option
- **vs MacBook Pro 14"**: 35% lower price, larger display, Windows ecosystem,
  but lower raw performance
- **vs ThinkPad X1 Carbon**: Larger display, better for creative work,
  comparable business features
### Market Position
- **Category**: Premium ultraportable laptops
- **Price Tier**: Upper-midrange ($1,200-1,500)
- **Target**: Business professionals and creatives prioritizing portability
- **Sweet Spot**: Users needing professional performance without dedicat-
ed GPU
```

This competitive (illustrative) framing helps AI agents understand when to recommend your product versus alternatives.

Experience-oriented metadata

Beyond specifications, capture the experiential aspects that influence decisions:

```
{
  "user_experience_attributes": {
    "unboxing_experience": {
      "quality_rating": 4.8,
      "notable_features": "Premium packaging, setup guide, quick-start accessories",
      "user_feedback": "Feels like a premium product from the moment you open it"
    },

    "keyboard_experience": {
      "type": "Backlit chiclet, 1.5mm travel",
      "typing_feel": "Responsive with good tactile feedback",
      "noise_level": "Quiet",
      "user_satisfaction": 4.6,
      "common_praise": "Comfortable for long typing sessions",
      "common_criticism": "Some users prefer deeper key travel"
    },
```

```
    "display_experience": {
      "visual_quality": "Exceptional (OLED, high contrast, vivid colors)",
      "viewing_angles": "Excellent",
      "outdoor_usability": "Good (400 nits brightness)",
      "eye_strain": "Low (anti-glare coating, blue light filter)",
      "user_satisfaction": 4.9
    },

    "audio_experience": {
      "speaker_quality": "Above average for laptop",
      "microphone_quality": "Good (AI noise cancellation)",
      "headphone_jack": "Yes (3.5mm)",
      "user_feedback": "Suitable for video calls and casual media consumption"
    },

    "build_quality_perception": {
      "materials": "Aluminum unibody, premium feel",
      "durability_perception": "High",
      "perceived_value": "Matches price point",
      "user_satisfaction": 4.7
    }
  }
}
```

This (illustrative) experiential data helps AI agents answer qualitative queries like "does this laptop feel premium?" or "is the keyboard good for long typing sessions?"

PXM technology stack for AI

Implementing AI-ready PXM requires integration across multiple systems:

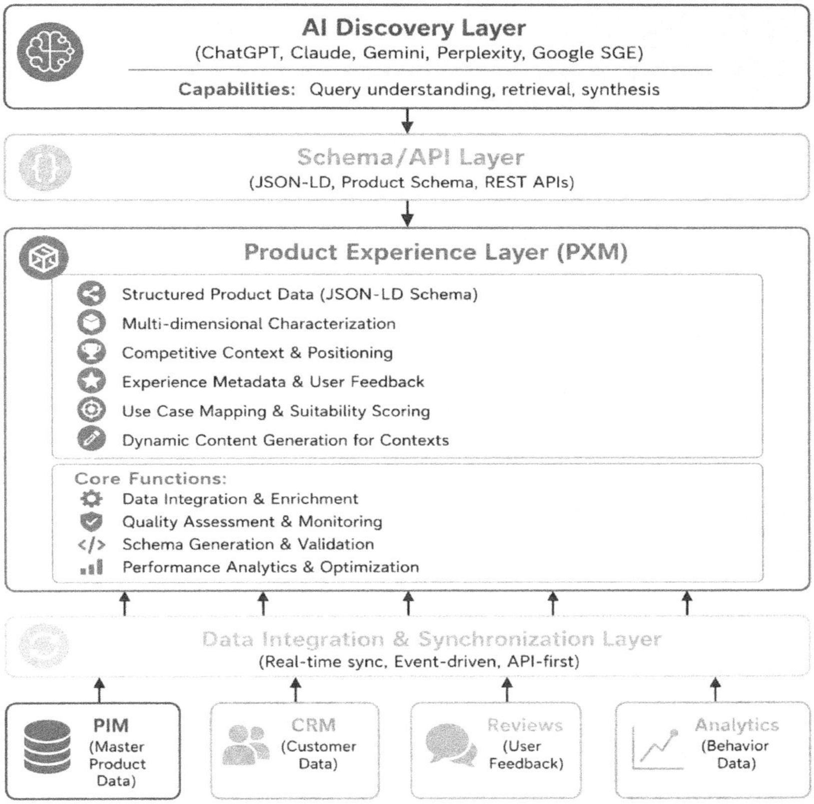

***Figure 7.1**: PXM technology stack for AI*

The core functions of PXM are as follows:

- **Data integration**: Aggregate product data from PIM, customer feedback from reviews, usage patterns from analytics, and customer profiles from CRM.
- **Enrichment**: Add multi-dimensional characterization, competitive positioning, use case mapping, and experiential attributes.
- **Context optimization**: Generate different content presentations based on query context, user intent, and channel requirements.
- **Schema generation**: Automatically create comprehensive schema markup from enriched product data.
- **Performance tracking**: Measure AI visibility, citation frequency, recommendation prominence.
- **Continuous improvement**: Identify gaps in product data, opportunities for enrichment, and optimization priorities.

Transitioning from basic PIM to AI-ready PXM

Most organizations have some form of PIM, even if it is just spreadsheets and a DAM system. Evolving to AI-ready PXM requires systematic transformation across people, processes, and technology.

PXM transformation roadmap across 12 months

Before diving into each phase, it is important to understand that transforming from basic PIM to AI-ready PXM is a stepwise process. Each stage builds on the previous one, ensuring your product data is not only complete and accurate but also structured, enriched, and optimized for AI discovery. The foundation you lay early will determine how effectively you can add context, emotion, and intelligence in later phases.

Phase 1, foundation, months 1 to 3

Goal: Establish a data quality baseline and basic AI-ready capabilities

The key activities are as follows:

- **Data completeness sprint**:
    - **Actions**:
        - Audit current attribute coverage by product category.
        - Define minimum required attributes for AI optimization.
        - Identify data sources for missing attributes.
        - Create data collection/enrichment workflows.
        - Implement automated completeness tracking.
    - **Resources required**:
        - Product manager (full-time).
        - Data analysts (full-time).
        - Data enrichment budget.
    - **Success metrics**:
        - Attribute completeness ≥95% for all products.
        - Zero products are missing critical attributes.
        - Automated monitoring dashboard is operational.
- **Schema implementation**:
    - **Actions**:
        - Create schema templates for each product category.
        - Develop automated schema generation from PIM data.

        - Implement schema on all product pages.
        - Validate using Google Rich Results Test.
        - Monitor schema errors and fix them systematically.
    - **Resources required**:
        - Technical SEO specialist.
        - Developer.
    - **Success metrics**:
        - 100% of products have valid schema markup.
        - Zero schema validation errors.
        - Schema properties ≥80% complete.
- **Technical infrastructure**:
    - **Actions**:
        - Implement or upgrade the PIM platform.
        - Create an API layer for product data access.
        - Establish real-time data synchronization.
        - Implement version control for product content.
        - Set up data quality monitoring and alerting.
    - **Platform options**:
        - Small (<500 SKUs): Plytix, Catsy.
        - Mid-Market (500-10K SKUs): Akeneo, Pimcore.
        - Enterprise (10K+ SKUs): inRiver, Salsify, Syndigo, Centric PXM.
    - **Success metrics**:
        - Product data accessible via API (<200ms response).
        - Sync latency <5 minutes across systems.
        - 99.9% uptime for product data services.

Phase 2, enhancement, months 4 to 6

Goal: Add AI-specific enrichments and optimizations.

The key activities are as follows:

- **Multi-dimensional characterization:**
    - Define dimension frameworks for each category.
    - Create scoring methodologies.
    - Develop enrichment workflows.

    - Integrate customer review data.
    - Implement competitive benchmarking.
    - **Success metrics**:
        - 80%+ products have multi-dimensional profiles.
        - Competitive data refreshed monthly.
- **Use case mapping**:
    - Identify primary use cases for each category.
    - Score product suitability for each use case.
    - Document reasoning for scores.
    - Create use-case-based content.
    - **Success metrics**:
        - All products are mapped to relevant use cases.
        - AI agents cite use case guidance in 40%+ recommendations.
- **Emotional data integration**:
    - Deploy emotional data extraction on reviews.
    - Conduct user experience studies.
    - Commission expert assessments.
    - Structure emotional attributes in product data.

Phase 3, optimization, months 7 to 9

Goal: Implement advanced PXM capabilities and measurement.

The key activities are as follows:

- **AI visibility tracking**:
    - Define query sets for product categories (100+ per category).
    - Implement an automated AI platform for querying.
    - Track mention frequency and prominence.
    - Analyze competitive visibility weekly.
    - **Success metrics**:
        - Visibility tracking covering 90% of target queries.
        - Month-over-month visibility improvement ≥5%.
- **Dynamic content generation**:
    - Develop content generation templates.

- Implement a rules engine for context adaptation.
- Create an A/B testing framework.
- Measure performance by context.
- **Success metrics**:
  - 75%+ content auto-generated with <5% error rate.
  - Context-optimized content performs 20%+ better.

Phase 4, intelligence, months 10 to 12

Goal: Implement AI-powered PXM intelligence.

The key activities are as follows:

- **Predictive optimization**:
  - Train ML models for visibility prediction.
  - Develop automated gap identification.
  - Create intelligent content recommendations.
  - Build predictive quality scoring.
  - **Success metrics**:
    - Prediction accuracy ≥80% for visibility outcomes.
    - Automated recommendations accepted ≥70%.
- **Automated quality management**:
  - Deploy continuous quality monitoring.
  - Implement automated issue detection.
  - Create automated correction workflows.
  - Establish quality score SLAs.

Emotional and functional data of a product

Traditional product information focuses heavily on functional specifications, what the product does, its technical capabilities, and its measurable features. However, purchase decisions, especially for consumer products, are driven as much by emotional factors as by functional ones. AI-ready PXM requires capturing both.

Understanding the functional-emotional spectrum

Functional data describes objective, measurable product attributes:

- Technical specifications.

- Features and capabilities.
- Performance metrics.
- Compatibility and requirements.
- Price and availability.

Emotional data describes subjective, experiential product attributes:

- How it makes users feel.
- Aesthetic qualities and design language.
- Brand associations and identity.
- Social signaling and status.
- Sensory experiences.
- Ease and pleasure of use.

Consider these two examples to understand the difference between types of data in practice.

Example: Wireless headphones (illustrative):

```
# Premium Wireless Headphones - Complete Profile
## Functional Data
- Driver size: 40mm neodymium
- Frequency response: 20Hz - 20kHz
- Active Noise Cancellation: Yes (up to 30dB reduction)
- Battery life: 30 hours with ANC, 40 hours without
- Bluetooth: 5.2 with aptX HD codec support
- Weight: 250g
- Price: $349
## Emotional Data
- **Design aesthetic**: "Minimalist luxury" - clean lines, premium materials
- **Brand perception**: "Professional quality without ostentation"
- **Comfort experience**: "Forget you're wearing them"
- **Sound character**: "Warm and detailed" - emphasized mid-
range, clear vocals
- **Use feeling**: "Confidence and focus" - isolation from distractions
- **Status signaling**: Subtle - recognized by audio professionals, not flashy
- **Unboxing experience**: Premium packaging, thoughtful organization
```

Why both matter: Functional specs alone might make these comparable to competitors. The emotional data sets them apart, explaining why someone would choose these over alternatives with similar specifications.

Example: Project management software (illustrative):

```
# Enterprise Project Management Platform - Complete Profile
## Functional Data
- Task and milestone tracking
- Gantt charts and Kanban boards
- Resource allocation tools
- Budget tracking and forecasting
- Role-based permissions
- API integrations (200+ tools)
- SOC 2 Type II compliant
- Pricing: $29-$79 per user per month
## Emotional Data
- **Professional identity**: "Built for serious operators"
- **Team perception**: Feels structured and disciplined
- **Leadership signaling**: Conveys organizational maturity
- **Interface feeling**: Clean, controlled, low visual noise
- **Adoption experience**: "Makes complex projects feel manageable"
- **Trust factor**: Enterprise-grade reliability and security
- **Cultural fit**: Appeals to process-driven, high-accountability teams
```

Why both matter: Functionally, this platform competes with dozens of similar tools. Emotionally, it signals control, rigor, and professionalism. For a VP of operations, that emotional positioning often outweighs marginal feature differences.

The following figure captures this duality: functional data forms the inner ring around every product, precise and structured like an engineering schematic, while emotional data forms the outer ring, warmer and more organic. Both feed into a single AI output. Without either ring, the product story reaching the AI agent is incomplete.

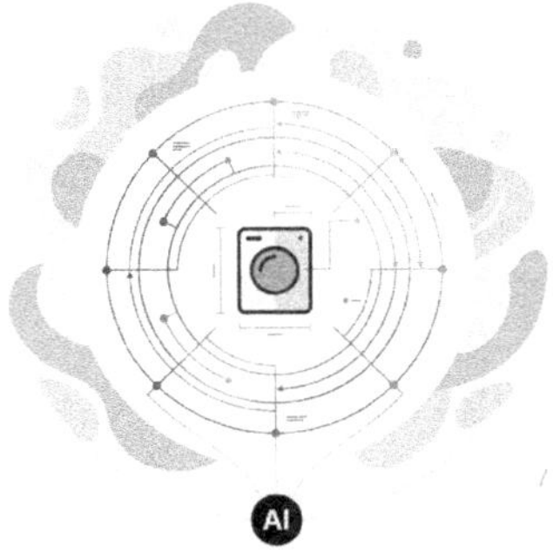

Figure 7.2: PXM is the system that structures both functional and emotional data for AI recommendations

Capturing emotional data systematically

Emotional data does not emerge by accident. It has to be observed, extracted, structured, and validated just like functional specifications. Organizations that excel at AI-ready PXM treat emotional insight as a research discipline, not marketing copy.

Customer review mining

Customer reviews are one of the richest sources of emotional data. Within thousands of reviews are repeated patterns of feeling, identity, and perception. The goal is not to cherry-pick flattering quotes. It is to identify recurring emotional dimensions and quantify them.

A systematic review analysis typically examines dimensions such as:

- Aesthetic perception (beautiful, sleek, cheap-looking).
- Tactile and physical feel (comfortable, solid, heavy, flimsy).
- Status and identity signaling (professional, flashy, prestigious).
- Overall experience (satisfying, frustrating, enjoyable).
- Confidence and trust (reliable, concerning, reassuring).

For each dimension, organizations analyze:

- Frequency of mentions.
- Sentiment associated with the term.
- Context in which it appears.
- Correlation with star ratings.
- Representative user quotes.

This produces an emotional profile that moves beyond anecdote. Instead of saying "customers love the design," you can state that 68% of positive reviews mention comfort and that comfort language strongly correlates with five-star ratings.

In addition to dimension analysis, teams extract quotable experience statements. Phrases such as "feels like a gentle hug" or "makes me feel focused" are not just testimonials; they are also expressions of the product's benefits. They are structured emotional signals that can be categorized, ranked by relevance, and tied to product attributes.

Over time, review mining reveals patterns such as dominant emotional themes, recurring metaphors, and even subtle anxieties. These insights can then be formalized into structured emotional attributes rather than left buried in free-form text.

Expert assessment integration

For certain categories, professional reviews add another layer of emotional credibility. Audio equipment, cameras, professional tools, and luxury goods often receive detailed expert analysis that blends technical evaluation with subjective experience.

Professional reviews typically provide:

- Measured performance data.
- Comparative positioning against competitors.
- Subjective sensory descriptions.
- Emotional characterization of the product's personality.
- Durability and long-term confidence signals.

For example, an expert might describe headphones as *rich and detailed, with an intimate soundstage that draws you into the music.* That description is not a specification, but it shapes how the product is perceived. When combined with objective measurements, it becomes a powerful hybrid of functional and emotional data.

Expert assessments help validate emotional positioning. They also add authority, which strengthens AI visibility and citation likelihood.

Ethnographic research and user studies

For deeper emotional understanding, leading organizations conduct qualitative research.

Short-term usage studies, interviews, and observational research reveal not only what users think but also how their feelings evolve. Emotional responses often follow a journey:

- Initial anticipation during unboxing.
- Early validation during first use.
- Routine comfort and reliability in daily use.
- Long-term attachment and trust.

Participants frequently reveal identity-based insights that would never appear in a technical specification. A user might say, "When I wear these, I feel like a serious professional," or "Putting them on signals to my brain that it is time to work." These statements capture identity signaling and ritual behavior, both of which strongly influence purchasing decisions.

Quantitative follow-ups can then measure how common these responses are. For example:

- Percentage of users who report feeling more professional.
- Percentage who associate the product with focus or confidence.
- Percentage who cite emotional benefits as more important than incremental feature differences.

This transforms emotional data from storytelling into measurable intelligence.

Structuring emotional data for AI

Emotional insight only becomes useful at scale when it is structured. Instead of burying feelings inside marketing paragraphs, advanced PXM systems codify emotional attributes into defined categories, such as:

- Aesthetic profile
- Tactile experience
- Emotional response
- Identity signaling
- Brand personality
- Experience journey

Each category can contain specific descriptors, dominant feelings, intensity ratings, representative quotes, and even known negative emotions such as anxiety about price or fear of damage.

This structure allows AI systems to retrieve not only what the product does, but how it feels, what it signals socially, and what identity it reinforces. It enables comparisons not just on features, but on emotional positioning.

When emotional data is structured this way, the product story becomes complete. AI systems can differentiate between two products with identical specifications because they understand the difference between *minimalist luxury for professionals* and *bold, expressive style for trendsetters*. That difference is often what drives the purchase.

Balancing functional and emotional for AI queries

Different queries emphasize different aspects:

- **Functionally-focused query**: "What are the technical specifications of [product]?" → AI should emphasize functional data, cite specific measurements.
- **Emotionally-focused query**: "Do [headphones] feel premium?" → AI should emphasize emotional/experiential data, cite user testimonials.
- **Balanced query**: "What are the best wireless headphones for professional use?" → AI should synthesize both: functional capabilities that meet professional requirements + emotional attributes that convey professionalism.

PXM implementation: Ensure your product data supports all query types:

- Complete functional specifications (for technical queries).
- Rich emotional/experiential data (for qualitative queries).
- Use case mapping that connects functional capabilities to emotional benefits.

- User testimonials that illustrate emotional experiences.
- Professional reviews that bridge the functional and emotional.

Example (illustrative):

```
"For professional use, these headphones excel both functionally and experien-
tially.
Functionally, they offer 30dB active noise cancellation, 30-
hour battery life,
and aptX HD codec support. Experientially, users describe them as creating a
'focused, professional mindset' and appreciate the 'understated quality' that
communicates competence without ostentation. The combination makes them
particularly suitable for professionals who value both performance and
professional presence."
```

Data quality as a ranking signal in AI discovery

Data quality is not just a technical concern; **it is a strategic advantage**. AI agents preferentially cite high-quality, comprehensive, well-maintained sources.

Data quality-AI visibility correlation

Product data quality is a critical factor in AI-driven discovery. AI systems consistently favor sources that are accurate, complete, consistent, precise, and up-to-date. Accuracy and completeness tend to drive citations more than any other factor, while precision, consistency, and freshness also contribute meaningfully. High-quality data is not just a technical necessity; it is a strategic advantage that directly affects how often products are recommended and cited by AI agents.

In practice, products with verified specifications and comprehensive attribute coverage are far more likely to be surfaced by AI. When information is clear, specific, and aligned across multiple platforms, AI agents can interpret, categorize, and reference it correctly. Fresh data ensures recommendations remain relevant, but even more important is the baseline of completeness and accuracy: without that, other optimizations have a limited impact.

Understanding how quality influences AI visibility

Brands can think about data quality across several dimensions. Completeness measures whether all critical attributes, such as specifications, dimensions, materials, and variants, are included. Accuracy ensures that those attributes reflect the true product. Consistency checks that information is uniform across channels, avoiding contradictions. Precision measures how specific and detailed claims are, helping AI systems distinguish between similar products. Finally, freshness ensures that the information reflects current offerings, pricing, and availability.

By focusing on these dimensions, organizations can create product data that AI agents can ingest, understand, and cite with confidence. Accuracy and completeness form the foundation: without these, AI agents may ignore or mischaracterize a product, no matter how well other elements are optimized. Precision and consistency increase the reliability of recommendations, while freshness keeps results current for customers and platforms alike.

Practical impact of high-quality product data

The effects of investing in data quality are immediate and compounding. Accurate, complete, and precise product information increases the likelihood that AI agents will cite a product correctly, provide the right recommendations, and surface it in relevant contexts. Consistent, fresh data reinforces trust, reduces characterization errors, and improves the overall discoverability of the brand.

For example, products with thorough and verified specifications are much more likely to be accurately recommended for technical queries or value-based comparisons. When emotional or contextual attributes are added, such as usability, lifestyle fit, or sustainability, AI agents can differentiate products beyond functional parity, reflecting the brand's intended positioning. Ultimately, organizations that prioritize high-quality, well-structured product data build durable advantages in AI-driven discovery, ensuring their products are visible, correctly represented, and more likely to be recommended.

Case studies of PXM AI-driven discovery

These case studies illustrate how organizations across industries applied PXM principles to boost AI-driven visibility. Each example highlights specific challenges, strategies implemented, and measurable outcomes, showing how data quality, emotional context, and structured product information translate directly into citations and recommendations.

Case study 1

The basic details are as follows:

- **B2B SaaS**: Data completeness drives visibility.
- **Company**: CloudSync (pseudonym), cloud storage platform.
- **Challenge**: Low AI visibility despite market leadership.
- **Timeline**: 4 months.
- **Initial state**:

- AI mention rate: 23% for category queries.
- Data completeness: 34% of critical attributes.
- Integration documentation: 27% complete.

Transformation

In the first two months, the company focused on laying a strong foundation. They cataloged all product integrations in detail, clearly defining primary use cases and ensuring every product was thoroughly documented. Feature descriptions were expanded to include precise specifications, making the data more complete and easier for AI systems to interpret.

Within a couple of months, these efforts began to pay off. The product catalog became significantly more comprehensive, and integration details were fully documented. AI systems began recognizing the improved data quality, resulting in more frequent mentions and increasingly accurate recommendations.

By the fourth month, the impact of these improvements was clear. AI visibility had increased substantially, with the company appearing more often in relevant queries and being recommended as a primary option for many products. Additionally, AI characterizations of the products became far more accurate, reflecting the underlying completeness and quality of the data. This case illustrates how systematically improving product data can dramatically enhance AI-driven visibility and recommendation reliability.

Key learning

Data completeness functions as a visibility threshold. Below it, AI agents lack sufficient signal to recommend accurately, regardless of the actual market position. Above it, citation rates rise consistently, and characterizations become reliable.

Case study 2

The basic details are as follows:

- **Consumer electronics**: Data quality as a foundation.
- **Company**: TechGear (pseudonym), electronics manufacturer.
- **Challenge**: Inaccurate AI citations are damaging brand trust.
- **Timeline**: 6 months.
- **Initial problem**: Customers complained that AI agents cited incorrect specifications:
    - Battery life: AI said "15 hours," actual was 12 hours.
    - Weight: AI said "2.8 lbs," actual was 3.1 lbs.
    - Outdated pricing and discontinued features.

- **Impact**:
    - Product returns: 18% (vs 11% industry average).
    - Support tickets about spec mismatches.
    - NPS declining 8 points YoY.
- **Root cause**:
    - Multiple conflicting data sources.
    - No single source of truth.
    - Audit found 1,247 discrepancies across 347 products.

Transformation

Over the first two months, the company focused on consolidating all product data into a centralized system. Every discrepancy was corrected, and a real-time synchronization process was implemented, reducing delays from weeks to mere minutes. This foundational step ensured that AI systems could access a single, authoritative source of information.

In the following months, the team implemented ongoing quality monitoring. Automated daily scans checked for inconsistencies, while AI citations were reviewed weekly, and alerts were generated in real time whenever issues arose. This continuous oversight maintained high data quality and prevented errors from creeping back in.

By the end of six months, the impact was clear: product data accuracy was nearly flawless, AI citations became highly reliable, and specification errors had been virtually eliminated. TechGear's experience demonstrates how centralizing data and maintaining rigorous quality monitoring can restore trust, improve AI-driven discovery, and ensure accurate representation across channels.

Key learning

AI agents preferentially cite high-quality sources. Once we established accuracy, citation rates increased significantly even without other optimizations.

Case study 3

The basic details are as follows:

- **Premium consumer brand**: Emotional data drives differentiation.
- **Company**: LuxeHome (pseudonym), premium home goods.
- **Challenge**: AI-recommended based only on specs, missing brand positioning.
- **Timeline**: 6 months.

- **Initial problem**: AI response (before):

  ```
  "For luxury bath towels:
  - Brand A - 700 GSM, $45
  - Brand B - 600 GSM, $38
  - LuxeHome - 650 GSM, $52
  All offer quality. Brand A has the highest GSM, Brand B has the best
  value, LuxeHome is a premium option."
  ```

- **Issue**: Characterized as just a "premium option" without differentiation. Competing only on specs.

Transformation

In the first two months, LuxeHome focused on developing emotional and experiential attributes for its products. The team analyzed over 1,200 customer reviews, conducted user experience studies with 30 participants over two weeks, engaged expert design and textile assessments, and documented the entire supply chain for transparency. This work established a rich layer of context beyond technical specifications.

During months three and four, this information was integrated into the structured product data. Emotional attributes, sustainability certifications, and guidance on ideal use cases were added to the schema, ensuring AI systems could understand and surface the brand's values alongside product details.

Six months after these enhancements, the results were striking. AI recommendations began consistently positioning LuxeHome as the go-to choice for "conscious luxury," clearly communicating the brand's values and unique positioning. Emotional attributes were regularly recognized and cited, and AI agents now conveyed the brand as a "sustainable luxury" option rather than just a premium product. LuxeHome's experience shows that embedding emotional and contextual data into structured product information enables AI systems to highlight brand differentiation, driving both visibility and preference in AI-driven discovery.

Key learning

Achieving functional parity only drives price-based competition. Embedding emotional and contextual data into structured product information enables AI agents to communicate brand values, differentiate the product, and influence preference, especially for queries framed around specific values or use cases.

Conclusion

The evolution from PIM to PXM is a fundamental shift in how organizations think about product data, becoming a competitive advantage. In the AI-driven discovery era, product information is the raw material from which AI agents construct recommendations, comparisons, and characterizations that shape purchase decisions.

Across every successful PXM transformation, the same patterns appear. High-performing organizations fix data quality first: completeness, consistency, and precision. They move systematically. Transformation is phased. Foundation. Enhancement. Optimization. Intelligence. They measure what matters: AI visibility, citation frequency, and characterization accuracy.

They capture emotion. Specifications make products comparable. Emotional and experiential data make them preferable. They treat quality as a strategy. In AI-driven discovery, accuracy and clarity determine who gets cited. Additionally, they collaborate. PXM excellence requires product, content, engineering, analytics, and brand teams to operate as a coordinated system.

For organizations beginning their PXM transformation, the path is clear. Assess the maturity of your PIM, the quality of your data, and your current level of AI visibility. Achieve high completeness and implement a structured schema.

Then expand its dimensionality. Add use cases, contextual positioning, and competitive differentiation. Integrate emotion deliberately. Capture experiential and identity-based attributes that explain why someone would choose your product. Measure and optimize. Track AI visibility, analyze how you are characterized, and close competitive gaps. Finally, scale intelligence. Introduce automation, predictive enrichment, and AI-assisted optimization. This is not a one-time project. It is a built-in capability. And the organizations that treat it that way will define the next era of product visibility.

The next chapter will examine how to dominate the Agentic Shelf with digital shelf analytics because in an agent-driven world, it is not enough to be indexed. You must earn your place on the shelf that actually gets shown.

CHAPTER 8
Dominating Agentic Shelf with Digital Shelf Analytics

Introduction

In previous chapters, we have explored the foundations of AI optimization, from understanding how AI agents work to implementing technical infrastructure to managing product experience for AI discovery. We have examined content strategies, data quality, and competitive positioning. However, there is a critical concept that ties all of these elements together: the **Agentic Shelf**.

The traditional retail shelf, whether physical or digital, gave brands visibility and choice. Walk down a supermarket aisle, and you see dozens of competing products. Visit Amazon, and you scroll through pages of search results. Brands competed for shelf placement, eye-level positioning, and featured placement. Success meant being seen among the options.

The Agentic Shelf operates fundamentally differently. When a consumer asks an AI agent for a recommendation, there is no shelf to browse. There are no *pages of results* to scroll through. There is often just one answer, or at most a short list of three to five options. The AI agent has already selected, compared, and recommended. The consumer never sees the other options that were filtered out.

This creates a winner-take-most dynamic unprecedented in commerce. If you are not in that AI-generated recommendation, you do not exist to that customer. A competitor did not beat you; you were simply never considered. The battle for visibility happens invisibly, in the AI's synthesis process, based on signals and data you may not even know you are sending.

This chapter explores how to dominate the Agentic Shelf through systematic digital shelf analytics adapted for AI-driven discovery. It covers the Agentic Shelf concept and why it is replacing traditional search pages, Share of Model as the critical new KPI for measuring brand health, and competitive benchmarking frameworks for understanding why AI agents cite specific competitors over others. It also addresses price and availability as hard signals in AI decision-making and strategies for closing the discovery gap between where you are and where you need to be.

For brand leaders, this chapter provides the measurement and competitive intelligence frameworks needed to win in AI-mediated commerce. For analysts and strategists, it offers concrete methodologies for tracking and improving AI visibility. For executives, it clarifies the new battleground where market share will be won or lost.

Structure

The chapter covers the following topics:

- Redefining digital commerce with the Agentic Shelf
- Measuring Share of Model
- Understanding why AI agents choose competitors
- Price and availability as hard signals
- Closing the discovery gap

Objectives

By the end of this chapter, readers will understand the concept of the Agentic Shelf and how AI-generated recommendations are replacing the traditional search results page as the primary battleground for visibility. They will be able to define and measure Share of Model as a new KPI for brand health in AI-driven discovery environments and analyze competitive citation patterns to understand why AI agents select certain products over others. Readers will also learn to identify the role of price, availability, and other hard signals in influencing AI recommendation decisions, diagnose and close the discovery gap between brand strength in traditional channels and performance on the Agentic Shelf, and develop a systematic digital shelf analytics framework adapted for AI-era monitoring, benchmarking, and optimization.

Redefining digital commerce with the Agentic Shelf

The shift from search to AI is not incremental. It is structural. What was once an open marketplace of links has become a curated shortlist generated instantly by an algorithm. To understand the strategic implications, we need to compare how visibility worked in the traditional search model versus how it operates on the Agentic Shelf.

From search results to AI recommendations

The traditional digital shelf, search engine results pages, category pages, and comparison sites provided transparency and choice. Consumers could see the full competitive set, browse options, and make their own comparisons.

Traditional search page model (illustrative):

```
User Query: "best project management software"
Search Results Page:
1. Brand A (Sponsored Ad)
2. Brand B (Sponsored Ad)
3. Comparison Article: "10 Best Project Management Tools"
4. Brand C Official Site
5. Brand D Official Site
6. Review Site: Brand E vs Brand F
7. Brand G Official Site
8. Industry Article
9. Brand H Official Site
10. YouTube Review: Brand I vs Brand J
User sees 10+ options on first page, can click multiple links,
scroll through pages 2-10, form own opinion through research.
```

Agentic shelf model (illustrative):

```
User Query: "best project management software"
AI Response:
"For project management software, I'd recommend considering:
1. **Brand C** - Best for mid-market teams needing customization
   - Robust workflow automation
   - Scales 20-500 users effectively
   - $24/user/month professional tier
   - Strong integration ecosystem

2. **Brand A** - Best for enterprise scale and security
   - Enterprise-grade security (SOC 2, ISO 27001)
   - Unlimited users, complex hierarchies
   - Advanced reporting and analytics
   - Starting at $35/user/month

3. **Brand E** - Best value for small teams
   - Simple interface, quick setup
   - Great for teams under 20
   - $12/user/month
```

```
    - Limited customization
Each offers different strengths depending on your team size,
budget, and specific requirements."
User sees 3 options, presented with AI's analysis already done.
No other brands visible in this interaction.
```

The difference is profound. In the traditional model, visibility meant appearing on page one, a goal achievable by dozens of brands. In the agentic model, visibility means being one of the three recommendations. Everything else is invisible.

The following figure makes the compression visible: where traditional search offered ten or more options on a single page, the Agentic Shelf has room for three. Everything outside those slots does not exist to the consumer standing in front of it.

***Figure 8.1**: AI recommendations compress an entire category into three visible slots*

Characteristics of the Agentic Shelf

Understanding the Agentic Shelf's unique characteristics reveals optimization opportunities and strategic imperatives. Five characteristics define how the Agentic Shelf operates and why it demands a fundamentally different approach from traditional search optimization:

- **Extreme selectivity**: Traditional search results showed ten organic results per page. AI agents typically recommend one to five options, and for users who historically browsed multiple pages of results, the compression is even more dramatic. Being good enough to appear in search results is no longer sufficient; a product must be definitively recommendable for specific use cases. Marginal differentiation that worked in traditional search, where the goal was earning a click among many visible options, is inadequate when competing for one of three recommendation slots. The strategic response is to focus on becoming the clear best choice for specific contexts rather than attempting to be acceptable across all of them.

- **Context dependence**: Traditional search results were relatively stable for a given query. The same search for *project management software* would yield similar results regardless of who performed it. AI recommendations vary significantly based on conversation history, implicit requirements inferred from how questions are phrased, specific constraints such as budget ranges and required integrations, the underlying problem the user is trying to solve, and signals about whether the buyer is an enterprise or a small business. Two users asking the same question but arriving with different contexts may receive entirely different recommendations. Optimization must therefore address multiple contexts and use cases rather than generic best-product positioning. Content should help AI agents understand clearly when a product is the right choice and when an alternative would serve better.

- **Synthesized positioning**: Traditional search allowed brands to control their positioning directly through title tags, meta descriptions, and page content. AI agents synthesize positioning from a much broader set of sources: official website content, third-party reviews and comparisons, user testimonials, competitive analysis articles, industry analyst reports, and social media mentions. The characterization that emerges is not written by the brand; it is constructed from the totality of available information. A brand that positions itself as the most powerful platform in its category may find that AI agents recommend it specifically for technical teams needing advanced customization while flagging its complexity for non-technical users. This synthesis reflects what users and analysts actually say, not just what the brand claims. Inconsistencies between official claims and external perceptions will surface in AI characterizations, making consistency across all information sources a strategic priority.

- **Comparative by default**: Traditional search required users to do comparison work themselves, visiting multiple sites and assembling their own evaluation. AI agents perform this comparison automatically, presenting explicit trade-offs and recommendations. Every recommendation inherently answers the question of why this option is over alternatives, and that comparative framing is built into the response, regardless of whether the user asked for a comparison. Vague positioning, such as "best-in-class" or "industry-leading," does not survive AI synthesis; it is replaced with specific, verifiable comparative statements. The appropriate strategic response is to develop honest, specific competitive positioning that acknowledges trade-offs openly and is clear about what the product is better at and what it is not optimized for.

- **Attribution variability**: Traditional search always showed a brand name and link, making visibility binary. AI attribution exists on a spectrum. A brand may receive prominent attribution as the primary recommendation, appear as one of several options without particular emphasis, receive a passing mention alongside competitors, or have its information synthesized into an answer without being named at all. The implication is that impact may exceed visible attribution. A brand's content can shape recommendations even when it is not explicitly cited, and conversely, being mentioned does not guarantee meaningful consideration. Measurement frameworks must therefore track both direct mentions through Share of Model metrics and indirect influence through category queries where a brand's information shapes the answer without its name appearing in it.

Economic implications

The Agentic Shelf creates fundamentally new economic dynamics that reshape competitive strategy.

Winner-take-most markets

When AI agents consistently recommend the same 2-3 brands in a category, those brands capture a disproportionate share of discovery, consideration, and ultimately sales. The market's tail becomes nearly invisible:

- **Traditional search**: Long tail thrives, hundreds of brands get meaningful traffic.
- **Agentic search**: Long tail collapses, visibility concentrates in the top few brands.

Market share concentration

In traditional search, even brands outside the very top tier could still attract meaningful visibility, as traffic was distributed across a wide range of results. Being lower in the rankings still meant that potential customers could discover your offerings. AI-mediated discovery works differently. Recommendations tend to focus heavily on the few brands recognized as authoritative or fully optimized. Beyond the top performers, visibility drops off sharply, leaving the "long tail" of brands with very little exposure. The implication is clear: a mid-ranked brand that once received steady traffic may now be effectively invisible unless it actively invests in high-quality data, structured information, and differentiation that AI systems can recognize.

Context as competitive advantage

Brands that own specific use cases or contexts can thrive even if they are not overall market leaders.

Market leadership is not monolithic anymore; it is contextual:

- **Brand A**: Leader for "enterprise project management".
- **Brand B**: Leader for "creative team collaboration".
- **Brand C**: Leader for "agile software development".
- **Brand D**: Leader for "construction project management".

Each captures a dominant share of its specific context, even if none dominates the overall market:

- **Implication**: Smaller brands can win by owning valuable contexts rather than competing for overall category leadership.

- **Strategic opportunity**: Identify underserved contexts where you can establish clear leadership. Better to own "best for X" in a valuable niche than be mediocre in a broad market.

Data quality premium

AI agents favor brands with superior data quality and clear positioning. When quality signals diverge between competitors, the higher-quality source gets recommendation preference.

Data quality advantage compounds:

- Better data | More citations | More user engagement | More reviews/signals | Better data.
- Poor data | Fewer citations | Less engagement | Fewer signals | Poorer data.

The gap widens over time. Early investment in data quality creates a lasting advantage.

Implication: Data quality is not just operational hygiene; it is a strategic competitive advantage. The quality premium in AI discovery exceeds that in traditional search.

Discovery tax

Brands not optimized for AI discovery pay an increasing "tax" in the form of:

- **Declining organic visibility** as discovery shifts to AI platforms.
- **Higher customer acquisition costs** as they must rely more on paid channels.
- **Lower consideration rates,** even when discovered through other means.
- **Longer sales cycles** as prospects are not pre-educated by AI.

This tax increases over time as AI-mediated discovery grows. Early optimizers avoid the tax; late movers pay an escalating penalty.

Measuring Share of Model

Share of Model (**SoM**) represents the percentage of relevant AI interactions where your brand is mentioned or recommended, becoming the new KPI for brand health. It is the AI-era equivalent of market share, but measured at the discovery layer rather than the transaction layer.

Defining SoM

Formula:

```
Share of Model (SoM) = (Number of relevant queries where your brand appears /
                        Total relevant queries measured) × 100
```

This deceptively simple formula requires careful definition of "relevant queries" and "appears."

Defining relevant queries

Relevant queries are questions or prompts where your product or service could reasonably be recommended. This includes:

Query category	Query patterns	Examples
Direct category queries	• "best [product category]" • "[product category] for [use case]" • "top [product category] tools" • "[product category] comparison"	• "best project management software". • "project management for construction teams". • "top project management tools for remote teams".
Use case queries	• "software for [specific use case]" • "how to [accomplish goal]" • "tools to help with [problem]"	• "software for managing client projects". • "how to coordinate team tasks". • "tools to help with project tracking".
Problem–solution queries	• "solve [problem]" • "improve [outcome]" • "manage [challenge]"	• "solve project deadline issues" • "improve team collaboration" • "manage multiple projects simultaneously"
Comparison queries	• "[your brand] vs [competitor]" • "[competitor] alternatives" • "products like [competitor]"	• "Asana vs Monday.com" • "Jira alternatives" • "products like Trello"
Feature-specific queries	• "[category] with [specific feature]" • "[feature] in [category]"	• "project management with Gantt charts" • "time tracking in project management software"

***Table 8.1**: Query categories and patterns for AI visibility measurement*

Defining "appears"

A brand "appears" when it is mentioned in the AI agent's response. However, not all appearances are equal.

The appearance types are as follows:

- **Primary recommendation (Weight: 10):**
    - Explicitly recommended as the top choice.
    - Featured first with a detailed description.
    - Phrased as "I recommend..." or "Best option is...".
- **Secondary recommendation (Weight: 7):**
    - Included in short list (typically 2-5 options).
    - Described with reasonable detail.
    - Presented as a viable alternative.
- **Tertiary mention (Weight: 4):**
    - Mentioned but not detailed.
    - Listed among many options.
    - Passing reference.
- **Category reference (Weight: 1):**
    - Category is mentioned, but the specific brand is not named.
    - Your information may inform a response without citation.

Weighted SoM calculation:

```
Weighted SoM = Σ(Appearance Weight × Frequency) / (Total Queries × 10) × 100
```

This accounts for the quality of mention, not just presence/absence.

SoM components

SoM breaks down into multiple sub-metrics that provide actionable insights.

Overall SoM headline metric

Total percentage of relevant queries where you appear at all. This is your primary health metric, the equivalent of "market share" for AI discovery.

Illustrative benchmarks by category maturity:

- **Mature category with clear leaders**: Top 3 brands typically have 40-60% SoM each (with significant overlap, as the same query can include multiple brands).
- **Emerging category**: Leaders might have 25-40% SoM.
- **Fragmented category**: No brand exceeds 30% SoM.

The interpretation is as follows:

- **SoM <10%**: Minimal presence, urgent optimization needed.
- **SoM 10-25%**: Emerging presence, significant opportunity.
- **SoM 25-40%**: Strong presence, competitive position.
- **SoM >40%**: Category leader for AI discovery.

Primary recommendation rate

Percentage of appearances where you are the primary (first/top) recommendation.

This measures **recommendation quality**, not just presence.

Formula:

```
Primary Rec Rate = (Primary recommendations / Total appearances) × 100
```

Example:

- Appears in 100 queries (40% SoM of 250 query universe).
- Primary recommendation in 30 of those queries.
- Primary Rec Rate: 30%.

The interpretation is as follows:

- **High SoM, low primary rate**: Frequently mentioned, rarely recommended first (also-ran positioning).
- **High SoM, high primary rate**: Frequent AND favored (market leader positioning).
- **Low SoM, high primary rate**: Niche leader, rarely mentioned but strongly preferred when relevant.

Weighted prominence score

Average prominence across all appearances.

Uses the appearance weight (1-10 scale) to measure quality:

```
Avg Prominence = Σ(Appearance Weights) / Total Appearances
```

The interpretation is as follows:

- **Score 8-10**: Consistently featured prominently.
- **Score 5-7**: Regular inclusion in lists.
- **Score 2-4**: Passing mentions, minimal detail.
- **Score <2**: Category references without brand citation.

Strategic insight: A brand can have moderate SoM but high prominence (strong but selective presence) or high SoM but low prominence (frequently mentioned but not detailed, weak positioning).

Context coverage

Breadth of use cases and scenarios where you appear.

Measures how many different contexts you are relevant to:

- **Context categories to track**:
  - **Company size**: Enterprise, Mid-market, SMB, Startup.
  - **Industry**: By vertical (construction, healthcare, technology, etc.).
  - **Use case**: Specific workflows or needs.
  - **Team type**: Engineering, marketing, operations, creative, etc.
  - **Complexity**: Simple vs complex requirements.
  - **Geographic**: Different regions/markets.
- **Coverage formula**:

  ```
  Context Coverage = (Contexts where you appear / Total contexts measured) × 100
  ```
- **Strategic implications**:
  - **Broad coverage (60%+ contexts)**: Generalist positioning, vulnerable to context-specific specialists.
  - **Focused coverage (20-40% contexts)**: Specialist positioning, strong in specific contexts.
  - **Narrow coverage (<20% contexts)**: Niche player, limited market but potentially dominant in niche.

Competitive displacement analysis

Queries where competitors appear instead of you. This identifies your biggest visibility gaps and competitive threats.

Analysis framework: For each competitor, measure:

- **Overlap**: Queries where both you and the competitor appear (co-consideration).
- **Displacement**: Queries where the competitor appears but you do not (lost opportunity).
- **Unique**: Queries where you appear but the competitor does not (your advantage).

Illustrative matrix:

```
                        You Appear    You Don't Appear
Competitor A Appears    45             38               (83 total appearances)
Competitor A Absent     22             145              (167 total absences)
                      (67 total)    (183 total)
Analysis:
- Competitor A has higher SoM (83/250 = 33% vs your 67/250 = 27%)
- Head-to-head overlap: 45 queries (you both appear)
- Competitive displacement: 38 queries (they appear, you don't)
- Your advantage: 22 queries (you appear, they don't)
Focus: Understand why Competitor A wins those 38 displacement queries.
What signals, content, or positioning do they have that you lack?
```

Measuring SoM

Measuring SoM starts with clarity. You cannot track what you have not defined. The first step is to build a structured query taxonomy that captures every meaningful moment where your brand should appear.

This taxonomy should reflect how real customers think. It spans intent, from informational queries like *what is project management software*, to comparisons, transactional searches, and problem-solution questions. It reflects specificity, from broad category terms to highly defined use cases. And it mirrors the buyer journey, from awareness to final decision.

The size of your taxonomy determines the strength of your insights. Fifty to one hundred queries provide directional signals. Two to five hundred deliver reliable measurements. A thousand or more unlock true competitive intelligence.

Developing the taxonomy is both creative and analytical. Teams brainstorm. Competitive research expands the field. AI helps generate variations. Queries are tested across platforms, filtered for relevance, categorized by intent and use case, and finally prioritized based on strategic importance.

Once defined, execution must be systematic. Queries are run across major AI platforms to measure real visibility in real recommendation environments. Coverage should include leading systems, recognizing that each platform behaves differently and weights signals uniquely.

For organizations with limited resources, sampling works. Rotate portions of the taxonomy weekly. Run full measurements monthly. Monitor critical queries in real time, especially brand comparisons and high-intent decision terms.

Execution can be manual for smaller datasets, with standardized phrasing and clean sessions to avoid contamination. Larger taxonomies benefit from semi-automation, using APIs and scripts to gather responses consistently while reserving human analysis for interpretation.

Every response becomes data.

You document whether your brand appears. You assess prominence: primary recommendation, supporting mention, or passing reference. You analyze positioning, framing, detail, and characterization. You note competitors mentioned, how they are described, and the trade-offs presented. You examine the structure: how many brands are recommended, and on what basis.

From this, metrics emerge.

The overall share of the model reflects how often you appear across the total query universe. Platform-specific SoM reveals strengths and weaknesses by ecosystem. Query-category analysis uncovers gaps in visibility for information, comparisons, or transactions. Prominence scoring adds depth, distinguishing between being listed and being leading.

Competitive benchmarking completes the picture. Applying the same methodology to competitors reveals displacement patterns, overlap zones, and contextual dominance.

Measurement without trends is static. SoM must be tracked over time.

Weekly sampling offers early warning signals. Monthly comprehensive analysis measures tactical effectiveness. Quarterly reviews reveal competitive movement and structural shifts. Year-over-year comparisons show whether your brand is gaining or losing strategic ground.

Share of Model is not a one-time audit. It is a living metric. It captures whether you exist on the Agentic Shelf and whether your presence is strengthening or eroding. What gets measured improves. What gets tracked systematically compounds.

Understanding why AI agents choose competitors

Traditional competitive analysis focused on comparing websites, features, pricing, and marketing strategies. AI-era competitive benchmarking requires understanding **why AI agents cite specific competitors** and what signals, content, and positioning drive those recommendations.

Competitive intelligence framework

Raw visibility numbers reveal who is winning but not why, and without that understanding, optimization efforts lack direction. A four-layer framework moves the analysis from surface observation to actionable insight, each layer building on the one before it.

Layer 1, SoM comparison

Measuring SoM across all major competitors using the same query taxonomy provides a baseline competitive landscape. This comparison immediately surfaces which brands AI agents favor most broadly and reveals the relative positions of market leaders, close competitors, growing challengers, and niche or declining players. The first strategic questions this data should prompt are which competitors consistently outperform you and why, which brands occupy a similar position and therefore represent the most direct competition for the next tier of growth, and which brands underperform in ways that reveal either cautionary patterns to avoid or valuable niches they have quietly claimed.

Layer 2, context analysis

Aggregate SoM figures tell only part of the story. Breaking down SoM by context reveals where each competitor wins and where you win, which is often more actionable than overall rankings. Segmenting by company size, for example, may show that a market leader dominates enterprise queries while you lead decisively in SMB queries and contest mid-market queries with a close competitor. Each of these positions carries a strategic implication. A competitor that owns the enterprise segment has established enterprise signals you currently lack. A segment you dominate reflects genuine strengths in the attributes AI agents associate with that context. A contested segment represents an opportunity for differentiation.

The same logic applies when segmenting by use case. A competitor may hold a commanding position in agile development queries while you lead creative teams, and a smaller brand not prominent in overall rankings may dominate a specific vertical, such as construction or field operations. These patterns reveal that niche specialization can produce strong contextual performance even without broad market leadership, and that the gap between your overall position and your position in specific use cases often points directly to where content investment will have the greatest impact.

Layer 3, citation pattern analysis

Understanding which content and signals AI agents cite when recommending competitors transforms competitive intelligence from observation into action. For each major competitor, the analysis should examine which specific pages, features, or categories of information appear most frequently in AI recommendations for that brand, and then compare those assets directly against your own equivalents.

A competitor that consistently wins enterprise queries may do so because AI agents repeatedly reference its security certifications page, enterprise case studies, advanced reporting documentation, integration directory, and transparent enterprise pricing structure. Comparing those assets against your own reveals not just that a gap exists but precisely where it exists: a basic compliance list versus detailed certifications with audit reports, three enterprise case studies versus dozens, a feature list versus documentation with use cases, a limited integration catalog versus a comprehensive one, and a contact-sales placeholder versus a published pricing tier.

The positioning language AI agents use to characterize each competitor makes the gap concrete. A competitor described as enterprise-grade, proven with large organizations, and offering extensive integrations occupies an entirely different position from a brand characterized as easy to use, affordable, and well-suited to small teams. Neither characterization is inherently negative, but they do not compete for the same queries. If the goal is to move into a segment currently owned by a competitor, the content, credentials, and signals required to earn that characterization must be built deliberately and specifically.

Layer 4, attribute advantage analysis

Identifying which specific attributes drive competitive advantage in AI recommendations requires examining the signals AI agents use to differentiate between brands across several distinct categories.

Authority signals encompass industry analyst recognition, awards, media coverage, and thought leadership, such as original research reports and speaking engagements. A competitor recognized by major analysts, holding multiple industry awards, and cited across dozens of media outlets carries an authority profile that AI agents weigh heavily. A brand with minimal analyst coverage, a single award, and sparse media presence will consistently lose authority comparisons regardless of product quality.

Data quality signals reflect how completely and accurately a brand's product information is represented across sources. Attribute completeness rates, specification detail, update frequency, and consistency across platforms all factor into how reliably AI agents can extract and cite product information. A competitor maintaining near-complete attribute coverage updated weekly presents a fundamentally different data profile from a brand with incomplete specifications updated quarterly.

Social proof signals include review volume and average rating, the size of the claimed customer base, testimonial quality, and community activity. A brand with thousands of reviews on major platforms and a large documented customer base gives AI agents strong, verifiable signals of market adoption. A brand with a fraction of that review volume, even with a comparable average rating, simply lacks the weight of evidence that AI agents use to assess market validation.

Content depth signals cover the breadth and comprehensiveness of documentation, the range of use cases addressed, the presence of problem-solution content, and the quality of educational resources. A competitor with hundreds of help articles, multiple industry guides, and dozens of use case pages has built a content library that AI agents can draw on across a wide range of queries. A brand with a fraction of that coverage will be invisible in the queries that richer content would otherwise serve.

Technical signals reflect the quality of API documentation, the size of the integration ecosystem, the depth of technical specifications, and the availability of developer resources such as portals and SDKs. For queries involving technical buyers, these signals function as proxies for product maturity and enterprise readiness. A brand with comprehensive developer documentation and a large, well-documented integration catalog occupies a categorically different position from one with basic API documentation and a limited integration list.

Taken together, these four layers of competitive intelligence move the analysis from knowing that competitors outperform you to understanding precisely which signals and assets drive that outperformance, making the path to closing specific gaps far clearer.

Competitive response strategies

Competitive intelligence is only useful insofar as it drives strategic decisions. Based on where gaps exist and where advantages already lie, four response strategies are available, each suited to different competitive situations. Based on competitive intelligence, choose your strategic response:

- **Strategy 1**: Direct competition:

  Direct competition is appropriate when the goal is to contest the same contexts where a competitor currently wins. This strategy requires building equivalent signals in areas where the competitor holds an advantage, matching their content depth, authority profile, and volume of social proof, and achieving parity on the key attributes AI agents use to differentiate between brands. The investment required is substantial, typically measured in years rather than months, and displacing an established leader in their strongest segment carries no guarantee of success. The opportunity, however, is a meaningful expansion of the addressable market and average deal size.

- **Strategy 2**: Flanking / context ownership:

  Flanking through context ownership is appropriate when direct competition would be costly, and the competitive map reveals underserved contexts where no brand has established a dominant position. Rather than contesting a competitor's stronghold, this strategy concentrates investment on owning specific contexts, building deep positioning, relevant content, targeted integrations, and community presence within a defined segment while accepting secondary status in segments the competitor already controls. The result is a narrower addressable market but one that is easier to defend and where the brand can achieve the kind of clear, consistent recommendation that broad competition rarely produces.

- **Strategy 3**: Differentiation emphasis:

  Differentiation emphasis is appropriate when genuine strengths already exist, but AI agents are not surfacing them consistently. This strategy does not require building new capabilities; it requires making existing advantages more explicit, more prominently documented, and more verifiable. If a brand implements faster, achieves higher user satisfaction scores, or delivers measurable value more quickly than competitors, that advantage needs to be expressed in specific, comparable terms that AI agents can extract and cite. The risk is that the advantage must be real and defensible; differentiation emphasis amplifies what is already true; it does not manufacture positioning.

- **Strategy 4**: Category expansion:

  Category expansion is appropriate when the competitive landscape in existing categories is sufficiently crowded that leadership in a new or emerging context offers a better return on investment. This strategy involves defining a market category or use case before competitors do, establishing thought leadership through original research and frameworks, developing features and content that address the specific needs of that context, and building the terminology and reference points that others will eventually cite. The timeline is long, and the risk is real, since a category that does not gain market traction produces little return, but the opportunity is leadership in a growing segment with significantly less competition than established categories carry.

Price and availability as hard signals

While content quality, positioning, and authority signals influence AI recommendations, **price and availability function as binary filters**. These hard signals can disqualify you from consideration before other factors even matter.

Understanding hard signals vs. soft signals

The details are as follows:

- **Soft signals (gradual influence):**
  - Content quality
  - Authority
  - Reviews
  - Feature depth
  - Brand recognition

  Effect: Incrementally increase or decrease the likelihood of a recommendation. Poor soft signals reduce recommendation probability, but do not eliminate you.

- **Hard signals (filter functions)**:
  - Price
  - Availability
  - Compatibility
  - Geography
  - Licensing

  Effect: Binary inclusion/exclusion. Fail a hard signal, and you are filtered out completely, regardless of how strong your soft signals are.

Price as a filter signal

How price filtering works: When a user query includes explicit or implicit price constraints, AI agents apply price as a filter before considering other factors:

Query with explicit price constraint:

"Best project management software under $25/user"

AI decision process (illustrative):

```
Step 1: Retrieve all project management solutions
→ [30 solutions retrieved from knowledge base]
Step 2: Apply price filter
→ Remove solutions with unclear pricing (7 eliminated - no decision possible)
→ Remove solutions exceeding $25/user (12 eliminated - above budget)
→ [11 solutions remaining]
Step 3: Apply soft signals (quality, authority, reviews, positioning)
→ Rank remaining 11 solutions
→ Recommend top 3
```

Critical insight: If your pricing is unclear or exceeds the constraint, you are eliminated before your excellent features, stellar reviews, or market leadership even matter. You lost not because competitors were better, but because you were filtered out.

Types of price signals

The types are as follows:

- **Fatal price signals (immediate filter-out):**
  - **No pricing information available:**
    - "Contact for pricing" / "Request quote".
    - No pricing page.
    - Pricing removed or hidden.
  - **Pricing significantly outdated:**
    - Last updated >12 months ago.
    - Contradictory pricing across sources.
    - Obsolete tier structure.
  - **Price exceeds stated constraint:**
    - User specified "$25/user max".
    - Your cheapest tier is $30/user.
    - Automatic elimination.

- **Pricing complexity preventing comparison:**
  - Requires a multi-step calculator.
  - Opaque bundling.
  - Variable pricing without ranges.

- **Disadvantage price signals (reduces ranking):**
  - **Unclear pricing tiers:**
    - Confusing differences between tiers.
    - Unclear what is included where.
    - Hidden limitations or caps.
  - **Price at the high end without a clear justification:**
    - Most expensive option without obvious differentiators.
    - AI cannot explain the premium price.
    - No clear value proposition for cost.
  - **Complex pricing requiring consultation:**
    - Custom pricing only.
    - Per-feature pricing with many features.
    - Dynamic pricing based on usage.
- **Advantage price signals (improves ranking):**
  - **Clear, specific pricing:**
    - "$49/user/month for Professional tier".
    - Simple tier structure (typically 3-4 tiers).
    - Transparent what is included.
  - **Transparent tier differences:**
    - Clear comparison of what each tier offers.
    - Obvious progression of value.
    - Easy to determine which tier fits needs.
  - **Value justification for premium pricing:**
    - Clear ROI articulation.
    - Specific advantages over alternatives.
    - Total cost of ownership transparency.

Price optimization strategies

Premium pricing requires justification that AI agents can extract and relay. A brand described simply as the most expensive option in its category loses every price-sensitive query. A brand whose content clearly explains that its pricing reflects enterprise-grade security, dedicated support, and advanced analytics unavailable in lower-priced alternatives gives AI agents the framing needed to recommend it accurately in contexts where those attributes matter. Achieving this requires value justification content that documents specific advantages, ROI data, or case study evidence, total cost of ownership comparisons, and explicit callouts of what is included that competitors charge extra for.

Mid-market positioning depends on tier clarity. When feature progression across pricing tiers is obvious and upgrade triggers are explicitly stated, AI agents can match users to the right tier rather than defaulting to a generic recommendation. Ambiguity about what is and is not included at each level creates the kind of inconsistency that erodes trust quickly.

Value and budget positioning work best when the price advantage is stated explicitly rather than implied. Content should specify what is included at the price point, how that compares to competitors at the same level, and what limitations apply. Transparency about limitations is not a weakness; it is a trust signal. AI agents making budget-conscious recommendations favor sources that give them complete, honest information over sources that obscure constraints. Clarity and honesty, across all three pricing positions, are what allow AI agents to make accurate recommendations rather than hedged or generic ones.

Availability as a binary signal

Unlike price, which influences where a product ranks within the recommendation set, availability determines whether it appears at all. A single availability failure, whether an out-of-stock status, a geographic restriction, or a platform incompatibility, is sufficient to remove a product from consideration entirely, regardless of how strong every other signal is. Understanding how this filter operates and how to ensure a product consistently passes it is a prerequisite for everything else in the recommendation optimization process.

How availability filtering works

Availability functions as an absolute filter in AI decision-making. When a user query signals purchase intent, AI agents first identify relevant products and then immediately filter by availability. A product that is out of stock is effectively invisible, regardless of how well it matches every other dimension of the query. The only exception is when the query explicitly asks about future products, in which case, unavailable items may be mentioned in a forward-looking context. For all other transactional queries, availability is binary: products that cannot be obtained now are excluded from recommendations.

Availability signal types

Availability issues that eliminate a product from consideration entirely include being out of stock without a restock date, carrying a discontinued status, being restricted from the user's geographic region due to shipping limitations or regulatory requirements, and being incompatible with the user's platform or operating environment. Any one of these conditions is sufficient to remove a product from an AI recommendation, regardless of its strengths on every other dimension.

Positive availability signals work in the opposite direction, actively supporting inclusion in recommendations. Immediate availability communicated clearly, whether through shipping timelines, access confirmations, or stock status, gives AI agents the signal they need to recommend with confidence. Specific lead times for backordered products, such as a defined ship date or restock date, are significantly more useful than vague status labels, because they allow AI agents to assess whether the wait is compatible with the user's needs. Alternative availability options, such as a different color that is in stock while the preferred one is backordered, or a previous model available while the current one ships later, keep a brand in consideration rather than ceding the recommendation entirely to a competitor.

Availability optimization strategies

The most critical availability optimization is accuracy. Availability status should reflect reality within minutes of any change, and showing a product as in stock when it is not is one of the fastest ways to erode the trust AI agents place in a source. Accuracy is not a technical nicety; it is a foundational requirement for remaining in the recommendation set.

For products with geographic limitations, clarity about which regions can purchase, what international shipping options exist, and what alternatives are available to users in restricted regions prevents AI agents from recommending a product to someone who cannot actually obtain it. Ambiguity here results in the same outcome as unavailability: exclusion.

Lead time communication should always favor specificity over vagueness. A defined ship date enables AI agents to make a judgment about whether the timeline meets the user's needs. A label like "temporarily unavailable" or "coming soon" provides no actionable information and is treated as effectively unavailable. The difference between a specific restock date and an indefinite status label is the difference between remaining in consideration and being replaced.

When the primary product option is unavailable, structuring content to surface alternatives explicitly keeps the brand present in the recommendation. A clearly documented relationship between an out-of-stock item and an available alternative, whether a previous model, a different configuration, or a rental or access program, gives AI agents a path to continued recommendation rather than a dead end that routes the user elsewhere.

Compounding effect of hard signals

Price and availability do not simply add to a product's competitive position; they gate it. A product with outstanding reviews, strong market authority, and a clear fit for the user's use case will still receive zero recommendations if pricing information is absent or availability is unclear. Soft signals, however compelling, cannot compensate for missing hard signals. They are evaluated only after hard signal filters have been applied.

The inverse is also instructive. A product with moderate reviews, reasonable authority, and an imperfect but acceptable fit for the use case will consistently outperform a superior product in recommendations if it offers clear pricing within the user's budget and confirmed immediate availability. It survives the filters and earns the right to compete on merit. The superior product, despite its advantages, never reaches that stage.

When hard and soft signals are both strong, the effect compounds in the other direction. A product that combines genuine quality and authority with transparent pricing, clear value justification, and confirmed availability earns consistent top placement across a wide range of queries. Each signal reinforces the others, and the recommendation becomes durable rather than situational.

The strategic implication is one of sequencing. Hard signals are table stakes, and optimizing soft signals before addressing them is a wasted investment. A brand that spends months improving content depth, earning reviews, and building authority while leaving pricing ambiguous or availability data unreliable will find that none of that work translates into recommendations. The correct order is to establish price clarity and availability accuracy first, then build on that foundation with the soft signal work that determines competitive position within the recommendation set.

Closing the discovery gap

The "discovery gap" is the distance between your current SoM and the level you need to achieve for sustainable business growth. Closing this gap requires a systematic improvement framework that prioritizes effort across multiple workstreams.

Discovery gap assessment

The steps are as follows:

1. **Quantify your current state**: Measure:
    a. Current Overall SoM.
    b. SoM by query category.
    c. SoM by context (company size, industry, use case).
    d. Primary recommendation rate.
    e. Competitive gaps (where competitors appear instead of you).
2. **Define target state**: Set realistic goals based on:
    a. Category maturity (emerging vs mature)
    b. Competitive intensity
    c. Resource constraints
    d. Business objectives

3. **Identify root causes of gaps**: Discovery gaps rarely have a single cause. Diagnosing them accurately requires examining six categories of root causes, each pointing to a distinct area of remediation:

Common discovery gap root causes	Specific Issues
Content gaps	• Missing use case coverage. • Incomplete industry positioning. • Lack of problem-solution content. • Thin educational resources.
Data quality issues	• Incomplete product information. • Outdated specifications. • Inconsistent data across sources. • Unclear positioning.
Authority deficits	• Minimal third-party validation. • No analyst recognition. • Limited social proof (reviews, testimonials). • Weak thought leadership.
Hard signal problems	• Unclear pricing. • "Contact us" barriers. • Availability not transparent. • Geographic limitations not communicated.
Positioning weaknesses	• Unclear differentiation. • Vague value propositions. • No owned contexts. • Generic messaging.
Competitive disadvantages	• Competitors have stronger signals in specific areas. • Missing features/capabilities. • Less comprehensive content. • Weaker brand recognition.

Table 8.2: Common discovery gap root causes and specific issues

Gap-closing framework and prioritization matrix

Organize initiatives by **Impact** (SoM improvement potential) and **Effort** (time/resources required):

```
High Impact, Low Effort → Quick Wins (Do First)
High Impact, High Effort → Strategic Investments (Plan Carefully)
Low Impact, Low Effort → Fill-Ins (Do When Capacity Available)
Low Impact, High Effort → Avoid (Rarely Worth It)
```

Quick wins

These initiatives deliver meaningful SoM improvement with minimal investment (high-impact, low-effort):

Initiative	Why this works	Implementation
Competitive comparison pages	• Captures "[your brand] vs competitor" high-intent queries. • Signals confidence and transparency. • Gives AI clear differentiation signals. • Demonstrates recency when updated regularly.	• Create detailed comparison pages for the top five competitors. • Include objective feature comparisons. • Be honest about trade-offs. • Update at least quarterly.
FAQ schema implementation	• Structured data AI agents can easily extract. • Captures question-based queries directly. • Demonstrates expertise through comprehensive Q&A. • Low-effort, high-impact enhancement.	• Identify the top 50 product/category questions. • Create a comprehensive FAQ page with schema markup. • Organize by topic clusters. • Update continuously based on real customer questions.
Pricing clarity and updates	• Removes hard-signal filter-out risk. • Enables inclusion in price-sensitive queries. • Builds trust through transparency. • Differentiates from competitors who hide pricing.	• Publish clear pricing for all tiers. • Specify inclusions and exclusions. • Reduce "contact us" barriers where possible. • Review and update at least every 90 days.

Initiative	Why this works	Implementation
Best for positioning	• Helps AI understand recommendation contexts. • Creates defensible owned niches. • Sharpens differentiation. • Simple to implement.	• Add "Best For" and "Not Ideal For" sections to key pages. • Be specific and candid. • Example: "Best for teams 20–200 needing customization; not ideal for teams wanting out-of-box simplicity".
Availability status updates	• Eliminates hard-signal disqualification. • Prevents AI from recommending unavailable products. • Builds a reliability advantage.	• Implement real-time availability updates. • Display clear backorder lead times. • Provide geographic availability transparency.

***Table 8.3**: Quick win initiatives for SoM improvement*

Medium-effort initiatives

These require more investment but deliver substantial SoM improvement (high-impact, moderate-effort):

Initiative	Why this works	Implementation
Industry-specific landing pages	• Captures industry-vertical queries. • Demonstrates domain expertise. • Provides relevant use cases and proof points. • Differentiates from generic competitors.	• Develop landing pages for the top 5–10 target industries. • Include industry-specific use cases. • Feature industry customer testimonials. • Highlight relevant integrations and compliance requirements.
Use case documentation expansion	• Captures problem-solution queries. • Demonstrates versatility. • Helps AI match products to specific needs. • Creates multiple "best for" ownership contexts.	• Document 15–20 specific use cases. • Explain how the product solves each. • Include examples and workflows. • Link clearly to relevant features.

Initiative	Why this works	Implementation
Integration documentation	• Captures integration-specific queries. • Signals ecosystem compatibility. • Provides technical credibility. • Reduces perceived implementation friction.	• Document top 30–50 integrations. • Include setup guides. • Highlight capabilities enabled by each integration. • Maintain regular updates for accuracy.
Problem-solution content library	• Captures "how to solve [problem]" queries. • Establishes authority. • Connects problems to your solution naturally. • Educational framing builds trust.	• Create 10–15 "How to solve [problem]" articles. • Position the product as a solution without over-promotion. • Include alternatives and comparisons. • Structure content for AI extraction.

***Table 8.4**: Medium-effort initiatives for SoM improvement*

Strategic investments

These require significant investment but create lasting competitive advantages (high-impact, high-effort):

Initiative	Why this works	Implementation
Comprehensive PXM implementation	• Foundation for all AI optimization. • Improves data quality across touchpoints. • Enables dynamic, context-specific content. • Compounds over time.	• Follow the full PXM transformation roadmap (see *Chapter 7, PXM Evolution and Managing AI Experience*). • Execute phased 12-month rollout. • Secure cross-functional alignment and executive commitment.
Thought leadership and authority building	• Generates third-party validation. • Establishes category expertise. • Creates citation-worthy original content. • Benefits from network effects over time.	• Publish an annual original research study. • Build conference and webinar speaking presence. • Invest in media relations and earned coverage • Develop an expert contributor program.

Initiative	Why this works	Implementation
Analyst relations program	• Analyst citations carry high authority weight. • Influences category framing. • Validates competitive positioning. • Builds long-term brand equity.	• Engage relevant analyst firms. • Participate in market evaluations. • Sponsor strategic research. • Build sustained analyst relationships.

***Table 8.5**: Strategic investments for SoM improvement*

Conclusion

Winning on the Agentic Shelf requires a fundamental restructuring of how brands achieve visibility in digital commerce. The compression from dozens of visible search results to a handful of AI recommendations creates winner-take-most dynamics where visibility concentrates among the top few brands in each context.

The Agentic Shelf rewrites the rules. Search once gave you ten chances. AI gives you three. Sometimes one. Visibility has collapsed. *Almost good enough* no longer exists. You are either recommended or invisible.

SoM is your new reality. It measures presence at the moment of decision. Not traffic. Not impressions. Recommendation. If the model does not surface you, the customer never sees you. SoM is now the frontline KPI of brand health.

Winning is contextual. You do not need the whole category. You need the moment. Own *best for remote teams*. Own *best for field crews*. Own a defined use case and dominate it. Precision beats breadth.

Hard signals decide survival. Price clarity. Availability accuracy. Get them wrong, and you are filtered out instantly. No brand story can rescue a product that fails the basics.

The discovery gap is operational, not existential. Close it with disciplined execution. Fix fundamentals. Optimize context. Track SoM relentlessly. Gains are measurable and achievable within a year.

Early movers compound. Authority compounds. Structured depth compounds. Every month you delay, competitors strengthen their position on the shelf that customers never see but always trust.

The brands that win the next decade of digital commerce will be those that dominate the Agentic Shelf, consistently appear in AI recommendations, own valuable contexts, and build authority that AI agents can trust. The invisible shelf determines your fate. Make yourself visible.

The next chapter will be a walkthrough on how to automate the deployment of GEO-optimized content across a multi-platform AI landscape. As optimization efforts mature and expand, manual processes become the primary constraint on growth. The next chapter addresses that constraint directly, providing the architecture, workflows, and automation frameworks needed to scale AI visibility operations without proportionally scaling headcount.

Chapter 9
Scaling GEO and Automating Visibility Across AI Platforms

Introduction

In previous chapters, we have explored the strategies, tactics, and frameworks for optimizing content for AI-driven discovery. We have examined how to structure product data, create quotable insights, implement schema markup, manage the Agentic Shelf, and measure Share of Model. These capabilities form the foundation of effective AI optimization.

However, there is a critical challenge we have not yet addressed: **scale**. The techniques described in earlier chapters, while effective, are often manually intensive. Creating answer-first content, implementing comprehensive schema, conducting competitive analysis, and monitoring AI visibility all require significant human effort. For organizations with hundreds or thousands of products, dozens of content types, and continuous updates, manual optimization becomes unsustainable.

Moreover, the AI landscape is constantly evolving. New platforms emerge, existing platforms update their models, query patterns shift, and competitive dynamics change. An optimization approach that requires weeks of manual work to implement cannot keep pace with this rate of change. What worked last quarter may be outdated this quarter. Manual processes create lag that undermines competitiveness.

The scaling paradox: The more successful your AI optimization becomes, the more products, content types, and platforms you need to optimize, creating an expanding workload that manual processes cannot sustain.

For technical leaders, this chapter provides the architecture and automation frameworks needed to scale AI optimization. For operations managers, it offers processes and workflows that balance efficiency with quality. For executives, it clarifies the infrastructure investments required to compete effectively as AI discovery becomes the dominant channel.

The organizations that will win in AI-driven discovery are not those with the most resources; they are those with the most efficient, automated, and scalable optimization processes. This chapter shows how to build them.

Structure

The chapter covers the following topics:

- Automating AEO and GEO content updates
- Platform-specific optimization
- Creating an AI brand voice
- Automating the audit process
- Maintaining data integrity during high-frequency updates

Objectives

This chapter addresses the scaling challenge through automation and systematization. It covers the design of automated pipelines for AEO and GEO content updates that maintain quality while reducing manual effort and platform-specific optimization strategies that account for the unique characteristics of different AI systems. It also examines how to create a consistent AI brand voice across all AI-generated descriptions of your brand, how to build automated audit processes that continuously monitor and improve quality, and how to maintain data integrity during high-frequency product updates.

Automating AEO and GEO content updates

Automation does not mean eliminating human judgment; it means systematizing repeatable processes so humans can focus on strategic decisions rather than routine execution.

Content update pipeline architecture

The six-stage automation pipeline is provided as follows:

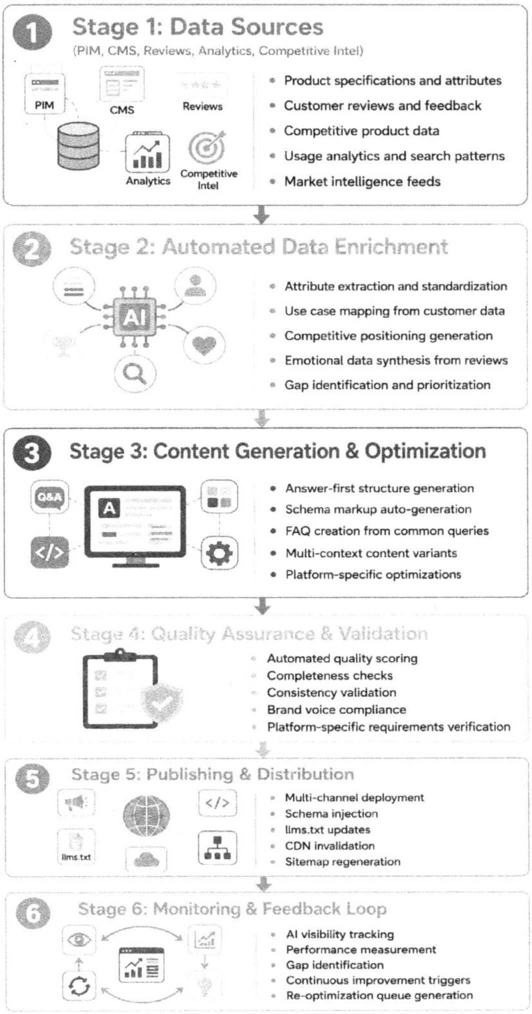

Figure 9.1: *Content update pipeline architecture*

An effective AEO automation architecture comprises six interconnected stages, as shown in the following figure:

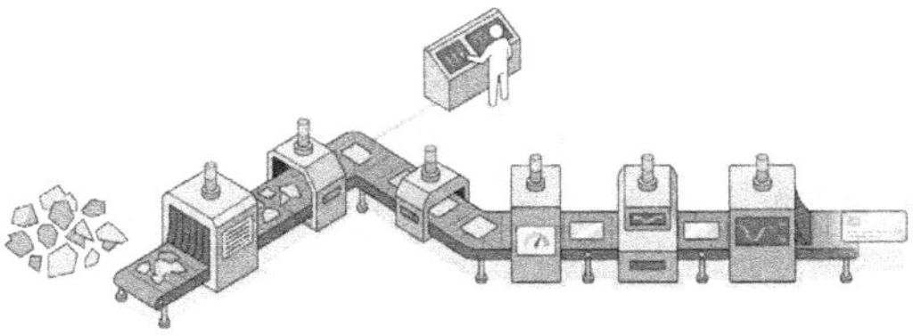

Figure 9.2: *The automation pipeline: six stages transform raw product data into AI-ready content at scale*

Stage 1, Unified data ingestion

Everything begins with aggregation. In most organizations, product truth is fragmented. Specifications live in the PIM. Marketing narratives live in the CMS. Reviews sit on third-party platforms. Search insights exist in analytics tools. Competitive intelligence is tracked in spreadsheets. None of these systems speak to one another natively.

Stage 1 creates a unified ingestion layer. All relevant sources feed into a structured staging environment: product specifications, pricing and availability, review data, search behavior, support tickets, competitive feature comparisons, SoM tracking, and usage analytics.

The system detects a change: a price adjustment, a new feature, a spike in reviews mentioning a specific use case. Minor changes are flagged differently from structural updates. This prevents unnecessary reprocessing while ensuring critical updates move quickly through the system.

The output of Stage 1 is not content. It is clean, validated, and synchronized data, ready for enrichment.

Stage 2, automated data enrichment

Raw data is insufficient for AI discovery. It must be structured, expanded, contextualized, and made machine-intelligent.

Enrichment operates across four dimensions:

- **Attribute standardization**: Unstructured descriptions are parsed into normalized specifications. Units are standardized. Terminology is aligned. Missing attributes are flagged or filled from trusted feeds. The result is completeness and consistency across the catalog.
- **Use case mapping**: Customer reviews, support logs, and search queries are analyzed to extract real-world contexts. Products are scored against use cases based on attributes and actual usage patterns. This produces defensible "Best For" positioning grounded in data, not marketing guesswork.
- **Competitive positioning modeling**: Products are systematically compared against competitors within their price tier and use-case cluster. Advantages, limitations, and "when to choose" guidance are generated based on structured feature analysis. This produces balanced differentiation frameworks that AI agents can interpret.
- **Emotional signal extraction**: Reviews are analyzed for emotional language, experiential descriptors, and social signaling. This produces structured emotional profiles that complement functional specifications. AI systems can now describe not only what a product does, but how it feels and who it resonates with.

At the end of Stage 2, the product is no longer a list of specs. It is a structured knowledge entity with functional, contextual, competitive, and emotional depth.

Stage 3, content generation and optimization

Once enriched, data becomes generative fuel. Manual content creation cannot scale across thousands of products and hundreds of contexts. Stage 3 converts structured intelligence into AI-optimized assets.

Three primary outputs emerge:

- **Answer-first content**: Content is generated to address high-intent query patterns directly, rather than with generic descriptions; pages open with decisive answers tailored to specific contexts. Variants are created for different query types: comparisons, use cases, stability concerns, pricing questions, and feature evaluations.
- **Structured data and schema**: Schema markup is generated automatically from enriched attributes. Offers, ratings, properties, FAQs, and availability are injected in standardized formats. Structured data updates automatically when source data changes, eliminating drift.
- **FAQ expansion**: Real customer questions extracted from support tickets, reviews, and search queries are converted into structured Q&A content. These FAQs address objections, clarify limitations, and provide direct responses optimized for AI extraction.

The system does not generate content blindly. Templates and positioning rules are human-approved. Competitive claims require validation. Edge cases trigger review. However, the heavy lifting is automated.

The result is scalable, context-aware, answer-structured content aligned with real search and AI behavior.

Stage 4, quality assurance and validation

Automation without validation creates risk. Stage 4 applies automated scoring across completeness, consistency, accuracy, brand voice alignment, and platform compliance. Products that fall below defined thresholds are flagged for review.

Checks include:

- Attribute completeness thresholds.
- Schema validation.
- Competitive claim defensibility.
- Tone alignment with brand standards.
- Logical coherence between functional and emotional positioning.

This stage prevents hallucinated advantages, unsupported claims, and inconsistent narratives from entering production. Quality becomes measurable, not subjective.

Stage 5, publishing and distribution

Once validated, content moves into controlled deployment. Publishing is multi-channel and synchronized:

- CMS updates.
- Schema injection.
- Sitemap regeneration.
- CDN invalidation.
- llms.txt updates.
- Feed distribution to relevant endpoints.

Critical updates, such as pricing and availability, trigger real-time pushes. Structural content improvements follow scheduled deployments.

This stage ensures that AI systems, search engines, and downstream aggregators receive fresh, structured, consistent information simultaneously.

Stage 6, monitoring and feedback loop

Optimization is incomplete without measurement.

The final stage monitors:

- Share of Model trends.
- AI visibility changes.
- Characterization accuracy.
- Competitive displacement.
- Query-level performance shifts.

When visibility drops, the system traces root causes: data gaps, authority deficits, competitive improvements, and hard signal errors.

Re-optimization queues are generated automatically. High-impact gaps return to the enrichment and content stages. The loop closes. Automation becomes cyclical, not linear.

Strategic impact of the pipeline

This six-stage architecture transforms content from static publishing into continuous intelligence refinement. Without automation, AEO becomes reactive and unsustainable.

With automation, every product update, review spike, pricing change, and competitive move becomes fuel for systematic optimization.

The pipeline ensures:

- Consistent data quality.
- Scalable contextual positioning.
- Rapid competitive response.
- Structured AI readability.
- Continuous visibility improvement.

Humans define strategy. The system operationalizes it. That is how AEO and GEO become durable competitive advantages rather than episodic initiatives.

Platform-specific optimization

AI platforms are not homogeneous; each has unique retrieval behaviors, ranking signals, and content preferences. Optimizing for one platform may not translate to others. Effective scaled optimization requires understanding and addressing platform-specific characteristics while maintaining operational efficiency.

Platform optimization comparison

The following table examines each platform in detail, covering retrieval behavior, content preferences, and the structural patterns most likely to earn citations:

Dimension	ChatGPT	Claude	Gemini	Perplexity
Market position	Broad consumer + business adoption.	Strong among technical/pro users.	Deep Google ecosystem integration.	Research-focused, citation-first.
Recency sensitivity	High (recent content weighted heavily).	Moderate (balanced with depth).	High (SEO freshness signals matter).	Very high (strong currency preference).
Citation behavior	Cites authoritative domains.	Nuanced, contextual citation.	Influenced by SEO + structured data.	Explicit, transparent multi-source citations.
Prefers	Structured, comprehensive content.	Balanced, nuanced analysis.	Technically optimized pages.	Data-rich, source-heavy content.
Penalizes	Thin, outdated content.	Overly promotional claims.	Poor technical SEO.	Unverifiable claims.

Dimension	ChatGPT	Claude	Gemini	Perplexity
	Freshness + structure + authority.	Balance + reasoning + transparency.	Technical SEO + schema + performance.	Data + attribution + recency.

***Figure 9.1**: Platform optimization comparison across key dimensions*

OpenAI ChatGPT

ChatGPT favors structured, comprehensive content from authoritative domains, with a strong preference for recently updated material. The following table outlines the key optimization parameters for this platform:

Category	Details
Primary retrieval sources	Bing web search, training knowledge base, and user context.
Recency weighting	Strong preference for content updated within 90 days.
Citation pattern	Authoritative domains, structured formatting.
Technical depth	Comfortable citing detailed specifications.
Ideal content length	800–1,500 words.
Preferred format	Lists and tables outperform pure prose.
Inferred ranking signals	Domain authority, freshness, completeness, structured data.
Strategic focus	Update frequently, include technical specs, and show authorship.
Structural pattern	Direct answer | summary | specs | analysis | comparison | FAQ.

***Table 9.2**: ChatGPT optimization parameters and strategic focus*

Anthropic Claude

Claude rewards balanced, analytical content that acknowledges trade-offs and explains reasoning transparently. The following table outlines the key optimization parameters for this platform:

Category	Details
Primary retrieval sources	Web search, knowledge base, document analysis.
Recency weighting	Balanced with depth and quality.
Citation pattern	Contextual, nuanced references.
Content preference	Trade-offs, limitations, reasoning.
Ideal tone	Balanced, transparent, analytical.
Inferred ranking signals	Quality depth, pros/cons clarity, contextual explanation.
Strategic focus	Include "Limitations" sections and explain why use cases fit.
Structural pattern	Overview | strengths | limitations | comparisons | decision framework.

***Table 9.3**: Claude optimization parameters and strategic focus*

Google Gemini

Gemini's retrieval is deeply integrated with Google's search infrastructure, making technical SEO and structured data particularly influential. The following table outlines the key optimization parameters for this platform:

<table>
<tr><th>Category</th><th>Details</th></tr>
<tr><td>Primary retrieval sources</td><td>Google Search + Knowledge Graph.</td></tr>
<tr><td>Recency weighting</td><td>High (SEO freshness signals matter).</td></tr>
<tr><td>Citation pattern</td><td>Influenced by structured data and traditional SEO.</td></tr>
<tr><td>Content preference</td><td>Schema-rich, technically optimized, mobile-friendly.</td></tr>
<tr><td>Technical emphasis</td><td>Core Web Vitals, mobile optimization, and page speed.</td></tr>
<tr><td>Inferred ranking signals</td><td>Backlinks, schema completeness, performance metrics.</td></tr>
<tr><td>Strategic focus</td><td>Perfect technical SEO + maximize structured data.</td></tr>
<tr><td>Structural pattern</td><td>Schema | direct answer | structured sections | FAQ schema | Offer schema.</td></tr>
</table>

Table 9.4: *Gemini optimization parameters and strategic focus*

Perplexity

Perplexity is the most citation-transparent of the major platforms, consistently surfacing its sources alongside answers and strongly favoring data-rich, frequently updated content. The following table outlines the key optimization parameters for this platform:

<table>
<tr><th>Category</th><th>Details</th></tr>
<tr><td>Primary retrieval sources</td><td>Multi-source web search.</td></tr>
<tr><td>Recency weighting</td><td>Very high.</td></tr>
<tr><td>Citation pattern</td><td>Always shows explicit sources.</td></tr>
<tr><td>Content preference</td><td>Data-heavy, statistics, research-backed.</td></tr>
<tr><td>Trust signals</td><td>Clear authorship, visible sources, timestamps.</td></tr>
<tr><td>Inferred ranking signals</td><td>Credible sources, statistical evidence, and update frequency.</td></tr>
<tr><td>Strategic focus</td><td>Include measurable data, cite studies, and refresh <14 days.</td></tr>
<tr><td>Structural pattern</td><td>Stats summary | benchmarks | comparisons | testing data | pricing verification.</td></tr>
</table>

Table 9.5: *Perplexity optimization parameters and strategic focus*

Cross-platform content strategy

Creating platform-specific variants for every product page is impractical at scale. The solution is a Universal content core with platform-specific enhancements applied programmatically. This approach is organized into a three-tier content system.

Tier 1, universal content

Create once, use everywhere.

The core elements are as follows:

- Product specifications and features.
- Pricing and availability (real-time).
- Primary use cases.
- Key differentiators.
- Fundamental value proposition.

The format requirements are as follows:

- Clean HTML structure.
- Comprehensive schema markup.
- Mobile-responsive design.
- Fast page load.
- Accessibility compliance.

This forms the foundation, approximately 70% of the content.

Tier 2, platform enhancements

Applied programmatically based on referrer/platform.

The enhancements are explained in the following table:

Platform	Enhancements
ChatGPT	• Boost "last updated" visibility. • Emphasize the recent developments section. • Highlight technical depth. • Surface third-party citations.

Platform	Enhancements
Claude	• Ensure the limitations section is present and prominent. • Add "trade-offs" framing to comparisons. • Include use case reasoning. • Provide decision frameworks.
Gemini	• Prioritize technical SEO perfection. • Maximize schema markup. • Optimize images aggressively. • Ensure Core Web Vitals are green.
Perplexity	• Elevate statistics and data. • Highlight source attribution. • Surface methodology. • Emphasize currency.

Table 9.6*: Tier 2 platform-specific content enhancements by AI system*

The implementation is as follows:

- Server-side enhancement based on referrer.
- CDN edge computing for performance.
- A/B testing platform-specific variants.
- Performance tracking by platform.

This represents approximately 20% of the content, enhancing the universal core.

Tier 3, platform-specific landing pages

Created manually for high-value scenarios. When to create platform-specific pages:

- Top-performing products (top 10% by revenue)
- Competitive battleground products
- New product launches
- Products with platform-specific advantages

The example is as follows:

- **Universal page**: `/products/ergodesk-pro`.
- **ChatGPT-optimized**: `/products/ergodesk-pro/technical-guide` (emphasizes specs and testing).

- **Claude-optimized**: `/products/ergodesk-pro/buying-guide` (emphasizes trade-offs and decision framework).

This represents approximately 10% of content / strategic investments.

Platform-specific measurement and optimization

Track Share of Model by Platform by weekly monitoring:

- SoM by platform (ChatGPT, Claude, Gemini, Perplexity).
- Primary recommendation rate by platform.
- Prominence score by platform.
- Platform-specific query performance.

Example dashboard:

```
Share of Model by Platform (Week of Jan 15, 2026)
Platform      | Overall SoM | Primary Rec % | Avg Prominence | Change (WoW)
--------------|-------------|---------------|----------------|-------------
ChatGPT       | 34%         | 18%           | 6.8            | +2%
Claude        | 28%         | 24%           | 7.2            | +1%
Gemini        | 31%         | 16%           | 6.5            | +4%
Perplexity    | 26%         | 21%           | 6.9            | +1%
--------------|-------------|---------------|----------------|-------------
Overall       | 30%         | 20%           | 6.9            | +2%
Key Insights:
- Gemini showing strong improvement (+4% WoW) - recent schema updates working
- Claude has highest primary rec rate despite lower SoM - strong positioning
- ChatGPT leads overall SoM - recency optimization effective
- Perplexity steady - data-focused content resonating
```

Platform-specific optimization cycle via monthly analysis:

1. Identify the platform with the lowest SoM.
2. Analyze why (content gaps, technical issues, positioning).
3. Implement platform-specific optimizations.
4. Measure impact over 4 weeks.
5. Scale successful tactics.

Creating an AI brand voice

AI agents do not just retrieve your content; they synthesize and rephrase it. This synthesis creates a "brand voice" that emerges from how AI systems characterize your products and company. Managing this voice requires strategic, consistent content creation.

Defining your AI brand voice

Defining the AI brand voice requires considering four voice dimensions.

Dimension 1, tone spectrum

Tone determines how formal or conversational your brand sounds when AI agents characterize it. The position you choose should reflect your industry norms, your audience's expectations, and the competitive space you are trying to occupy.

```
Formal ←——————————————————→ Casual
```

The details are as follows:

- **Formal position (70-100% formal):**
  - Enterprise-grade project management solution.
  - Comprehensive workflow automation platform.
  - Professional collaboration software.
- **Balanced position (40-60% formal):**
  - Powerful project management that teams actually enjoy.
  - Project management built for growing companies.
  - Professional tools without the complexity.
- **Casual position (0-30% formal):**
  - Project management that does not suck.
  - Finally, a project tool your team will use.
  - Project management without the headaches.
- **Decision criteria:**
  - Industry norms (B2B vs B2C).
  - Target audience sophistication.
  - Brand personality goals.
  - Competitive positioning.

Dimension 2, complexity spectrum

Complexity determines how technical or accessible your brand language feels to the reader. The right position depends on your audience's sophistication, the inherent complexity of your product, and how much differentiation technical depth can provide in your category.

```
Technical ←————————————————→ Accessible
```

The details are as follows:

- **Technical position (70-100% technical):**
  - Leverages machine learning algorithms for resource optimization.
  - RESTful API with OAuth 2.0 authentication.
  - Implements directed acyclic graph dependency management.
- **Balanced position (40-60% technical):**
  - AI-powered scheduling that optimizes team workload.
  - Secure API integration with major platforms.
  - Visual dependency tracking that prevents bottlenecks.
- **Accessible position (0-30% technical):**
  - Automatically suggests the best person for each task.
  - Connects with the tools you already use.
  - See which tasks need to be done first.
- **Decision criteria:**
  - Audience technical sophistication.
  - Product inherent complexity.
  - Competitive differentiation needs.
  - Support and onboarding implications.

Dimension 3, confidence spectrum

Confidence determines how assertive or measured your claims feel when AI agents relay them. The appropriate position depends on the strength of your evidence, your market standing, and the skepticism levels of your target audience.

```
Assertive ←————————————————→ Measured
```

The details are as follows:

- **Assertive position (70-100% assertive):**

- The best solution for enterprise project management.
- Industry-leading automation capabilities.
- Outperforms competitors in every category.

- **Balanced position (40-60% assertive):**
  - A strong choice for mid-market project management.
  - Advanced automation competitive with market leaders.
  - Better value than alternatives in its tier.
- **Measured position (0-30% assertive):**
  - A capable option for teams needing customization.
  - Solid automation features for the price point.
  - Worth considering alongside other options.
- **Decision criteria:**
  - Evidence strength (can you back claims?).
  - Market position (leader vs challenger).
  - Risk tolerance (legal/regulatory).
  - Audience skepticism levels.

Dimension 4, personality spectrum

Personality determines how serious or playful your brand comes across in AI-generated characterizations. The right position reflects your brand values, the conventions of your category, and the expectations your audience brings to the interaction.

```
Serious ←——————————————————→ Playful
```

The details are as follows:

- **Serious position (70-100% serious):**
  - Professional project management platform.
  - Enterprise workflow management system.
  - Mission-critical collaboration software.
- **Balanced position (40-60% serious):**
  - Project management that means business.
  - Professional tools, human-friendly design.
  - Serious about results, not complexity.

- **Playful position (0-30% serious):**
    - "Project management that sparks joy".
    - "No more project management pain".
    - "Work better, stress less".
- **Decision criteria:**
    - Brand personality and values.
    - Category conventions (can you differentiate?).
    - Audience expectations.
    - Risk and stakes of decisions.

Once the four dimensions are defined, the combination becomes a voice profile that can be documented, tested against existing content, and used to evaluate whether the language AI agents are currently using to characterize your brand reflects the positioning you intend. If AI systems consistently describe your product in terms that skew more formal, more technical, more cautious, or more serious than your target profile, the gap reveals where your source content needs adjustment. Voice management is ultimately a content consistency problem: the characterizations that AI agents synthesize are only as intentional as the inputs they draw from.

Automating the audit process

Continuous auditing ensures quality does not degrade as scale increases, enabling the organization to identify and fix issues before they affect AI visibility. A structured audit framework organized across three time horizons, daily, weekly, and monthly, distributes the monitoring workload appropriately and ensures that technical failures are caught within hours while strategic trends are assessed with the cadence they require.

Daily audits focus on technical and operational health, with the objective of catching issues within 24 hours of their occurrence.

Schema validation runs a nightly crawl of all product pages, extracts schema markup, validates it against Schema.org standards, and checks both required and recommended properties. The target is full schema presence across all pages, near-zero validation errors, and a high completeness rate. Missing schema on more than a small fraction of pages, or validation errors above a minimal threshold, should trigger immediate triage with resolution expected within hours rather than days. Recurring issues warrant root cause analysis rather than repeated fixes.

Broken link detection crawls content pages and checks both internal and external links, flagging redirects and errors, and generating a prioritized repair list. The standard for internal links is zero breakage on product pages. Even a small number of broken internal links on high-traffic pages should trigger immediate remediation, while redirect accumulation warrants attention before it compounds.

Image availability and optimization audits verify that all product images return valid responses, meet file size targets, carry descriptive alt text, implement lazy loading, and include image schema markup. Each of these elements contributes independently to both page performance and AI extractability.

Price and availability consistency audits compare live page data against the PIM, match displayed availability against actual inventory status, and verify that timestamps reflect recent updates. Any price inconsistency on an active product or any instance of a product marked in stock when it is unavailable should be treated as a critical failure requiring immediate correction. These are the hard signals that gate AI recommendations entirely.

Weekly audits shift focus from technical health to content quality and competitive positioning.

Content freshness assessment identifies pages that have not been updated within a defined window, prioritizes them by a combination of traffic volume, time since last update, and competitive intensity, and generates a ranked queue for editorial attention. High-traffic pages that have gone without updates for an extended period represent the highest-priority cases, since stale content on heavily visited pages carries the greatest risk of eroding AI visibility.

Completeness scoring evaluates each product page against a defined set of required and recommended attributes, checks schema property coverage, identifies missing use case documentation and competitive positioning content, and flags products that fall below the threshold. The output is a ranked enrichment queue that directs content investment toward the gaps most likely to affect recommendation outcomes.

AI visibility tracking executes the query taxonomy, records mention rates and positioning quality across platforms, calculates SoM by platform, and flags week-over-week changes that exceed a defined threshold. Significant SoM movements in either direction warrant investigation. Gains reveal which recent optimizations are working; losses signal emerging competitive threats or content degradation.

Competitive gap analysis tracks competitor SoM by query category, identifies the queries where competitors appear instead of your brand, analyzes the signals driving those wins, and generates prioritized optimization recommendations. The prioritization logic weights gap size against query value and competitive intensity, ensuring that effort concentrates where the return is greatest.

Monthly audits operate at the strategic level, assessing overall quality and health, and measuring the return on optimization investment.

Comprehensive quality scoring aggregates all quality dimensions into a single score for each product, assessed across data completeness, data accuracy, content quality, and AI visibility, each weighted to reflect its relative contribution to overall performance. Products scoring below a defined threshold are flagged as priority candidates for optimization. Trend analysis across monthly scores reveals whether overall quality is improving, stable, or degrading and provides the evidence base for setting improvement targets and allocating resources.

ROI assessment closes the loop between optimization activity and business outcome. It tracks time invested by initiative, correlates that investment against Share of Model improvement, attributes revenue to AI-driven channels, and calculates return per initiative. Over time, this analysis identifies which categories of work produce the highest returns and informs the prioritization of future optimization cycles.

Maintaining data integrity during high-frequency updates

As update frequency increases, the risk of data inconsistencies, errors, and quality degradation grows. Systematic data-integrity processes prevent automation from amplifying mistakes.

Data integrity framework

The four-pillar approach are as follows:

- **Single Source of Truth** (**SSOT**).
- Change detection and validation.
- Update frequency management.
- Quality gates and rollback.

Pillar 1, Single Source of Truth

Challenge: Product data is spread across multiple systems (PIM, CMS, e-commerce platform, marketing databases), leading to conflicting information.

Solution: Establish PIM as the master data repository with unidirectional data flow.

The SSOT architecture is provided as follows:

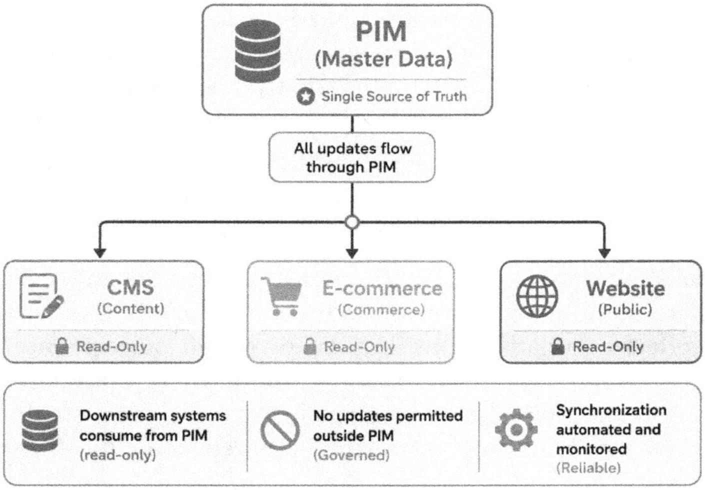

Figure 9.3: PIM as a single source of truth architecture

The implementation is as follows:

Step	Phase	Key actions
1	Designate PIM as master	• All product specification updates occur in PIM. • Downstream systems sync from PIM (one-way). • No exceptions; even urgent updates go through PIM.
2	Implement data flow controls	• API-based sync from PIM to downstream systems. • Prevent manual editing downstream. • Lock downstream fields to prevent drift. • Alert on unauthorized changes.
3	Migration and validation	• Identify existing inconsistencies. • Resolve conflicts using an authoritative source. • Migrate clean data into PIM. • Validate downstream sync accuracy.
4	Governance and training	• Document SSOT policy clearly. • Train content and product teams. • Implement approval workflows in PIM. • Conduct regular compliance audits.

Table 9.7: SSOT implementation steps for PIM-led data governance

The SSOT benefits are as follows:

- Eliminates conflicting data.
- Simplifies the update process.
- Enables automated sync.
- Provides an audit trail.
- Reduces error rates.

Pillar 2, change detection and validation

Challenge: Changes can introduce errors or break dependencies if not properly validated.

Solution: Automated change detection with validation before propagation.

Change detection workflow: When a product data update is received, the first step is to compare the incoming data against the current state, identify which fields have changed, and classify the magnitude of the change. Minor changes, such as small price adjustments, inventory level updates, minor copy edits, or image optimizations, can be approved automatically and propagated without human review. Moderate changes, including larger price adjustments, new product variants, specification updates, or feature additions and removals, are queued for review before propagation. Major changes, covering significant price movements, product discontinuations, category reassignments, or complete content rewrites, require explicit approval from a senior stakeholder and a business impact analysis before any downstream action is taken.

Before any change is accepted, it passes through a validation sequence covering three layers. Data format validation confirms that incoming values use correct data types, that required fields are present, that values fall within acceptable ranges, and that no corrupt or malformed data has entered the pipeline. Dependency validation checks that any referenced products, categories, or image URLs exist and resolve correctly, that links are valid, and that schema compatibility is maintained. Business rule validation confirms that the change respects margin floors, reasonable inventory levels, product lifecycle rules, and valid category assignments.

Once validation is complete, an impact assessment identifies every downstream system affected by the change. A price update, for example, may require automatic updates to the product page and schema markup, cache invalidation at the CDN layer, updates to comparison tables across a potentially large number of pages, and manual review of any marketing emails already queued that reference the old price. The assessment should estimate propagation time and explicitly flag any systems requiring human intervention rather than automated handling.

With the impact understood and approval obtained at the appropriate level, propagation begins by updating the PIM master record and triggering downstream system synchronization. Propagation status should be monitored actively rather than assumed, with confirmation that updates have been applied correctly before the process is considered complete. Cache invalidation should be triggered wherever stale content could otherwise persist.

Post-propagation verification closes the loop. Spot-checking updated content in its live state, confirming that no dependencies have broken, revalidating schema markup, and verifying that AI platforms are returning the updated information ensure that the change has fully taken effect across the systems that matter most for visibility and recommendation accuracy.

Pillar 3, update frequency management

Challenge: Different data types require different update frequencies. Real-time for some, daily for others.

Solution: Tiered update frequency aligned to data volatility and business needs.

Update frequency tiers: Different data types change at fundamentally different rates, and treating them all with the same update cadence creates either unnecessary processing overhead or dangerous staleness. The following tiers align update frequency to the volatility and business impact of each data type:

Update frequency	Update types	Implementation approach
Real-time (<5 minutes)	• **Price**: Critical for competitiveness and regulatory compliance. • **Availability**: Prevents overselling and customer frustration. • **Inventory levels**: Support purchase decisions. • **Promotional offers**: Time-sensitive.	• Event-driven sync (webhook on change). • API-based updates. • CDN invalidation. • Real-time monitoring.
Hourly	• **Stock levels (non-critical products)**: Less time-sensitive inventory. • **Shipping estimates**: Based on location and availability. • **Competitive price monitoring**: Market intelligence.	• Scheduled jobs every hour. • Batch processing. • Incremental updates only.
Daily	• **Product specifications**: Rarely change, but critical accuracy. • **Reviews and ratings**: Aggregate daily. • **Image updates**: New images, optimizations. • **Category assignments**: Taxonomy changes.	• Overnight batch processing (2-4 AM). • Full validation during off-peak. • Comprehensive change logs.
Weekly	• **Marketing copy**: Strategic content updates. • **Use case content**: New applications or scenarios. • **Competitive positioning**: Market changes. • **FAQ content**: New questions and answers.	• Scheduled for low-traffic days (weekends). • Full content review process. • A/B testing of changes. • Performance monitoring.
Monthly	• **Strategic positioning**: Major market shifts. • **Category expansion**: New product lines. • **Brand voice refinement**: Messaging evolution. • **Template updates**: Content structure changes.	• Coordinated with the marketing calendar. • Stakeholder review and approval. • Comprehensive testing. • Phased rollout.

Table 9.8: Update frequency tiers by data type and volatility

Update frequency decision matrix:

```
Data Type      | Volatility | Business Impact | Frequency
---------------|------------|-----------------|----------
Price          | High       | Critical        | Real-time
Availability   | High       | Critical        | Real-time
Inventory      | Medium     | High            | Hourly
Specifications | Low        | High            | Daily
Reviews        | Medium     | Medium          | Daily
Marketing Copy | Low        | Medium          | Weekly
Use Cases      | Low        | Medium          | Weekly
Strategy       | Very Low   | High            | Monthly
```

Pillar 4, quality gates and rollback

Challenge: Automated updates can rapidly propagate errors at scale.

Solution: Quality gates before publication and rollback capability.

Pre-publication quality gates: Automated updates can propagate errors faster than any manual process can catch them. Quality gates intercept problems before they reach publication, with each gate targeting a distinct category of risk:

Gate	Purpose	Validation checks	Failure action
Gate 1: Automated quality checks	Ensure technical and content integrity before publishing.	• Schema validation passes. • Required fields present. • Correct data format. • Links valid. • Images load successfully. • Voice compliance score >60.	Block publication and flag for review.
Gate 2: Consistency verification	Prevent cross-system or cross-channel inconsistencies.	• Price consistent across all touchpoints. • Availability matches inventory. • Competitive claims remain accurate. • Category assignment valid.	Block the publication and alert the team.

Gate	Purpose	Validation checks	Failure action
Gate 3: Business rules compliance	Ensure commercial and regulatory alignment.	• Price maintains minimum margin. • Promotional pricing includes an end date. • Discontinued products removed from active marketing. • Regulatory requirements met (warnings, certifications).	Block publication and escalate.

***Table 9.9**: Pre-publication quality gates and failure actions*

Passing the pre-publication gates confirms that content is ready to deploy, but verification does not stop at publication. Post-publication monitoring and rollback procedures ensure that problems introduced by a live deployment are caught and reversed before they cause lasting damage:

- **Post-publication verification**:
  - Immediate verification (0-5 minutes):
    - Content deployed successfully.
    - Pages render correctly.
    - Schema validates.
    - No 404 errors.
    - Images load.
  - Short-term verification (1-24 hours):
    - Traffic patterns are normal (no drop-off).
    - Conversion rates maintained.
    - No spike in support inquiries.
    - AI platforms are retrieving updated data.
- **Rollback procedures**:
  - Critical errors (Rollback immediately, automatically):
    - 5% pages return errors after deployment.
    - Conversion rate drops >25% within 1 hour.
    - Schema validation failures >10%.
    - Site-wide performance degradation.
  - Warning conditions (Alert for manual decision):
    - Conversion rate drops 10-25% within 4 hours.

- Traffic drops >15% (not explained by seasonality).
- Support inquiries spike >30%.
- AI visibility drops >20% within 48 hours.

Conclusion

Scaling AI optimization requires moving from manual processes to automated systems that maintain quality while dramatically reducing effort. Organizations that master automation can optimize thousands of products across multiple platforms while competitors struggle to maintain dozens.

The scaling imperative is clear: manual optimization cannot keep pace with the rate of change in the AI landscape, the expansion of product catalogs, or the proliferation of AI platforms. Automation is not optional; it is essential for competitive survival.

The organizations that win in AI-driven discovery will not be the loudest; they will be the most operationally disciplined. Their advantage will come from building efficient, automated, and endlessly scalable optimization systems.

They will update thousands of products with the same precision and consistency as updating a single page. They will optimize for multiple AI platforms without multiplying effort, using architectural approaches rather than manual duplication. Their brand voice will remain coherent and intentional across all AI-generated summaries, recommendations, and comparisons. Quality issues will be identified and resolved before they ever impact visibility. When platforms shift or new AI systems emerge, they will not scramble; they will adapt quickly because their foundations were built for change.

In an AI-mediated market, operational excellence becomes a competitive advantage. The investment required is substantial. Pipeline development, platform-specific strategies, brand voice systems, audit automation, and data integrity processes require significant upfront effort. However, the alternative, attempting to scale manual optimization, is extremely difficult.

The next chapter will explore preparing for the future of AI-driven discovery, including multimodal AI, voice interfaces, and the next generation of AI agents that will further transform how consumers discover and evaluate products. It also looks beyond optimization tactics to the structural shifts ahead, including the transition to Agent-to-Agent commerce, where AI systems transact directly with one another on behalf of human buyers.

CHAPTER 10
Future-proofing Brands for the Next AI Shift

Introduction

Throughout this book, we have explored the transformation of search and discovery driven by AI agents, from understanding how AI systems retrieve and synthesize information, to implementing AEO and GEO, to managing product experience and competitive positioning, to scaling these capabilities across platforms. We have provided frameworks, strategies, and tactics for succeeding in the current AI-driven discovery landscape.

However, the landscape is not static. The AI agents of today, ChatGPT, Claude, Gemini, and Perplexity, represent just the beginning of a much larger transformation. The shift from traditional search to AI-mediated discovery is itself only one phase in a longer evolution toward ambient, autonomous, and agent-driven commerce.

The organizations that will thrive in the coming decade are not those that perfectly optimize for today's AI systems; they are those that build adaptable capabilities and strategic frameworks that can evolve with whatever comes next, preparing for an uncertain future. This chapter provides the foundation for that adaptability.

Structure

The chapter covers the following topics:

- Transition to Agent-to-Agent commerce
- Multimodal search is the next wave
- Ethical AI and data privacy
- Building a resilient discovery stack
- Guide to continuous AI search auditing

Objectives

This final chapter looks forward. It examines the transition to **Agent-to-Agent** (**A2A**) commerce, where AI agents transact on behalf of users, and the next wave of multimodal search that integrates video, image, and voice. It also addresses the critical challenges of ethical AI and data privacy that will shape regulatory and consumer expectations, strategies for building a resilient discovery stack that does not depend on any single platform, and a practical ongoing audit checklist for continuous optimization.

Transition to Agent-to-Agent commerce

The current state of AI-driven discovery involves humans asking AI agents for recommendations. The next evolution removes humans from the transaction loop entirely: AI agents will autonomously research, evaluate, and purchase on behalf of their users.

Understanding the three-stage evolution

Let us look at the various stages of the evolution.

Stage 1

Current state: Human | AI Agent | Human decision.

Today's model:

```
User: "I need project management software for my team"
AI Agent: "Based on your needs, I recommend these three options:
1. ProjectFlow - Best for mid-market teams needing customization
2. Asana - Best for ease of use and templates
3. Monday.com - Best for visual project tracking
Each has different strengths depending on your priorities..."
User:
- Evaluates the three recommendations
- Visits each website
- Reads reviews
- Compares features and pricing
- Makes decision
- Completes purchase
```

The characteristics are as follows:

- AI provides information and recommendations.
- Human does research, comparison, and decision-making.

- The transaction happens outside AI interaction.
- Human retains full control.

Stage 2

Near future: Human | AI Agent | Autonomous decision.

Emerging model:

```
User: "Set up project management software for my team that integrates
with our existing tools (Salesforce, Slack, Google Workspace), stays
within our $5,000 annual budget, and can be implemented this month"
AI Agent (Autonomous Actions):
1. Researches all available options
2. Filters to those matching requirements:
   - Salesforce integration ✓
   - Slack integration ✓
   - Google Workspace integration ✓
   - Annual cost ≤ $5,000 ✓
   - Implementation timeline ≤ 30 days ✓
3. Narrows to 4 compatible solutions
4. Compares pricing and feature sets
5. Evaluates implementation timelines (checks vendor APIs)
6. Verifies integration capabilities (tests authentication)
7. Checks current promotional pricing
8. Reads recent reviews for each option
9. Schedules demos automatically (if authorized)
10. Presents recommendation with detailed reasoning
11. If fully authorized: Completes purchase and initiates implementation
12. Configures initial setup based on team structure
User receives:
- Final recommendation with complete analysis
- Demo scheduled (calendar invite sent)
- If authorized: Purchase completed, onboarding email received
```

The characteristics are as follows:

- AI conducts substantial research autonomously.
- AI negotiates pricing and schedules interactions.
- Humans provide high-level requirements and authorization.
- Significant time savings for the user.

Stage 3

Further future: **Agent-to-Agent** (**A2A**) commerce.

Future model:

```
User's Personal AI Agent:
"My user needs project management software with the following
verified requirements [sends structured data about team size,
budget, existing tools, timeline, feature priorities, compliance
requirements]"
Vendor AI Agents (Multiple vendors, simultaneous):
ProjectFlow AI Agent:
- Analyzes requirements against capabilities
- Generates detailed proposal with pricing
- Provides API access for capability verification
- Offers implementation timeline guarantee
- Includes customer success metrics
- Proposes contract terms
Asana AI Agent:
- [Similar process with their strengths/pricing]
Monday.com AI Agent:
- [Similar process with their strengths/pricing]
User's AI Agent (Evaluation Process):
1. Receives all vendor proposals simultaneously
2. Conducts technical verification via APIs
   - Tests claimed integrations
   - Verifies capacity limits
   - Confirms feature availability
   - Validates performance benchmarks
3. Negotiates with each vendor:
   - Requests volume discounts
```

```
   - Asks for extended trial period
   - Negotiates implementation support
   - Seeks contract flexibility
4. Evaluates proposals systematically:
   - Feature match: 95% vs 88% vs 92%
   - Total cost: $4,200 vs $5,800 vs $4,900
   - Implementation time: 5 days vs 14 days vs 7 days
   - Risk assessment: Low vs Medium vs Low
5. Presents top recommendation to user with complete analysis
6. With approval or full autonomy: Executes purchase
7. Manages entire onboarding process
8. Monitors performance against vendor promises
9. Escalates issues automatically
10. Handles renewals and optimization
User involvement:
- Sets high-level requirements once
- Reviews and approves recommendation (or grants full autonomy)
- Uses the software (AI handles everything else)
```

The characteristics are as follows:

- Fully autonomous negotiation between AI agents.
- Human involvement is minimal (requirements + approval).
- Verification-based evaluation (not persuasion-based).
- Ongoing management and optimization by AI.
- Dramatically reduced friction in B2B purchasing.

Implications for brand strategy

The transition to A2A commerce fundamentally changes how brands compete.

Shift 1, from visibility to verifiability

In A2A commerce, brands compete not on persuasive marketing but on verifiable facts.

Traditional marketing claims (unverifiable) are as follows:

- The leading project management platform trusted by thousands.
- Industry-leading features and capabilities.
- Best-in-class customer support.

- Seamless integrations with popular tools.
- Quick and easy implementation.

A2A-optimized positioning:

```
{
  "claim": "Supports teams of 5-500 users",
  "verification_method": "API endpoint returns current capacity limits",
  "verification_url": "https://api.example.com/capabilities",

  "claim": "Integrates with Salesforce, Slack, Google Workspace",
  "verification_method": "Integration directory with authentication test",
  "verification_url": "https://api.example.com/integrations/verify",

  "claim": "Average implementation time: 2-4 weeks",
  "verification_method": "Historical data from 500+ implementations",
  "verification_url": "https://api.example.com/metrics/implementation",

  "claim": "99.95% uptime SLA",
  "verification_method": "Real-time status page and historical data",
  "verification_url": "https://status.example.com/api"
}
```

Shift 2, from content to APIs

AI agents will prefer structured, programmatic access over scraping web pages:

- **Current optimization:**
  - Rich website content
  - Schema markup
  - SEO-optimized pages
- **A2A optimization:**
  - Product information API.
  - Real-time pricing and availability API.
  - Capability verification endpoints.
  - Integration testing APIs.
  - Performance metrics API.
  - Customer success data API.

Shift 3, from persuasion to negotiation

AI agents will negotiate on behalf of users, requiring brands to support programmatic negotiation.

The traditional human sales process is as follows:

1. Marketing generates interest.
2. Sales engages the prospect.
3. Discovery call (understand needs).
4. Proposal presentation.
5. Negotiation (multiple rounds).
6. Contract execution.
7. Onboarding.

A2A negotiation capabilities needed are as follows:

- Dynamic pricing API:
  - Volume-based pricing.
  - Term-length discounts.
  - Bundle opportunities.
  - Seasonal promotions.
  - Competitive matching policies.
- Flexible terms API:
  - Contract length options.
  - Payment terms flexibility.
  - Cancellation policies.
  - Trial extensions.
  - Service level agreements.
- Customization API:
  - Feature à la carte options.
  - Custom integration development.
  - White-label opportunities.
  - Priority support options.
- Rapid response:
  - Real-time quote generation.

- Instant contract generation.
- Automated approval workflows.

Preparing for A2A commerce

Organizations should begin preparing now, even though widespread A2A adoption is 3-5 years away.

Step 1

Develop machine-readable product information. Action items are:

1. **Create a comprehensive product API:**
   - All specifications programmatically accessible.
   - Real-time pricing and availability.
   - Integration capability verification.
   - Performance metrics exposure.
2. **Implement verification endpoints:**
   - Allow AI agents to test claims.
   - Provide proof of capabilities.
   - Enable integration testing.
   - Offer sandbox environments.
3. **Expose customer success metrics:**
   - Implementation timelines (verified).
   - Customer satisfaction scores.
   - Support response times.
   - Uptime statistics.
4. **Provide comparison-ready data:**
   - Standardized feature descriptions.
   - Industry-standard benchmarks.
   - Competitive positioning (honest).
   - Total cost of ownership calculators.

Step 2

Build negotiation infrastructure. Prepare for AI-to-AI negotiation:

1. **Dynamic pricing engine:**
    - Rule-based discount structures.
    - Volume pricing tiers.
    - Term-length incentives.
    - Competitive response pricing.
2. **Automated contract generation:**
    - Template-based contracts.
    - Configurable terms.
    - Digital signature integration.
    - Rapid approval workflows.
3. **Decision-making APIs:**
    - Can approve deals within parameters.
    - Escalate outside parameters.
    - Track negotiation history.
    - Learn from successful deals.

Step 3

Establish trust signals for autonomous agents. Trust mechanisms for A2A:

1. **Verifiable credentials:**
    - Industry certifications (verifiable).
    - Security audits (accessible).
    - Financial stability (transparent).
    - Legal compliance (documented).
2. **Third-party validation:**
    - Independent test results.
    - Analyst ratings (machine-readable).
    - Customer reviews (verified).
    - Industry awards (verifiable).

3. **Performance guarantees:**
    - SLAs with monitoring.
    - Money-back guarantees.
    - Performance bonds.
    - Insurance backing.
4. **Reputation systems:**
    - Transaction history.
    - Dispute resolution record.
    - Customer retention rates.
    - NPS scores (verified).

Multimodal search is the next wave

The next evolution of AI search integrates video, image, and voice in ways that fundamentally change optimization requirements. Text-only optimization is becoming table stakes; multimodal optimization is the frontier.

Multimodal search means AI systems can accept and process multiple input types (text, image, voice, video) and provide responses in multiple formats. This creates discovery pathways and optimization requirements.

Visual search optimization

Scenario: User photographs a desk setup and asks, "Find me a desk like this one but in a smaller size for my apartment."

The AI process is as follows:

1. Analyzes the image to identify the desk type, size, and style.
2. Extracts visual features (color, material, design aesthetic).
3. Understands context (home office setup, modern aesthetic).
4. Applies constraints from the query (smaller size, apartment-suitable).
5. Searches for visually similar products matching the criteria.
6. Returns recommendations with visual comparisons.

Visual search optimization requirements

Let us look at the requirements for the visual search optimization.

High-quality images are foundational

Visual search begins with image quality. If your images are low-resolution, inconsistent, or incomplete, AI systems struggle to identify and recommend your product accurately. As a baseline, images should be at least 2000 pixels on the longest edge and professionally lit with consistent color temperature and minimal shadows. Backgrounds should be clean and uncluttered, so the product, not distractions, dominates the frame.

Coverage matters as much as resolution. A single hero image is not enough. Each product should include multiple angles: straight-on front views, left- and right-side profiles, a top or overhead perspective, and close-up detail shots of key features. Include at least one lifestyle image that shows the product in realistic use. For a product like the ErgoDesk Pro, this means capturing it at standing and seated heights, from the side to show depth and cable management, from above to highlight the surface and controls, and in detailed close-ups of mechanisms and stability components. A lifestyle image of someone using the desk in a home office setting adds context, while size references and color variants ensure clarity.

Comprehensive coverage reduces ambiguity. It allows AI systems to "see" the product from every meaningful perspective.

Metadata is visibility

Images are not just visual assets; they are data assets. File names should be descriptive and specific, replacing generic labels like "IMG_0234.jpg" with names that clearly describe the product, position, and context. Alt text should be equally precise, describing dimensions, configuration, environment, and distinguishing attributes in natural language.

Embedded metadata strengthens discoverability. EXIF and IPTC fields can include product names, specifications, searchable keywords, color profiles, and physical dimensions. Accurate color representation ensures consistency across platforms, while dimension data reinforces scale. The more structured context you provide, the easier it is for AI systems to interpret and match your product correctly.

Optimize for visual similarity

AI vision systems rely on visual similarity signals. If your product has distinctive features, they must be visible. For a standing desk, that means clearly showing the height adjustment mechanism, the control panel, cable management solutions, surface texture, and structural stability. If these features are hidden or obscured, AI may fail to differentiate your product from generic alternatives.

Context strengthens similarity recognition. Show the product alongside familiar objects to communicate scale. Include subtle measurement overlays if appropriate. Demonstrate the product in use with standard equipment such as monitors or laptops. Maintain aesthetic consistency across your product line to make your brand visually recognizable across platforms.

Consistency builds machine recognition over time.

Design for AI vision accessibility

AI systems need clarity. Products should be fully visible, unobstructed, and free from text overlays that obscure key details. Avoid aggressive cropping that removes important structural elements. Keep backgrounds minimal to reduce visual noise.

Contextual cues help AI systems interpret purpose. Show the product in realistic environments. Include humans or common objects to establish scale. Demonstrate actual use scenarios rather than staged ambiguity. If multiple colors or finishes are available, photograph each variant consistently and label it clearly in metadata.

Lifestyle imagery should feel authentic. Real people in real environments outperform generic stock imagery because they provide richer environmental signals and usage cues.

Voice search optimization

Scenario: User asks smart speaker, "What is a good standing desk for a small apartment under $500?"

The AI process is as follows:

1. Processes spoken query.
2. Understands constraints (small apartment, price <$500).
3. Retrieves matching products.
4. Synthesizes a concise spoken response.
5. Delivers an answer optimized for voice (speakable, brief).

Voice search optimization requirements

Let us look at the requirements for voice search optimization.

Conversational structure wins

Voice search changes how content must be written. Keyword fragments and spec sheets do not translate well to spoken responses. Instead of writing *ErgoDesk Pro – 48" Electric Standing Desk. 48"W x 30"D, dual motor, 150lb capacity, $479,* write the way someone speaks: *The ErgoDesk Pro is a 48-inch wide electric standing desk that costs $479 and works well in small apartments. It fits comfortably in tight spaces and supports up to 150 pounds.*

Natural language matters. Write in complete sentences. Avoid keyword stacking. Include context in every sentence. Front-load important information so the first line answers the question clearly.

Design FAQs for speech, not screens

Voice queries are full questions, so your answers should be too. *Price*? becomes *How much does the ErgoDesk Pro cost?* Hence, the response should be complete: *The ErgoDesk Pro costs $479* *and is currently in stock with free shipping. The price includes the desk frame, desktop surface, control panel, and cable management tray.*

Voice answers should typically run 20 to 40 words, something that can be spoken in under 12 seconds. Deliver a complete thought in the first sentence. Add supporting detail in a second sentence if needed. Avoid long, multi-paragraph responses.

A strong voice answer is direct and quantified. *Most people assemble the desk in 20 to 25 minutes. It operates at about 50 decibels, quieter than normal conversation. It fits two 24-inch monitors side by side*. Clear, specific language performs better than vague claims.

Optimize for featured snippets

Many voice assistants read directly from featured snippets. Structure answers accordingly. Use the question as a heading, *Is the ErgoDesk Pro stable at full height?*, and follow with a concise, evidence-backed paragraph of 40 to 60 words.

Lead with a direct answer. Then provide measurable proof. For example: *Yes, the ErgoDesk Pro is stable at full height. Independent testing measured less than 2mm of lateral movement at 48 inches with a 100-pound load, which is within industry standards. Customer reviews show that 89% of users report no wobble.*

Additional context can follow for human readers, but the first paragraph must stand alone.

Prepare for local intent

Voice search often carries local intent: *Find standing desk stores near me*, or *Where can I buy an ErgoDesk Pro in Seattle?* That requires accurate business listings, consistent name, address, phone information, region-specific references in content, and location pages if you operate in multiple markets. Local optimization ensures you surface when proximity matters.

Make commerce voice-ready

Voice commerce demands clarity. State prices explicitly: *The total cost is four hundred seventy-nine dollars*. Specify whether it is a one-time payment or a monthly payment. Make availability unambiguous: *In stock now. Ships in three to five business days. Available for immediate delivery.*

The purchase process should be simple, minimal-step, and compatible with voice commands. Confirmation should be clear and easy to read aloud.

Video search optimization

Scenario: User watches a YouTube review of standing desks and asks, *Show me desks similar to the one at minute 3:42 in this video.*

The AI process is as follows:

1. Analyzes video at specified timestamp.
2. Identifies product features, use case, and context.

3. Extracts visual and spoken information.
4. Searches for similar products.
5. Returns matches with video comparisons.

Video search optimization requirements

Let us look at the requirements for video search optimization.

Build a structured, comprehensive video content strategy

Video search optimization begins with structure. AI systems do not simply *watch* videos; they parse them. Clear sequencing, logical segmentation, and explicit topic coverage increase the likelihood that your content will be surfaced, quoted, or referenced.

Product overview videos should typically run between two and three minutes and follow a deliberate arc. Open with a strong hook and a concise product introduction. Move quickly into three to five key feature highlights, then demonstrate the product in real-world use. Provide context for comparing alternatives, clarify ideal use cases and target customers, address pricing and availability, and close with a clear call to action.

Audio clarity is critical. Narration must be crisp and intelligible for voice-search compatibility. Reinforce spoken points with on-screen text and ensure timestamps are included for major sections. Visual demonstrations should clearly show features in action rather than relying on abstract claims. Real-world use examples strengthen both viewer engagement and AI interpretability.

Installation and setup videos require even more structure. These longer videos, typically five to ten minutes, should begin with a clear unboxing segment, followed by tools and requirements, then a step-by-step assembly walkthrough. Troubleshooting common issues and demonstrating first use are essential. Maintenance tips add long-term value and reduce customer friction. Both spoken and on-screen instructions should be synchronized, and sections should be timestamped to enable quick navigation.

Use case videos expand discoverability by targeting specific audience segments. Rather than producing a single generic review, create multiple focused videos aligned with the primary customer scenarios. For example, a video positioning the ErgoDesk Pro for small apartments should emphasize compact dimensions and show the desk in a realistic apartment setting, ideally with a testimonial from an actual user. A productivity-focused home office video should highlight workflow benefits and day-in-the-life usage. An assembly-focused video should capture the unboxing experience and first impressions. Each use case video becomes its own searchable asset.

Optimize every metadata layer

Video SEO is not cosmetic; it is structural. Titles must be explicit and intent-driven. Generic labels like "Desk Review" lack search context. A title that includes product name, primary benefit, price positioning, and year signals relevance and recency to both users and algorithms.

Descriptions should function as structured summaries. Include a concise product overview, a clear explanation of who the product is for, and detailed timestamps that map to the video's sections. Specifications should be written in text form, not just spoken in the video, so they can be indexed. Pricing, shipping details, and warranty information provide additional contextual signals. Links should be clearly labeled, and disclosures should be transparent.

A complete, manually edited transcript significantly strengthens discoverability. Auto-generated captions are often inaccurate, especially when it comes to product names and technical specifications. A clean transcript with accurate timestamps, correct terminology, and properly spelled brand names increases the likelihood that AI systems can extract precise information.

Use chapter markers to enable AI referencing

Chapter markers are not just user-friendly; they are machine-friendly.

Time-coded sections allow viewers to jump directly to relevant segments, improving watch time and satisfaction. More importantly, they allow AI systems to reference specific portions of your content. If your video includes clearly labeled chapters such as introduction, unboxing, assembly, features overview, in-use demonstration, comparison testing, pros and cons, recommendations, and pricing, each section can be indexed independently.

This segmentation enables timestamp-based recommendations, improves engagement metrics, and increases the likelihood that your video will surface for highly specific queries.

Cross-modal consistency

Consistency across all messaging channels is critical to building a coherent and trustworthy brand presence. Every key point you make about your product should be reinforced across text, images, video, and voice interactions. For example, the ErgoDesk Pro is consistently positioned as ideal for small apartments. On the website, the copy emphasizes that at 48 inches wide, it is 20% more compact than standard desks. Images reinforce this by showing the desk in a small apartment and including visual size comparisons. Videos demonstrate the desk in tight spaces and measure it against a standard 60-inch desk. Voice-based FAQs mirror this language, explaining, *The ErgoDesk Pro works great in small apartments because it is 48 inches wide, which is significantly smaller than the typical 60-inch desk.*

Across all these modalities, the same features, use cases, pricing, availability, limitations, and competitive positioning must be highlighted. By repeating the same messages consistently, you ensure that every touchpoint, whether human or AI-driven, communicates the same story, strengthening brand clarity and enhancing discoverability.

Ethical AI and data privacy

As AI becomes more powerful and autonomous, ethical considerations and data privacy become critical not just for regulatory compliance but also for building lasting consumer trust and brand reputation.

Privacy paradox

The challenge is as follows:

- AI agents need data to provide personalized, relevant recommendations.
- Users are increasingly concerned about data collection, use, and sharing.
- Regulations (GDPR, CCPA, AI Act) impose strict requirements.
- Brands must balance: Useful AI experiences vs. Privacy protection.

The opportunity is:

- Privacy-first practices build trust.
- Transparency differentiates ethical brands.
- Compliance creates a competitive moat.
- User control increases loyalty.

Privacy-preserving AI optimization

Effective AI optimization does not have to come at the expense of privacy. These five principles guide organizations to use data responsibly while enabling intelligent, trustworthy AI-driven insights:

- **Data minimization**: Organizations should collect only the information necessary for AI optimization, such as product specifications, pricing and availability, aggregated usage statistics, general customer satisfaction data, and publicly available competitive information. Individual user browsing behavior, personally identifying information, detailed purchase histories, irrelevant demographic data, or precise location information should be avoided. By focusing on aggregated and anonymized data, AI platforms can make informed recommendations without compromising individual privacy.

- **Transparency**: Brands must be explicit about what data they collect and how they use it. This involves providing clear, human-readable disclosures about product performance metrics, customer satisfaction scores, and technical product specifications. It also requires clarifying what data is never collected, such as personal messages, individual browsing activity, or sensitive financial information. Users should understand that AI agents access only structured, aggregated product data and are never provided with personal user details.

- **User control and consent**: Users must be able to control their data and how it is shared. This includes offering granular consent options, such as allowing AI platforms to access reviews, contribute anonymized satisfaction ratings, or share product configurations as case studies. Opt-out mechanisms should be simple, with one-click removal, confirmation of deletion, and retroactive consent withdrawal. Clear communication about the impact of these choices ensures users retain control over their personal information.
- **Security**: All data must be protected with robust security measures, including encryption in transit and at rest, secure API communications, and strict access controls with multi-factor authentication. Organizations should maintain detailed audit logs, perform regular access reviews, and conduct security audits, penetration testing, and continuous vulnerability scanning. In the event of a breach, detection and user notification must occur promptly, accompanied by transparent remediation procedures.
- **Privacy-preserving analytics**: Insights should be derived without exposing individual users. Techniques such as differential privacy, federated learning, and edge processing ensure that personal data remains anonymized and is often never sent beyond the user's device. Aggregated data is reported only when groups are sufficiently large, outliers are suppressed, and statistical ranges are used to prevent identification. These methods enable AI optimization while safeguarding privacy.

Ethical AI principles

Beyond privacy, brands must consider the broader ethical implications of AI optimization across five interconnected principles.

Accuracy and truthfulness are the foundational requirements. AI agents synthesize and relay product information to users who rely on it to make decisions, which means misrepresentation at the source propagates directly into user harm. Accurate, current specifications should be maintained as a baseline, with errors corrected immediately and limitations acknowledged honestly. Exaggerating capabilities, omitting known constraints, providing outdated information, or mischaracterizing competitors are not just ethical failures; they undermine the trust that AI agents place in a source over time.

Fairness and non-discrimination require that the content and signals shaping AI recommendations do not produce discriminatory outcomes. Regular audits using diverse review panels help identify whether recommendation patterns exclude particular groups or whether product content contains language that inadvertently disadvantages certain users. Inclusive representation across imagery, accessibility features, language availability, and accommodation of different abilities reflects both ethical practice and broader market reach. Competitive positioning should be honest and verifiable, acknowledging competitor strengths rather than relying on misleading comparisons that would not survive scrutiny.

Transparency applies across product operations, pricing, and contractual terms. Users interacting with AI-recommended products deserve to understand how key features work, where AI or machine learning is involved, how their data is used, and where product limitations lie. Pricing transparency means stating all costs clearly, eliminating hidden fees, disclosing renewal pricing upfront, and providing advance notice of changes. Contracts and terms should be written in plain language with clear cancellation processes, explicit data ownership provisions, and straightforward explanations of usage restrictions.

User autonomy means supporting informed decision-making rather than engineering around it. Content should present genuine alternatives, surface trade-offs honestly, and avoid artificially limiting the choices available to users. Dark patterns, including manufactured urgency, false scarcity signals, deliberately obscured cancellation paths, and difficult opt-out mechanisms, are incompatible with ethical AI optimization and, increasingly, with regulatory requirements. Complete information, accessible comparison data, and visible reviews that include negative feedback alongside positive are the practical expressions of this principle.

Accountability requires that responsibility for accuracy and impact be explicitly assigned rather than diffuse. Claims should be verified before publication and audited regularly thereafter. Errors should be corrected quickly and transparently. A clear escalation path for concerns, timely responses, and fair resolution processes demonstrates that accountability is operational rather than aspirational. Documenting ethics guidelines, decision frameworks, and escalation procedures, and designating specific ownership at a senior level, ensures that ethical commitments survive organizational change and can be reported on publicly.

Regulatory compliance

AI optimization must be designed with evolving regulatory requirements in mind, and the regulatory landscape is expanding in scope and enforcement intensity across multiple jurisdictions.

Understanding the regulatory landscape begins with recognizing that obligations vary significantly by region. In Europe, GDPR imposes strict consent requirements, data minimization obligations, and significant penalties for non-compliance, while the AI Act introduces a risk-based framework with transparency obligations and prohibitions on manipulative AI practices for certain system categories. In the United States, the **California Consumer Privacy Act** (**CCPA**) establishes consumer rights around data access, deletion, and opt-out of data sale, with similar frameworks in Virginia, Colorado, and other states introducing their own assessment requirements and enforcement mechanisms. Brazil, China, India, and many other jurisdictions have enacted or are developing their own data protection regimes, each with varying requirements that organizations operating internationally must track and address.

Implementing compliance programs requires moving from regulatory awareness to operational processes. Privacy impact assessments should evaluate data processing activities, identify privacy risks, document mitigation measures, and be updated as practices evolve.

A comprehensive data inventory should map all data collected, document the purposes for which it is processed, trace data flows across systems, and classify sensitivity levels. User rights response mechanisms must be capable of processing access requests, managing deletion requests, providing opt-out mechanisms, and meeting response deadlines imposed by applicable regulations.

Designing for compliance means treating privacy as an architectural requirement rather than a retrospective control. Privacy by design embeds protective defaults into systems and processes from the outset, reducing the risk that compliance gaps emerge as products scale. Data minimization disciplines, including collecting only what is necessary, enforcing retention limits, and implementing automatic deletion, reduce both regulatory exposure and the surface area of potential harm.

Ongoing monitoring ensures that compliance does not drift as regulations evolve and organizational practices change. Annual compliance assessments, data protection impact assessments for significant processing activities, and regular policy effectiveness reviews maintain currency. Regulatory monitoring should be continuous, with policy updates communicated clearly to users and operational practices adapted accordingly. Compliance is not a one-time achievement; it is a sustained organizational capability.

Building a resilient discovery stack

The greatest risk in AI optimization is dependence on any single platform. AI platforms rise and fall, algorithms change, and new competitors emerge. Organizations that build their discovery strategy on a single platform create existential vulnerability.

A resilient discovery stack diversifies across platforms, channels, and content types while maintaining operational efficiency.

The following figure frames the journey: the landmarks built across this playbook, structured data, content authority, technical infrastructure, and measurement form the path forward. What lies on the horizon is not yet fully defined, but it is navigable precisely because the foundations beneath it are solid.

***Figure 10.1**: The foundations built across this playbook form the path toward whatever the next AI shift brings*

Discovery stack architecture

The following architecture illustrates how a resilient discovery stack distributes presence across seven layers, from AI platforms at the top to industry-specific directories at the base. No single layer should dominate, and strength at each level reinforces visibility across the others:

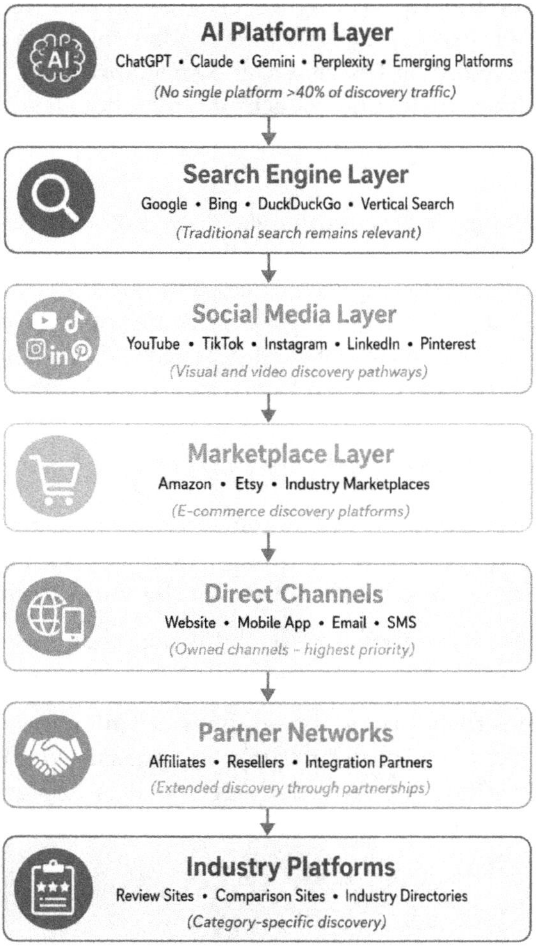

Figure 10.2: *Discovery stack architecture*

Platform diversification strategy

Knowing that diversification is necessary is not the same as knowing how to achieve it. The following five-step framework moves from diagnosis to execution, providing a structured path from current-state dependency to a balanced, resilient discovery portfolio.

Step 1, assess current state

Diversification planning begins with an honest assessment of where discovery traffic currently originates and what concentration risks that distribution creates. A portfolio in which a single AI platform accounts for nearly half of all discovery traffic has exceeded a safe dependency threshold, regardless of how well that platform is currently performing. When that same portfolio shows a major traditional search engine declining year over year while an emerging AI platform is growing rapidly from a small base, the structural shift underway becomes clear. Direct and owned channel traffic sitting well below a healthy target compounds the risk further, since any algorithmic change, policy shift, or competitive displacement on a dominant platform translates directly into a material traffic loss with no owned channel buffer to absorb it. The current state assessment should quantify each source's share, its trajectory, and the risk level it represents, then surface the implications plainly: where dependency is excessive, where decline is structural rather than cyclical, and where growth opportunities are being underexploited.

Step 2, define target diversification

With the current state understood, the next step is defining a target distribution across a realistic twelve-month horizon. The goal is not to abandon high-performing platforms but to reduce the share of any single source below a concentration threshold while deliberately growing presence on emerging platforms and owned channels. Reducing dependence on a dominant platform is best achieved not through active de-optimization but through natural relative decline as other channels grow. Each emerging AI platform warrants a distinct approach reflecting its particular strengths: some reward nuanced, trade-off-aware content; others favor technical SEO precision and schema completeness; others respond to data-driven content with clear source attribution. Owned channels, including email lists, direct navigation, brand search, and community, require parallel investment, since they carry no platform dependency risk and provide a stable foundation regardless of how the AI discovery landscape evolves.

Step 3, build platform-agnostic assets

The most durable diversification investments are assets that deliver value across multiple platforms simultaneously rather than being optimized for any single channel. Comprehensive product data, including complete specifications, accurate pricing and availability, honest capability descriptions, and verified customer success metrics, serves AI platforms, search engines, marketplaces, and direct channels alike. High-quality visual content, covering multiple product angles, demonstration videos, lifestyle imagery, and authentic user-generated content, supports visual search, social platforms, marketplaces, and email in parallel. Authoritative written content in the form of detailed product guides, original research, and thought leadership earns citations from AI platforms, organic rankings from search engines, and engagement from social and email audiences. Third-party validation through customer reviews, analyst ratings, industry awards, and media coverage functions as a trust signal across every platform category. Customer success stories, documented with quantified outcomes and updated regularly, provide use case evidence for AI recommendations, long-tail content for search, and proof points for sales and marketing. The common thread across all five asset types is that they are owned, compounding, and platform-independent.

Step 4, develop quick-adaptation processes

The AI discovery landscape is evolving quickly enough that the ability to assess and respond to new platforms rapidly is itself a competitive advantage. A structured evaluation process moves through continuous monitoring, initial assessment, and implementation in a defined sequence with clear decision criteria at each stage. Monitoring tracks platforms reaching meaningful user scale, the emergence of commercial and shopping features, signals of user intent, and competitor presence. When a platform crosses a monitoring threshold, an initial assessment of one to two weeks covers user demographics, platform capabilities, commercial model, and competitive dynamics, followed by a minimal viable pilot to generate early performance data. A go decision triggers a phased implementation beginning with account setup and core content migration for the highest-priority products, followed by platform-specific optimization, testing, and competitive benchmarking, with a scale-or-exit review at the end of the initial period. Speed matters: the time from trigger to live presence should be measured in weeks, not quarters.

Step 5, maintain traditional channels

Diversification into AI platforms does not justify abandoning traditional channels, which continue to deliver meaningful returns and serve as the foundation on which AI optimization itself is built. Traditional search engines remain significant discovery sources and are declining gradually rather than collapsing, with positive ROI likely to persist for several years and ongoing SEO investment directly benefiting AI visibility through the same structured data and content quality signals that both channel types reward. Direct website traffic represents the highest-value visitor segment, since demonstrated intent and full control over the experience make it the most valuable owned channel and the most important buffer against platform dependency risk. Email marketing combines high ROI with complete platform independence, making list growth a priority investment regardless of how the discovery landscape shifts. Social media contributes to discovery, community engagement, and content distribution, with investment concentrated on the platforms that deliver the highest return for the specific audience. Marketplace presence should be maintained wherever buyers are already actively shopping, since incremental discovery and revenue within those environments come at relatively low marginal cost. The principle across all traditional channels is maintenance rather than abandonment, with selective increased investment in the owned channels that reduce platform risk most directly.

Guide to continuous AI search auditing

A practical, actionable checklist for ongoing AI optimization.

Daily monitoring

Daily monitoring is the foundation of operational health. These automated checks run continuously in the background and should require no manual intervention unless an alert is triggered:

- **Technical health:**
  - Schema validation (zero errors on product pages).
  - Site availability (99.9%+ uptime maintained).
  - Page speed (Core Web Vitals passing - LCP <2.5s, FID <100ms, CLS <0.1).
  - Broken link detection (zero critical broken links on key pages).
  - Image availability (all product images loading correctly).
- **Data accuracy:**
  - Pricing current and consistent (PIM sync verified).
  - Availability status is accurate (inventory sync confirmed).
  - Inventory levels updated (real-time or <5min lag).
  - No conflicting product information (cross-source consistency).
- **Critical alerts:**
  - llms.txt accessible and current.
  - API endpoints responding (product, pricing, availability).
  - No security issues flagged (SSL valid, no vulnerabilities).

Weekly monitoring

Weekly monitoring shifts focus from technical health to visibility and content performance. These checks require light human review and should feed directly into the editorial and optimization queue for the following week:

- **AI visibility tracking:**
  - **Share of Model (SoM)** measured across platforms (ChatGPT, Claude, Gemini, Perplexity).
  - New mentions or citations identified and cataloged.
  - Citation quality assessed (prominence, accuracy).
  - Competitive positioning monitored (vs. top 3 competitors).
- **Content quality:**
  - New content published meeting frequency goals (minimum 2 pieces/week).
  - Content freshness maintained (updates completed on schedule).

- Quality scores reviewed (all content >70/100).
- Voice compliance validated (automated checks passing).

- **Performance metrics:**
  - AI-attributed traffic tracked by the platform.
  - Conversion rates monitored (AI vs. other channels).
  - Lead quality assessed (AI-sourced leads).
  - Revenue impact measured (attribution to AI discovery).

Monthly audits

Monthly audits provide the strategic context that daily and weekly monitoring cannot. These reviews require dedicated time from cross-functional stakeholders and should produce a prioritized action plan for the month ahead:

- **Comprehensive quality review:**
  - Full product catalog audit (completeness >95%, accuracy >98%).
  - Schema implementation review (all products compliant).
  - Content inventory analysis (gaps identified and prioritized).
  - Competitive benchmark update (SoM by competitor, trends).
- **Strategic assessment:**
  - Platform-specific SoM trends analyzed (growth/decline by platform).
  - Query coverage gaps identified (missing use cases, features).
  - Content performance reviewed (top/bottom performers).
  - ROI assessment completed (cost per acquisition by channel),
- **Improvement planning:**
  - Quick wins identified and prioritized (high-impact, low-effort).
  - Medium-term initiatives planned (quarter roadmap).
  - Long-term strategy reviewed (annual goals on track?).
  - Resource allocation assessed (team, budget, tools).

Quarterly strategic reviews

Quarterly reviews step back from operational detail to assess market position, technology evolution, and capability maturity. These sessions should involve senior leadership and produce decisions about resource allocation, platform investment, and strategic direction:

- **Market position assessment:**
  - Overall SoM trend analyzed (vs. 3, 6, 12 months ago).

  - Competitive position evolution tracked (market share correlation).
  - Market share correlation assessed (SoM → actual sales).
  - Category leadership status evaluated (are we in the top 3?).
- **Technology evolution:**
  - New AI platforms evaluated (emerging competitors, capabilities).
  - Platform capability changes assessed (new features, algorithm updates).
  - Technology stack reviewed (tools effective? gaps identified?).
  - Infrastructure upgrades planned (automation, monitoring, analytics).
- **Capability maturity:**
  - Team skills assessed (training needs identified).
  - Process efficiency evaluated (bottlenecks identified).
  - Automation coverage reviewed (what else can be automated?).
  - Tool effectiveness measured (ROI by tool).
- **Strategic planning:**
  - Annual goals progress reviewed (on track? adjustments needed?).
  - Budget allocation optimized (shift resources to high-ROI activities).
  - Initiative prioritization updated (based on performance).
  - Risk assessment conducted (platform dependencies, competitive threats).

Annual comprehensive audit

The annual audit is the most thorough review in the cycle, covering the entire discovery stack, competitive landscape, financial performance, and long-term roadmap. It should be treated as a dedicated strategic exercise rather than an extension of routine monitoring:

- **Complete discovery stack review:**
  - All components are assessed for effectiveness (every channel, platform, tool).
  - Platform dependencies analyzed (diversification adequate?).
  - Resilience validated (can we survive platform loss?).
  - Future-readiness evaluated (prepared for next 2-3 years?).
- **Competitive intelligence:**
  - Comprehensive competitor analysis (top 5 competitors deep-dive).
  - Market dynamics assessment (category growth, trends, disruption).
  - Emerging threat identification (new competitors, business models).
  - Opportunity landscape mapping (white space, underserved segments).

- **ROI and business impact:**
  - Complete financial analysis (full-year costs and returns).
  - Attribution modeling reviewed (AI discovery | revenue).
  - Customer acquisition cost trends (by channel, over time).
  - Lifetime value impact assessed (AI-acquired customers vs. others).
- **Strategic roadmap:**
  - 3-year vision articulated (where are we headed?).
  - Annual priorities defined (what must we achieve this year?).
  - Resource requirements planned (team, budget, technology).
  - Success metrics established (how will we measure progress?).

Conclusion

We began this book by recognizing a fundamental shift: the transition from traditional search to AI-driven discovery is one of the most significant changes in commerce since the rise of the internet. Throughout these chapters, you have gained the knowledge, frameworks, and capabilities to succeed in this new landscape. However, the most important lesson is this: AI optimization is not a destination. It is a continuous journey.

As AI systems evolve and platforms rise and fall, the fundamentals remain the same. Quality wins. No matter how algorithms change, AI consistently favors accurate, comprehensive, well-structured information over thin or misleading content. Invest in quality, and the returns compound.

Authority compounds, too. Real expertise, credible third-party validation, and sustained thought leadership create durable advantages that outlast platform shifts. What you build today continues to work for you tomorrow. User focus is decisive. Adaptability is power. And trust is leverage.

You understand the AI discovery landscape, how AI agents operate, and what drives their recommendations. You have the frameworks to optimize content, execute technically, position competitively, and plan strategically. You have the capabilities to implement structured data, refine content, measure Share of Model, and build automation. You have a clear roadmap for the next three to five years.

What remains is execution. The shift from traditional search to AI-driven discovery is disruptive, but disruption is leverage. Those who understand AI systems, optimize for AI-driven discovery, and build scalable, adaptable processes will capture outsized value.

As the long tail compresses, leaders widen the gap. As visibility becomes algorithmic, preparation becomes power. The transformation of discovery is not coming; it is here. The playbook is in your hands. The journey begins now.

Index

A

S

T

V

Z

www.ingramcontent.com/pod-product-compliance
Lightning Source LLC
LaVergne TN
LVHW060544061126
851857LV00017B/1898
* 9 7 8 8 1 6 9 6 1 9 3 7 0 *